Lutherans On The Yangtze

Hong Kong - Macau - Taiwan

Volume II
1949-2013

Refugees from Nationalist China at the Rennie's Mill refugee camp on Junk Bay, in a then–remote area of Hong Kong. Men and women were part of the Concordia Bible Institute, organized in 1950 by Gertrude Simon (seated far right), herself a refugee from the Missouri Syond Lutheran mission in China.

Front Cover: Students in assembly at newly opened Kwun Tong Lutheran School in 1961. As with all schools in Hong Kong, uniforms bearing the school insignia were standard dress.

Back Cover: Savior Lutheran Mission at 232 TaiPo Road in Sham Shui Po served as first chapel, youth facility, Sunday school, primary school, and residence of the Hong Kong Mission.

Lutherans On The Yangtze

Hong Kong - Macau - Taiwan

(Jangtzee Lutheraner) Tome 2

A centenary account of the Missouri Synod
in Greater China
1949-2013

By David G. Kohl
Concordia University, Portland, Oregon

In consultation with Dr. Hank Rowold
Concordia Theological Seminary, St. Louis, Missouri

One Spirit Press
Portland, Oregon

Copyright © 2014 by David G. Kohl

All rights reserved.
Printed in the USA

ISBN: 978-1-893075-63-4
Library of Congress Number: 2014903947
Dewey: 266.251

Cover Design One Spirit Press

Book Design One Spirit Press, LLC
Photographic editing Ellen Lewis

Lutherans on the Yangtze is an independently researched unauthorized production and does not represent in any way an official connection with or endorsement by the Lutheran Church - Missouri Synod or its officials. The author takes full responsibility for accuracy of contents and observations expressed.

This book may not be reproduced by electronic or any
other means which exist now or may yet be developed,
without permission of Spirit Press, except in the case
of brief quotations embodied in critical articles and reviews.

One Spirit Press, LLC
Portland, Oregon

Preface

Nearly forty years spent establishing chapels, schools, clinics, and orphanages by a core of 65 missionaries along the Yangtze River were brought to an abrupt halt at the conclusion of the Chinese civil war. Along with over a million social, economic, and political refugees, foreign mission forces exited Mainland China *en mass* during the year leading to Mao Tse-tung [Mao Zedong]'s October 1949 declaration of the People's Republic of China.

Volume One of this account records in nine chapters the exploits and projects of those Missouri Synod men and women in six major locations in Hupeh [Hobei] and Szechwan [Sichuan] provinces, and the involvement of nearly 3,000 Chinese converts.

Volume Two continues the saga. Although disheartened by their forced exodus, three determined women and one pastor marooned in Hong Kong discovered refugees speaking the Mandarin language, the dialect of their previous work. While awaiting passage home, they realized there was essential work for them to do there, an opportunity to witness the gospel, and refused re-assignment to other "safe" areas of Asia. The four launched into humanitarian and evangelistic work at two hillside relocation camps - a rural location at Rennie's Mill and an urban shop front in Kowloon. Additionally, they organized the handicraft skills of over 150 destitute refugees, enabling many families to earn a meager income through local and overseas sales.

Within a year, a Bible School was training new believers as Bible students and eventual roles as pastors, teachers, and evangelists. When refugees were able to obtain visas and leave the British Colony, relocation in Taiwan or nearby Macau created a need for foreign missionaries in those places. A wave of enthusiastic proselytization establishing 19 congregations, and Primary and Middle schools followed. Seminaries were opened in both Hong Kong and Taiwan. Medical mission work led to founding a tuberculosis sanitarium and hospital in remote Junk Bay. The Lutheran Hour radio broadcasts offered correspondence schools. local rallies, and increased membership.

Veering from a course of working only with refugee Chinese, the mission and a group of expatriate Christians founded an English-speaking congregation in 1962 and located their sanctuary five years later within the structure of an innovative K-12 International school. Since the era of the Vietnam War, that International school has become a recognized leader among world-class schools and inspired four additional schools in the region.

Local Chinese language congregations organized independent sister Synods in Hong Kong and Taiwan in the 1970s. In Macau and Hong Kong, church leaders established social services, especially quality schools for the Deaf and Blind and assistance for the challenged and elderly. In recent years, the teaching of English and attendant friendship evangelism in Mainland and offshore China mark a new direction in mission outreach, a practice in which lay volunteers serve as part of teaching teams.

The revelation of surviving Christian communities in China following the ending of Cultural Revolution in 1976, and resulting "normalization," has energized a new generation of Christians to witness and live their faith openly in a modernizing and emerging China.

Details of these developments are the substance of this volume. I think you'll find it a remarkable story of individual determination, of group problem-solving, and of developing creative solutions to the challenge and opportunities of Christian witness in a changing Asia.

Rev Martin Chiang at Savior Lutheran Mission, 232 TaiPo Road in Sham Shui Po. The street chapel, near Shek Kip Mei and the refugee area, served as school, church, activity center, literature center, and living quarters.

Among the individuals interviewed for this volume (from top left): Andrew Chiu; Paul Strege; Roy and Betty Karner with Ruth Proft; Karl and LaVerne Boehmke; the author with Daniel Lee; Carl Hanson, Ted Englebrecht, Josh Lange and Stephen Oliver; John Chu; John Mehl, Travis Scholl, and Hank Rowold; Carol halter; Manfred and Jutta Berndt; Len and Ruth Galster.

Table of Contents

Preface	v
Table of Contents	vii
Alumni interviewees	vi, viii
Acknowledgements and Credits	ix

Chapter Ten	Establishing the Hong Kong Mission 1949-1950	1
Chapter Eleven	Growth of the Hong Kong Mission in the 1950s	21
chapter Twelve	Maturity and Diversification - the 1960s	61
Chapter Thirteen	Transitions and Partnership The Lutheran Church Hong Kong Synod	83
Chapter Fourteen	English and International Developments-1962-2012	105
Chapter Fifteen	Macau - Not the Least of These	125
Chapter Sixteen	Planting the Seed in Taiwan -The Missionary Stage	143
Chapter Seventeen	Taiwan Progress and Transition - 1962-1983	155
Chapter Eighteen	Regrouping, Trauma, and Hope - 1983-2012	173
Chapter Nineteen	Looking Back - Looking Forward	185

List of Maps

Pearl Delta - Hong Kong, Canton, & Macau	x
Hong Kong Territory	6
Locations of the LCMS and LC-HKS enterprise	84
Macau Peninsula LCMS Locations	126
Taiwan - LCMS Locations and the CELC	144
Lutheran Hour Locations and the Taiwan Mountains	150
Missouri & Hupeh compared; Illinois & Taiwan compared	171

Glossary – See Volume One

Index (Individual)	216
Index (Volume Two)	219
Bibliography	226
Colophon	233

Alumni" of the LCMS mission: Ardon Albrecht; Natalie Seltz and Carol Kreyling; Paul Kreyling; Carol with Dusty Reinbrecht Knisely; David, Jane, and Mel Kieschnick; Joel and Iantha Scheiwe; Harold "Blackie" Schmidt; Richard and Lois Meyer.

Acknowledgements and Credit

When the idea first occurred to me that the centennial history of the Missouri Synod's enterprise in the Chinese world was an important and meaningful story to explore, my naiveté and curiosity would soon lead into a matrix of individuals, family members, a complex of offices, boards, institutions, and archives. Sadly, I was to confirm a general unawareness of the Mission within "our beloved Synod." As I discovered and unearthed connections and collections, I came to the humble awareness that mine was a blessed project.

I so appreciate the knowledge, expertise, and friendship of Hank Rowold. The chapters on Taiwan, in particular, represent his input. The alumni of the Taiwan Mission, Chevanurch, have even elected me as a member (I am told this is an honor). Regarding Hong Kong, the casual network of "Hong Kong leavers" meeting irregularly over dim sum or Lunar New Year feasts have inspired me with detailed memories. HKIS alumni are held together by the vision of Bill Mahlke, the alumni association so long headed by Ken Koo, and the Dragontrain e-group established by Judy Porter Rower. You former students, many now friends, represent the halcyon days of my teaching career. *Doh jay*

Collections of church periodicals at Concordia University Portland and Concordia Seminary in St. Louis have been invaluable. The archives of donated notes, photographs and memorabilia housed by Concordia Historical Institute are a treasure chest, of which Laura Marrs has provided the key. I am grateful for the loan of photographs and enthusiastic help of Gerald Pershbacher and the International Lutheran Hour. In Hong Kong, I am grateful to LCMS Hong Kong staff - Ted Englebrecht, Carol Halter, Carl Hanson, Josh Lange, John Mehl, Joel and Iantha Schiewe, Ed Stroschein, and Josh Lange. Members of the Lutheran Church Hong Kong Synod have provided both interviews and print literature, especially Daniel WC Lee, Dante Yeong, Sam Yeung, and Allen Yung. Dr. Andrew Chiu and his daughter Mary have become both good friends and superior sources. If I attempted to include recognition of all the phone calls, e-mails, and packages I have received, I would run out of space, and still probably overlook many helpful people - in and beyond the LCMS.

The photographs that illuminate this story have been provided by missionaries, their families, and archival collections in the U.S, Taiwan, and Hong Kong. Many were photo-shopped by Ellen Lewis. A partial list of sources includes the Andres family (Gertrude Simon), Lorraine Behling Sonnenberg, Karl and LaVerne Boehmke, Bob and Arlene Christian, Bill and Evelyn Dingler, Len and Ruth Galster, Carol Halter and Lutheran handicrafts, Roy and Betty Karner, the Kieschnick family, Ruth Proft, the family of Fred Schalow, and Paul and Caroline Tuchardt.

Several photographs included in this volume (pages 2, 4, 12, 18, 22, 28, 32, 34, 40, 42, and 213) were stamped "Lutheran World Federation" on the reverse. They are the work of Cheng Chink-woon (1919-1988) who gave up a career as an art photographer to help promote the charitable work of the LWF in the 1950s with Hong Kong's refugee population.

I am so fortunate to have attempted this project at this moment in time, and am grateful to several wonderful workers, now sainted. Unknown to me until I started in 2007, I celebrate the friendships of Lorraine Behling, Paul Kreyling, Ed May, and Ruth Proft, as well as long-time co-workers Manfred Berndt and Paul Tuchardt. Many hours over coffee and other libations with Carl and Jo Brandhorst, Nathan Brandt, Bob and Arlene Christian, Len Galster, Bruce Richards, and Warren Schumacher have helped me develop and refine the telling of this story. Without the patience and consistency of Suzanne Deakins and One Spirit Press, the book would not exist.

My hope is that you find the story to be a case study and example of what personal committed involvement can accomplish in meeting overwhelming challenge head-on, a testimony to individual determination, and to the power of any one person acting in faith.

Chapter 10 Establishing the Hong Kong Mission – 1949-1950

Arrivals
1949 -   (all via the "St Paul")
    Simon,   Gertrude
    Holtje   Wilbert
    Boss,   Martha
    Behling   Lorraine

1950 Hinz   Herb

Departures
1950
    Holtje   Wilbert & Geri + Paul

Missouri Synod Board of Foreign Missions staff data will be listed at the beginning of each chapter throughout this book. These are unofficial and are only as accurate as the available research materials or anecdotal notes available.

Pearl Delta - Hong Kong, Canton, & Macau

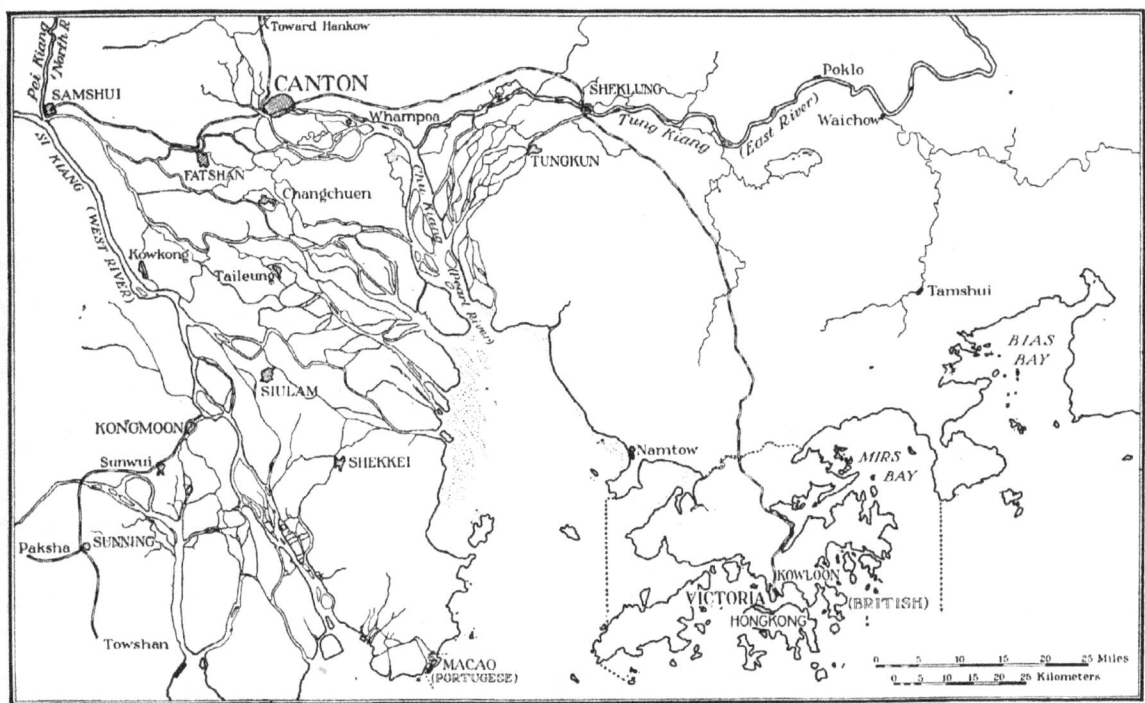

The Pearl River Delta, where China's East, West, and North Rivers merge, marks a 90-miles estuary from Canton (Kwangchow)[Guangzhou] to British Hong Kong. At the western mouth of the bay sita historic Macau. The majority of Overseas Chinese living in South East Asia and America hail from the villages and counties between Portuguese Macau and Canton, often grouped and known as Toishanese. Both Hong Kong (in 1997) and Macau (in 1999) were peacefully reunited with the Peoples Republic as Special Administrative Regions (SARs).

For the love of Christ controls us, because we have concluded this: that He died for all, that those who live might no longer live for themselves but for him who for their sake died and was raised. Therefore, we are ambassadors for Christ, God making His appeal through us. We implore you on behalf of Christ, be reconciled to God. 2 Corinthians 5: 14, 20 (ESV)

Chapter 10

Establishing the Hong Kong Mission – 1949 -1950

In late 1949, four Missouri Synod missionaries stranded in Hong Kong by the civil war in China found themselves in the midst of a tidal wave of human flotsam as Communist troops were "liberating" the Mainland. Mao Tse-tung [Mao Zedong] declared the People's Republic of China (PRC) in Peking [Beijing] on October 1, 1949. Communist forces stopped at the Shum Chun River (now ShenZhen) on Oct 17, recognizing the British Colonial Hong Kong boundary, establishing the "bamboo curtain" separating Communist and non-Communist Asia. Refugees arrived daily by plane, train, boat, but mostly on foot.

The tale of these three women and one pastor re-discovering and forming a new mission venture would lead to two Chinese Lutheran Synods, forty local schools, five International Schools, and a distinctive Social Services system.

The Hong Kong Setting

Hong Kong's historic and geographic character is important to understanding the formation of the LCMS mission. The territory (the prized British Crown Colony on the southeast China coast until 1997) occupies about 396 square miles at the mouth of the Pearl River, whose three branches drain the southern 20% of China. The sheltered deep water harbor became Britain's prize, gained after the First Opium War. The nearly barren rocky peaks, sub-tropical islands and lush peninsulas were nearly unoccupied at the time of British possession in 1842.

The Colony of Hong Kong rapidly became a haven for traders, diplomats, missionaries, and pirates. To romantics, it is the "Pearl of the Orient." The protected harbor is the finest on the China coast, approached via the East Lamma channel. Settlement grew rapidly, preceding Shanghai as a shipping, commerce, and financial center. Reunited with China peacefully as a Special Administrative Region (SAR) in 1997, the Territory of Hong Kong is composed of four major land areas. The main components are Hong Kong Island, the Kowloon Peninsula across the mile-wide harbor, the adjacent New Territories, and the outlying islands.

The main island of Hong Kong (78 sq km) was the original British Crown Colony (BCC). Eleven miles long, running east to west, and varies from two to five miles wide,

Chapter 10   Establishing the Hong Kong Mission – 1949 -1950

Centuries-old traditional villages and farmland typify the New Territories, the landmass leased from China by Britain in 1898. During the major waves of refugee migration beginning in 1949, the region became populated with refugee camps administered by the Hong Kong Government, in cooperation with the United Nations and several international charitable organizations.

comparable to New York City's Manhattan. The island rises from fish-laden waters to several peaks, the highest being Victoria at 652 m), known locally as "the Peak." Most building sites on the island are on the north side, facing the harbor, and are primarily on harborfront landfill. There rise today, the tall residential towers of North Point, Causeway Bay, Wanchai, and Victoria, the business district known as "Central."

The Kowloon Peninsula (12 sq km) across the mile-wide harbor was also ceded to Britain in 1860, following the Second Opium War. Larger areas of flat land have made "Kowloon side" the area of greatest building expansion and population concentration. In 1898, nearly 380 square miles of additional mountains, bays, farmland, small villages, and 235 islands also became British with the 99-year lease. These are the "New Territories" and "Outlying Islands." About 12% of Hong Kong was arable, dotted with traditional ancestral walled villages. Several communities of boat-dwelling clans fished in coves and inlets.

Only appropriately-named Boundary Street separates Kowloon from the New Territories, near the area of the first LCMS mission. Of 235 islands, just the larger dozen are inhabited. These include Lantau, Lamma, Peng Chau, and Cheung Chau, where LCMS mission families had lived during the Japanese occupation in China. From the time of the "handback" in 1997, several parts of Lantau Island were developing into the new Chek Lap Kok airport, Disney World, and several residential areas, composed of high-rise towers, set jewel-like amidst greenways and country parks.

Forty miles east, across the estuary of the Pearl River, lies the much older and smaller former Portuguese colony of Macau. That river drains the southern 20% of China. Canton or Kwangchow [Guangzhou] lies 90 miles northwest up the Pearl River, past Whampoa. Until 1842, it was the sole port within China open for restricted trade with Europe, America, and Asian merchant fleets.

Missouri in Hong Kong

Hong Kong was not on the usual transportation route for missionaries bound for interior China. Through rail service to Northern China was not completed until 1936. The first phase of LCMS activity in Hong, from 1937 until 1942, is told in Chapter Eight, bought about by the events of Japanese occupation and War.

Missionary Vic Hafner was sent to Hong Kong in late 1948 by Hankow seminary president Alfred Ziegler, with the goal of finding a rental property there for the Synod. The purpose of obtaining a location in Hong Kong was to have a permanent address so that any LCMS missionary could obtain exit visas as China's civil war was progressing. At that time, no one could enter Hong Kong without a visa, and no one could get a visa unless they had a guaranteed place to stay, since the Colony was already overpopulated with refugees from the Chinese "War of Liberation."

A hostel was in operation by May, 1949, when the Bringewatt family stayed there, evacuating from Chungking on their way to the States. In June, the Hafners were re-assigned to the Philippines and the hostel was discontinued. After serving in the Philippines, Hawaii, Wisconsin, and Taiwan, the Hafners would return in 1962 to serve in Hong Kong for ten years.

"There Is Work to Be Done Here"

When Rev. Wilbert Holtje and Gertrude Simon evacuated from Chungking aboard the St. Paul on November 29, they found temporary housing at an LWF hostel, awaiting onward passage out of Hong Kong. A huge humanitarian crisis became apparent among the multitudes of refugees pouring into the area daily. Population in the colony had dwindled from 1.5 million pre-war residents

Chapter 10 Establishing the Hong Kong Mission – 1949 -1950

Refugees or "squatters" found or made shelter in both rural and urban locations, finding niches of unoccupied space, or becoming part of large refugee camps throughout the British Colony.

 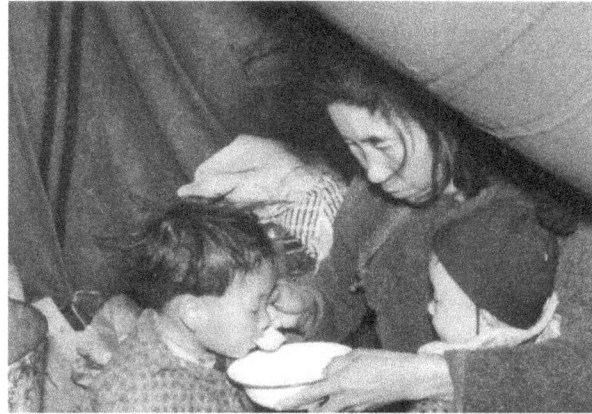

Martha Boss and Lorraine Behling found housing at the Basel Mission home on Tai Po Road. In February, 1950, they convinced visiting Missions Director O.H.Schmidt to authorize their work. Pictured at Kai Tak aerodrome are Behling, Rev. Wilbert Holtje, unidentified, O.H.Schmidt, Gertrude Simon, Boss, and Paul Chang.

to 600,000 in 1945, but doubled, and doubled again within two years. Hong Kong had quickly become the "Berlin of the East."

No one was turned back at the Lo Wu or Man Kam To crossing points for the first six months of 1950. Nearly all refugees were KMT bureaucrats or military. Colonial government maintained neutrality. Hong Kong and neighboring Macau were the first destinations of displaced intellectuals, businessmen, government workers, and Kuomintang military, but many parents, wives, and children had to be left in China. Thousands of families never reunited.

During this waiting period, Miss Simon met a local Chinese missionary wife, Mrs. Chao, who took her one day to see Baptist work among the displaced and destitute. When Simon heard the refugees speaking Mandarin, her dismay over potentially leaving her beloved China vanished. Her resolve to stay on in Hong Kong would change Lutheran history in Asia, and at home.

On December 9, Martha Boss and Lorraine Behling were evacuated into Hong Kong on the St. Paul in the daring rescue from Chengdu described in the last chapter. They soon reunited with Holtje and Simon. The women first found housing at the Presbyterian mission. Soon, all four missionaries secured lodging at the Basel Mission Home, a Swiss-based Lutheran society. They would live at 58 Tai Po Road, on the Kowloon side just north of Boundary Street near the Sham Shui Po refugee area, where pre-war Quonset huts housed displaced mainlanders. Nearly 50 other refugee missionaries of various denominations were also living there. Room #9 was to be the women's bedroom, office space, and church office for the next six months. Rev. Holtje used a small room on the verandah.

Determined to serve war-ravaged immigrants, the four missionaries resisted a LCMS re-assignment to India or New Guinea, and exchanged several cables with St. Louis about future plans. They had only temporary visas from the Hong Kong government at the time. Missionary Holtje was experienced in working with orphans, in education, in medical work and administration from his four years in Enshih. He knew Mandarin through two years of intense study. As the sole ordained minister, his duties included preaching the word, and administering the sacraments, but in refugee-occupied Hong Kong, his tasks would soon multiply.

Not merely housemates, the three women became a dynamic working team. Simon and Boss had been schooled as deaconess nurses. Behling had earned a master's degree in religious education from Concordia Seminary, St. Louis - the first woman to do so. She would officially become a deaconess after she left HK in 1959. The LCMS deaconess is a dedicated assistant in ministry, with a firm grounding in Scripture. Women are charged to care for the health, education, and welfare needs of the poor and needy, regardless of faith-status. As professional church workers, they could perform all of the roles of a minister/missionary except preaching from the pulpit and administering the sacraments. Yet with all their training, they had little preparation for the enormity of what lay ahead.

A Dislocated People

Refugees in Hong Kong in 1949 represented nearly every socio-economic level whereas the Chinese known to the LCMS Mainland missionaries had been primarily laboring class urban and rural peoples. All the significant patterns that affect historic interaction between the Chinese and the Western world were at play. Many are paired factors, such as *yin-and-yang*; good and evil; warm and cold; south and north; day and night; male and female; Christian and pagan. It may seem disingenuous to stereotype a people or nationality. Yet there are distinct patterns and trends which particularly apply to certain groups - the French are particular about their cuisine; Italians show their emo-

Chapter 10   Establishing the Hong Kong Mission – 1949 -1950

Hong Kong Territory

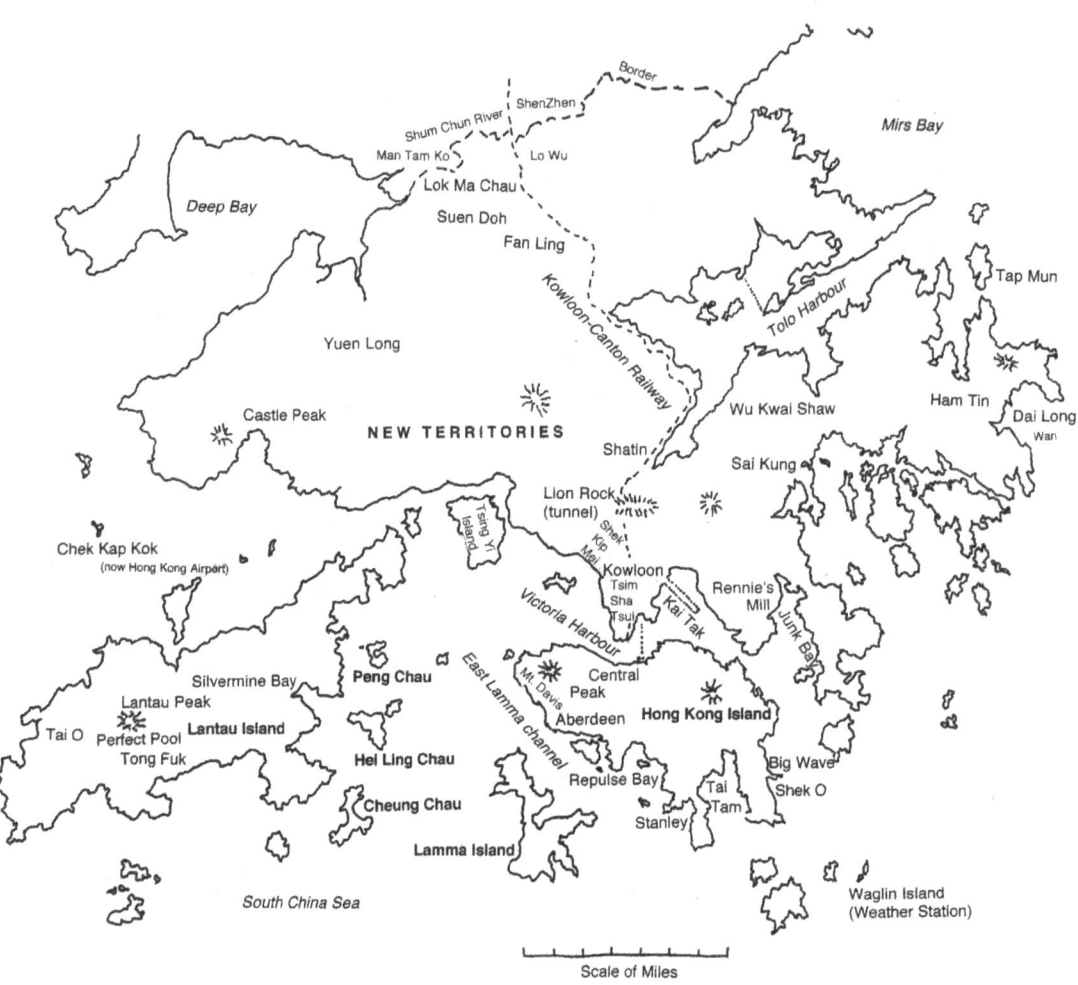

Map of Hong Kong, the British territory from 1842-1997, handed back to China and now a SAR. Nearly 400 square miles, the mountainous islands and peninsulas and a very indented coastline make a spectacular landscape, with less than 12% of land naturally level enough for habitation. Hong Kong Island is approximately the size of Manhattan. At the shore of the South China Sea, the territory is subject to monsoonal weather and often in the path of typhoon in the fall.

tions freely; Germans are highly structured; Americans tend to be entrepreneurial; survivors of the Great Depression are thrifty, etc. So it was with traditional Chinese culture, suddenly challenged by the chaos and dislocation of millions of people forced into the precarious life of homelessness.

In retrospect, we benefit today from the observations and studies of sociologists and anthropologists of the past 100 years. Western stereotypical views of the Chinese had deteriorated for decades. Prevailing attitudes were predominantly euro-centric, colonial, judgmental, and insensitive. This viewpoint was about to be challenged and slowly transformed.

The Chinese are fiercely loyal to family and clan. Confucian structure dictates obedience to family, clan, tribe, province, nation, and head of state - be he Emperor, President, or Chairman. While one's first obligation is always to the Confucian teachings, the Chinese are a friendly and warm people. Most love and pamper their young children almost to a fault. Chinese are accomodating and hospitable to travelers, and deeply loyal and committed to friendships. The deep association of family, servants, compradores, fellow workers, and fellow believers is well documented. Many of these practices became impossible for the refugees.

Gone was the design of the family home or temple, laid out for privacy and protection. High walls surrounded whole villages of precincts of family courtyard houses, in which all rooms face a central plaza - no windows to the outside. Misaligned doorways prevented any breech of privacy. As sons marry, rooms are re-assigned for the next generation. Prosperity is not displayed on an ostentatious exterior or colorful facade, hence a certain monotone coloration to most Chinese communities. Mud and brick walls topped with black or grey rooftiles made a drab cityscape. The only taller buildings are temples or pawnshops. The desperation for any shelter in Hong Kong's camps and hillsides upset all normalcy for families.

Loyalty and kinship, so basic to Chinese culture, was reinforced by linguistic groupings. Over 300 spoken dialects and language groups lead to colloquialism and clannishness. Yet the people are also unified by the written language - 5000 memorized characters constitute basic literacy. Drawn or brushed abstract and stylized designs or characters are standard in their general meaning, but without any hint of pronunciation. A competent telegraph operator needed to know 60,000 of these to be considered efficient.

The written word has always held great respect, and the Chinese are voracious readers. Historically, most news and local information was hand written on paper and pasted on public walls for all to read, and reading the postings was a communal activity. Over ten Hong Kong newspapers, with as many points of view, supplied local and world news to the literate and mostly well-educated Chinese, stable or itinerant.

Refugees came from the Cantonese-speaking Pearl Delta, but many more were Mandarin speakers, alien to the local Hong Kong language, citizenry, and government. Added to political differences, the language barriers between Northerners and Southerners were problematic.

Learning has always been highly regarded. Story-telling holds a powerful role in education, as does memorization and recitation. Chinese culture is about wisdom, hence the traditional respect for parents and the elderly. Innovation, problem-solving and mathematical acuity are highly valued. This may be the result of learning patterns based on concepts and characters rather than lineal thinking and phonetic language of the West. Rote learning and memorization were standard learning techniques. Memorization often substituted for reading. Foreign observers of

Chapter 10   Establishing the Hong Kong Mission – 1949 -1950

At Rennie's Mill, a chapel of straw, thatch, and bamboo was erected, soon to become a social center of the refugee camp. Gertrude Simon began the Concordia Bible School within months, a hub of energy for believers to earn more about Jesus Christ. One goal was to return to the homeland and witness their new faith

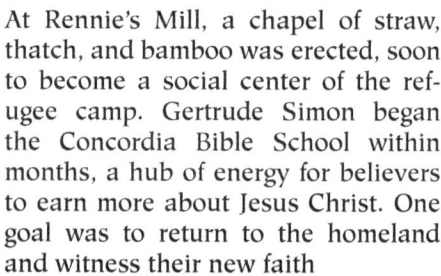

the Chinese often equated illiteracy with stupidity and the use of *pidgin*, "chinglish," or any patois as a sign of mental inferiority. The great wealth of common sense and reasoning based on Confucian, Taoist, and Buddhist philosophies would be put to the test.

For the millions of refugees, survival took precedence in their topsy-turvy new world. Men and women eked out any income by doing any physical labor job, literally earning pennies per day. It was to be a long stretch until Hong Kong's vast new labor supply would be able to find any income-producing activity

Wariness towards change had typified the continuity of Chinese culture over 5000 years. Farming methods, settlement patterns, architectural practice, and cuisine have millenia of traditions which reinforce behind them. As refugees scrambling for survival, new situations called for solutions or invention. New ways, ideas, and variation from tradition is challenging The industrious Chinese were forced into desperate applications, totally alien to their previous lives.

Historically, frugality is universal in the Chinese world and wealth is security. For refugees, that stability was annihilated. More than ever, nothing was wasted by the displaced, be it food, fuel, clothing, anything useable for construction of shelter, even human and animal excrement. The new Hong Kong Chinese survived by their wits and will to live. They generated new levels of recycling and alternate usage. Outside or government aid would eventually develop, but not before the challenge and aftermath of initial survival.

The Mission Is Launched!

Two months before the mission board sanctioned any work, the four missionaries-in-transit seized the moment. Although displaced themselves, they interpreted turmoil as opportunity. Local schools needed instructors to teach scripture history (which was part of the British-mandated curriculum). By January 15, Lorraine was teaching at Heung Kong College, a middle school adjacent to the Basel Mission Home. In partial exchange, Principal Chen Shu Kui also granted permission for the missionaries to hold worship services on Sundays, using a room with street access. He himself had been educated in a missionary school, but his family was Buddhist and believed that through ancestor worship tradition, China could be freed from the Communists. While there was to be no rent at the college, it was understood that LCMS missionaries would continue teaching some English classes for Heung Kong College.

One of the college teachers was Jason Mui, whose son was a local basketball star. Mr. Mui became a loyal friend, and supported a campus ministry and evening Bible class at the school. The Lau family also became supporters. Already Christians from the mainland, their son John was soon baptized as well. Mr. Lau was a builder who would later help construct several chapels. Later in the 1960s, the Mui and Lau families would help Rev. Holt establish a mission in San Francisco's Chinatown, which became the Church of the Holy Spirit.

In February 1950, Director O.H. Schmidt, of the Board of Foreign Missions, flew into Kai Tak airport to be greeted by the four excited and determined missionaries. Their Chinese interpreter, 23-year old evangelist Paul Chang, was also in the greeting party. Even though many "authorities" predicted that Hong Kong would soon fall to the Communists, Rev. Schmidt recognized the mission potential, and a decision was made to formally open a LCMS mission in Hong Kong. On March 26, the first regular public worship service was conducted in a classroom at Heung Kong College by Rev. Holtje and the three women. There were 26 attendees. Sermons were delivered in Mandarin, and translated into Cantonese. Sunday school brought in many curious children. Official establishment came at the 26th Synodical Convention

Chapter 10   Establishing the Hong Kong Mission – 1949 -1950

Refugees doubled the population of Hong Kong within a year. Crowding intensified and life in the camps settled into a semi-permanent routine while they awaited visas to Taiwan, America, and in SE Asia. Gertrude Simon (pictured with Rev Chen Hui-jen and family back in China), founded the Concordia Bible School in the thatched chapel at Rennie's Mill.

in Milwaukee in June, 1950.

The four pioneer missionaries took on a full plate. The mission, as they saw it, was to try to maintain contact with the remnant Chinese Christians on the mainland; evangelize in the streets to both Mandarin and Cantonese speakers (Rev. Holtje would do *wai-tang* and preach anywhere); teach English; conduct worship and Sunday school; inform the churches back in the States about their needs, potential, and activity; and begin social services—educational, medical, and welfare.

Preaching in the streets around the Basel Mission Home and Heung Kong College was often a spontaneous event. The missionaries, with children from the Sunday school, would start singing on the sidewalk and attract a crowd, which they'd then educate with large Bible pictures. Passersby expressing curiosity were invited to come into the classroom at the college for worship.

The gospel was explained through interpreter Paul Chang, from the Basel Mission. In his ambition and love for God, Evangelist Chang was able to translate the message into Mandarin, Cantonese, and the language spoken by Hakka communities. Chang sought out evangelical opportunities where Holtje could preach. The two set up loudspeakers on Tai Po Road. They found a bare wall and painted an image of Jesus on it. The picture drew a lot of people for street evangelism. Some of those were American sailors in port.

Chang also helped connect the missionaries with teaching possibilities at St. Peter's Commercial School, where they taught Bible class to a group of 60 boys and 10 girls. Paul located an unused soy sauce factory for Sunday school sessions. Martha Boss also taught a class in a funeral home amid the caskets. Paul had helped make the arrangements with the owner, Mr. Huang, who wanted to learn more about Christianity. Paul became a mainstay and evangelist of the mission, later translating Lutheran Hour sermons into Cantonese. In a few years, he would leave Hong Kong to pastor True Light Lutheran Church in New York City. (See page 41)

Beyond Hong Kong

An occasional letter from missionaries R.J. Mueller in Shanghai, or Elmer Thode and Fred Schalow, still in Hankow, reported on the status of the mainland stations. In 1950, these were operated by loyal indigenous laymen and evangelists. Schools were still operating in Ichang and Wanhsien, but the whereabouts of any Hankow seminary graduates was mostly unknown.

In China, several policies were established at a Peking meeting of various Christian leaders with Premier Chou En-lai [Zhou Enlai] in May 1950. Essentially, the discussion produced the document, "How Shall the Church Go Forward?" Recommendations were that the church should work harmoniously with and support the new government leadership. Christians should participate in the struggle for independence, democracy, peace, unification, and the prosperity of China. These goals could be accomplished if the church helped eradicate all imperialism; avoid old feudal ways and capitalistic practices; practice self-criticism; and support the new Land Reform Program which divided and re-allocated farmland.

The church was to be self-governing, self-supporting, and self-propagating—a long-established missiological vision. This meant no foreign personnel and no external funding. Worship, training indigenous leaders, and promoting education of the masses were the goals. The church should also support labor, good literature, and music; help with medical services; and emphasize the care and raising of children. "Missionaries who are law-abiding and not the 'running dogs of the imperialists' may remain in China, but no new missionaries are welcome at this time."

Chapter 10   Establishing the Hong Kong Mission – 1949 -1950

Basic needs of housing, food, and clothing came through hardscraple survival and the services of various welfare agencies. The refugee influx included Chinese of all social and educational classes, equalized by circumstance.

To reach supporters in America, Lorraine Behling began mimeographing a bi-monthly newsletter in April of 1950, *The Hong Kong Letter*. Her publication featured news about the work of the mission, individual stories of new Chinese believers, listings of needed materials, and "thank yous" for donations. The first two issues were mailed directly by sea mail from Hong Kong, but Lorraine then approached her brother-in-law, Rev. Harold Ott of Bridgeman, Michigan, for help. His Walther League youth group at Immanuel volunteered to duplicate and mail the bi-monthly letters, which they did for the next nine years. This saved countless dollars in overseas postage and saved Behling thousands of hours of folding and addressing the newsletters. Lorraine's brother Robert supplied stencils, paper, and envelopes. Circulation grew from 300 to over 3000 copies by 1960.

Rennie's Mill

Work and witness among encamped refugees began almost immediately on the streets and on the grounds of the Tung Hwa hospital. The government relocated these homeless to a hillside location in a temporary camp on Mt. Davis near Pok Fu Lam on Hong Kong island. It was March 28, during the rainy season.

Speaking Mandarin, the missionaries decided to do work in this hillside camp. Three evenings each week, at least two of the four missionaries visited, talked, and listened. Martha Boss used a flannel board to tell Bible stories, while Lorraine Behling led singing and began a study class on the Gospel of John. Paul Chang built a small hut on the trail at the foot of Mt Davis. Inside, were Christian books and tracts. People also went to hear Pastor Holtje and Evangelist Chang give lectures. Sunday services attracted about 35 people. Holtje began teaching a catechism class.

In mid-1950, the government halted its open immigration policy, restricting to 50 the number of new immigrants each day. On June 27, the Mt. Davis refugees were relocated again, to remote Rennie's Mill Camp on the site of an early 1900s Canadian flour mill. Overlooking an isolated bay in the New Territories, the isolated camp was perched on the hillside which today is Tiu Keng Leng, facing Devil's Hill.

Initially, over 3000 refugees lived in shelters of straw, cardboard, or tarpaper. New homeless families arrived daily. Formerly prosperous and well-educated families had been uprooted, bringing nothing but a *kang* (shoulder pole) of goods with them over the border. In this Nationalist camp, most refugees had been associated with the Kuomintang (KMT), now defeated, without a country, and distrusted by Communist sympathizers.

Presenting the gospel to refugees proved to be quite different from former work within China. The people were tired, lonely, and separated from their clans, families, and home villages. Their structured world had vanished and traditional support systems no longer existed. Huddled in very close proximity were people from several provinces and language groups, different educational levels, and varied economic classes. There were teachers, professors, scholars, businessmen and bankers. Without job or income, they were equally in a survival mode, desperate for food and shelter. In the crowded conditions of the camp, they had endless hours of open time.

Many had lost all family links. In this milieu of humanity, many were ready for a new start, reluctant but willing to accept help from non-Chinese sources, overcoming tradition and a century of anti-foreignism. Ancestral gods and military heroes had failed them. Many young refugees were open and receptive to the Christian message.

In June, hostilities erupted on the distant Korean Peninsula, which for the next three years, would pit the North Koreans, with PRC backing, against South Korea, with

Chapter 10 Establishing the Hong Kong Mission – 1949 -1950

LCMS missionaries from 1938-41 lived in the arcaded house #29 on Cheung Chau. Martha and Lorraine brought Rev. Holt to the island for a brief "holiday" in 1950, hoping to restore his health, amidst the charms of the fishing village and famous Pak Tai temple. His tuberculosis would send him back to America in June, 1951, for 3 years of recovery.

its American and United Nations support. A strict embargo was placed on any possible war-related shipping through Hong Kong. Most local industry was affected. Unemployment skyrocketed, and the plight of the homeless became even worse. Empty ships awaiting any cargo littered the harbor.

The missionaries continued to work at Rennie's Mill, now numbering over 7000 inhabitants. To reach the barren location on Junk Bay required over an hour of travel by taxi, bus, and *sampan*. The camp was destined to become the major venue of LCMS work among refugees for years to come. The site would become resettlement estates in 1962, eventually demolished for a new town in 1995.

Colonial government erected tarpaper tents and provided two meals (bowls of rice) a day for each refugee. The government also allocated spaces for church groups—Catholic, Baptist, Christian Missionary Alliance, etc. The Lutherans constructed a 25' x 50' simple bamboo mat chapel and reading room, with a thatch roof, naming it St John's Chapel. In the rear of this shed, Gertrude Simon set up simple living quarters, so that she could live and work among the people. She felt a kinship with the Mandarin Chinese that came from her almost 25 years of teaching and nursing in China. Living at the camp also eliminated the long commute from Kowloon.

Concordia Bible Institute

Miss Simon opened an evangelism school on August 18, 1950, with permission from Rev. Holtje, but with no funds, materials, or curriculum. It was named Concordia Bible Institute. Simon set a goal of training 500 Bible students who would be ready to return to the mainland one day as evangelists, although it was also recognized that Communism might be the future of China. Her syllabus was hand-written. Rev. Holtje planned to go there on certain days and also conduct Sunday services. Paul Chang was to stay at the camp half of each week. After just three weeks, both men became ill, and Miss Simon was left alone to run the school.

Using her nursing training, she also began seeing patients three days a week, treating them mostly for ringworm, scabies, trachoma, malaria, and dysentery. She lacked medicines and even simple bandages. On August 22, a hillside fire consumed almost 40 straw and tarpaper huts. Although flames surrounded St. John's Chapel, the thatched matshed was spared in what many knew was a miracle.

Education and Baptism

Behling and Boss started a correspondence Bible reading course, from their room at Basel Mission House. An English Bible class began twice a week on the rooftop garden of the Tropic Island Hotel in Kowloon. Space there was granted by the manager, Mr. Chow, in exchange for English lessons taught to his 27 bellboys—no "key money" and no rent! Young people's meetings were also held on the rooftop, where slides on the Apostles Creed from the Churchcraft division of Concordia Publishing House (CPH) were shown.

Several of these young people began corresponding with individual Walther Leaguers in the States, as part of the League's Bible Reading Mission project. The Hong Kong Letter continued linking supporters in the U.S. with people and projects in Hong Kong. Worship and Sunday school were still conducted weekly at Heung Kong College. Three Sunday school classes—one in Mandarin and two in Cantonese were taught by local teachers.

Rev. Holtje conducted the first baptisms on the 6th of June—eleven refugees from Rennie's Mill and eight from Kowloon. In the group were Andrew Chiu, Silas Chang, and Harold Jen, all destined to become pastors. As they began to accept Christ as their Savior, they were given, or selected, a biblical name. When the Chu brothers were baptized, they were re-named James and John, like the biblical brothers. Over time, other popular

Chapter 10 Establishing the Hong Kong Mission – 1949 -1950

Savior (Saviour) Lutheran Mission opened its first rented space in October 1950 at 232 Tai Po Road, near Heung Hong College and the Basel Home. In the midst of crowded Sham Shui Po on the fringe of Shek Kip Mei, the chapel was used day and night for services and educational programs, youth activities, and the opening of Concordia Lutheran School in 1953.

Tracts explaining Christian beliefs.

names were Daniel, Paul, Silas, Titus, Timothy, Luke, Andrew, Phillip, Stephen, and Peter.

To supply learning materials, hectograph copies were tediously produced in the women's flat. This antiquated process involves a pan of gelatin upon which a sheet of absorbent paper was laid to pick up an image from the surface of the purple goo. A borrowed mimeograph machine was set up in the bedroom/office, which the missionaries also called "Concordia Publishing House." They churned out 300 copies each of *Luther's Catechism* and its explanation by early LCMS theologian August Selle. These had been translated earlier by missionary Richard Muehl, and further edited by Paul Chang. Hymnbooks for services at Heung Kong College and Rennie's Mill were also printed, as well as Bible Reading Class materials.

Through *The Hong Kong Letter*, Lorraine requested donations of used Sunday school leaflets from stateside churches. These arrived in large numbers and were sorted to be used not only in Sunday School and Bible classes, but also in reading rooms, which were set up at the Tropical Island Hotel rooftop and out at Rennie's Mill. The full color pictures were often cut out and re-pasted onto posters. LCMS missionaries in the Philippines were doing the same thing.

Rev. Holtje conducted worship services in Mandarin and English, which Paul Chang translated into Cantonese. All four missionaries became involved at various levels of learning written and spoken Cantonese. Language work was challenging. Spoken Mandarin and Cantonese are totally different; only the written ideographic characters are understandable to all reading groups.

Martha Boss was involved everywhere. She divided her time between Rennie's Mill and Kowloon, teaching classes in both venues and helping Gertrude with medical services. Evening classes during the week, weekend daytime classes, and visits to the camp took up any time leftover from her work with the correspondence course. Her cot was the sorting table for Sunday school leaflets and donated clothing. It is rumored that she did actually get a few hour's sleep.

Seeing that the refugees had no way to earn money, Boss and Simon began encouraging women and children to develop embroidery skills, with the hope of selling napkins and other items to tourists. At the time, no such products from "Red China" could be imported or sold in the USA. Soon, the deaconesses were writing home about the needs of the refugees to "earn their rice." Many individuals and some LWML groups in America began to order and purchase these handicrafts.

With some reluctance, Boss and Behling allowed themselves a week "holiday" on Cheung Chau Island in August. This was an hour's ride on the Hong Kong-Yaumati ferry. Holtje also went to Cheung Chau hoping to restore his health, not realizing that he had contracted tuberculosis. Simon couldn't, or wouldn't, leave Rennie's Mill, as she was fully engaged with the start of the Concordia Bible school. It was to open in September; and did so with as many students as could fit into the cramped single room at Rennie's Mill that also served as worship space for St. John's Lutheran congregation.

Savior Lutheran Mission

Autumn seemed to bring a "perfect storm" of challenges. In September, the Tropic Island Hotel closed, so the rooftop was unavailable. The relationship with Heung Kong College became strained due to its own special needs. A typhoon severely damaged the new Rennie's Mill chapel and Miss Simon's Bible School. Both Paul Chang and Rev. Holtje were seriously ill with tuberculosis. Geri Holtje and her two children had arrived from the U.S. June 19, and were shocked at the reverend's condition. In September doctors advised that Holtjes needed to return to America, where he could recuperate at the

Chapter 10	Establishing the Hong Kong Mission – 1949 -1950

After ten months, the Hong Kong mission was operating programs in Kowloon and at Rennie's Mill, where a wood chapel was to replace the original thatched mat shed. Gertrude Simon lived in small quarters behind the building that was both St. Johns church and Concordia Bible Institute. Rev. Herb Hinz, center lower photo, replaced the ailing Rev. Holt. Reinforcements would not be sent for over a year.

Walther League operated TB sanitarium at Wheat Ridge, Colorado. The family sailed October 6, and would not return for nearly three years. Complicating the situation, the doctor limited Chang to preaching one sermon per week, due to his weakness.

Yet in the midst of all this change, remarkably good things were happening. Four days before the Holtjes sailed, he baptized 23 individuals at Heung Kong College and eight more at the refugee camp, bringing the total of newly baptized Chinese to 84. Principal Chen from Heung Kong College began taking Bible lessons, against the wishes of his traditional family. Gertrude Simon had opened the Concordia Bible Institute (CBI). (The Holtjes would return to HK in late 1953; the Bible Institute would become Concordia Seminary; the Rennie's Mill clinic would become Haven of Hope sanatarium; and Martha Boss's crafters would become Lutheran Handicrafts.)

A storefront with an upstairs room in a new building at 232 Tai Po Road was procured after much negotiation, replacing arrangements at the Basel Mission Home. About 200 people could sit on the main floor, with four more rooms and a courtyard in back. Upstairs were five rooms besides a kitchen, bath, and verandah. Approval from the mission board to rent it arrived the same hour that the Holtje's sailed for America. The first worship service there was held October 15, 1950, conducted by the three women and Paul Chang. Missionary Herb Hinz flew in the next week to replace Rev. Holtje. Rev. Hinz had spent two years with the LCMS in Free China at Enshih and Wanhsien, and in the US Panama Canal Zone as chaplain. He had returned to the U.S. and was about to begin a mission among the Chinese of San Francisco when called to replace ailing Missionary Holtje. It was a good fit of his experience and the situation in Hong Kong. He would remain with the LCMS and LCHKS until his death in 1981.

Savior Lutheran Church was thus launched as sanctuary, school, mission office, warehouse, residence, and the mother church of the LCMS in the colony. It had been a remarkable ten months.

Significant Sources:

Behling, Lorraine, *The Hong Kong Letters, 1950-1959*
Carroll, John, *A Concise History of Hong Kong, 2007*
Lutheran Witness, *1952-1960*
Royal Observatory, *Typhoon, Hong Kong, 1971*

Interviews with Lorraine Behling and Paul Holt

Salvation

Chapter 11 Growth of the Hong Kong Mission in the 1950s

Arrivals
1950	Hinz	Herb (earlier in China since '43)
1952	Proft	Ruth
	Thode	Elmer & Frieda Thode (earlier in China since '26)
1953	Holt (Holtje)	Wilbert & Geri (earlier in China since 1945; HK in 1950)
1954	Karner	Roy & Betty
1955	Winkler	George & Florence
1956	Kieschnick	Mel & Jane
1959	Seltz	Eugene & Clara (earlier in China since 1929)
	Gihring	Ralph & Dorothy (business manager; Japan since 1957)
1960	Schmidt	Harold & Ruth
	Galster	Len & Ruth

Departures
1959	Behling	Lorraine

Death
1959	Gihring	Ralph	(age 30 - polio)

Concordia Bible Institute at Rennie's Mill in 1951. Classes were taught, primarily, by Herb Hinz (far left) and Gertrude Simon (third from right). In five years, 105 students would graduate, many migrating to Taiwan or America. Several went on to become Pastors and leaders of the Hong Kong Synod.

"I have been crucified with Christ. It is no longer I who live, but Christ who lives in me. And the life I now live in the flesh I live by faith in the Son of God, who loved me and gave himself for me."

Galatians 2:20 (ESV)

Chapter 11

Growth of the Hong Kong Mission in the 1950s

Every day in 1951, an estimated 5000 refugees continued to pour across the Hong Kong border. This migration was called the Red Tide. Uprooted and disoriented Chinese refugees lived in shelters of cardboard, tin sheeting, or straw and thatch on the many hillsides and any open spaces on the Kowloon peninsula and Hong Kong Island. Some streets became unofficial camps, as did open areas under stairways and any available protected space. Over one million new dwellers inundated social services. They climbed over the wire fences; they crawled past guard posts, they came in *sampans* and ferries from Macau. Some were able to move on to Taiwan, Southeast Asia, or the Americas. Others would never leave Hong Kong.

Refugees Everywhere

Anxiety over the future of the British colony dominated most aspects of daily life. Fear was that any day Communist forces could and would overtake this remaining piece of Chinese soil. There was no guarantee of permanence, and most decisions about mission planning assumed a transitory and uncertain future. Many other Protestant groups had chosen to bypass Hong Kong altogether.

In November 1951, the American Consulate surmised that the Communist Chinese were not going to take over the British Crown Colony, and issued a statement indicating that is was probably safe for expatriate families to return.

A massive surge of refugees during a four-month period in 1952 further taxed the Colony's ability to absorb them. Immigration officials began limiting new arrivals to 50 per day. Government forcibly detained and returned thousands to the mainland. Hong Kong residents brought food and clothing to fenced-off throngs awaiting deportation. Yet, an estimated 60,000 were able to enter during that time.

This was indeed an epic humanitarian tragedy. Rickety shacks of wood or sheet metal scraps were precariously anchored on granite outcrops; flimsy tents of tarpaulin or tar-paper were held up with bamboo poles; squatter settlements filled steep gullies and watercourses; any flat rooftop was usurped for flimsy "lean-to" tenements; maggot-infested sheds were strewn about urban areas in terraces of poverty; the ancient wall-less Kowloon walled city harbored humanity in a miserable sinkhole of open sewers and dark

Chapter 11　　　　　　　　　　　　　Growth of the Hong Kong Mission in the 1950s

A great influx of new refugees came to Hong Kong in 1952, as a result of famine conditions across the border. New settlers found living spaces atop roofs and amidst the ravines of islands and the peninsula. World relief organizations continued supplying food and clothing. Residents also found fresh daily produce in the large street markets, which had always been part of the Hong Kong cityscape.

narrow refuse-strewn alleys. Sanitation and clean water were nearly non-existent. Any edible morsel—even grass or tree bark—was a sought-after prize. Few had any money or valuables to barter; most came with just the clothes on their backs; there was little possibility of employment. Proud, once energetic intellectuals of the middle and upper classes were reduced to doing any manual labor, or the demeaning activity of begging.

In addition to food shortages for the new arrivals, Hong Kong's water system quickly proved to be inadequate for the burgeoning populace. Old catchments or nullahs ringed the slopes of Hong Kong Island, diverting typhoon rainfall into several pre-war reservoirs. Water at the camps usually came through a single spigot, at which long lines of refugees with cans or buckets patiently awaited their turn. Drinking water had to be boiled . . . always!

Various systems of water rationing were introduced; sometimes available just four hours each day. Until 1964 when a water supply from China became guaranteed, water rationing was a constant reality, occurring for more than 300 days some years. Common activities—laundry, personal hygiene, and food preparation—were impacted. Industrial use of water took priority over domestic demands. In the later 1950s, a separate system of seawater was piped in to use for toilet-flushing, reducing the strain on the fresh-water reservoirs by 30%.

Yet within a year, the four LCMS missionaries and evangelist Paul Chang had established Sunday school and worship services. They began active refugee work, initiated a Bible School and Bible Reading Correspondence course, started a bi-monthly newsletter, provided first-aid, received and sorted donated clothing and Sunday school materials. At the same time, they taught English and Bible classes at four Anglo-Chinese schools in order to use space rent-free in which to meet with groups of curious youngsters and adults.

Rev. Holtje had baptized two more groups of new Christians for a total of 173 souls in the mission, before his October departure. Several future church workers were in the first group. One newly baptized member from a group at Stanley prison, John Yunnan Wei, took up residence in Portuguese Macau, 40 miles southwest across the Pearl River estuary, and began witnessing and organizing about 60 people in a refugee camp. Life and ministry were provisional, with the belief that the refugee situation was short-term, and that both Chinese and expatriates would soon return to their home countries.

That was not to be.

Rennie's Mill Camp

Population in the isolated camp at Junk Bay had risen in a year from 7000 to 20,000, the result of the heavy influx in 1952. PRC guards had looked the other way as hoards of new refugees streamed past the barbed wire border and the mile-wide "closed area." Mandarin was the language of most newcomers, limiting refugee assimilation into Cantonese-speaking Hong Kong. Rennie's Mill was the largest of the nationalist camps, and sometimes the target of mischief from local Communist sympathizers, hence the concern of Colonial authorities.

Each day at camp began with the ringing of the chapel gong. Assembled refugees filed into the chapel classroom, prayed, sang hymns written on a large chart, and read in unison from their own mimeographed copy of the Gospel of St. John. Daily memorization of selected verses was followed by prayers for faith, hope, health, and the relief of China. Included were prayers for missionaries Holtje and Schalow, for those Christians still held by the PRC, and for an opportunity for return to the mainland.

Refugees were allotted one cup of cooked rice twice each day on a government ticket system. People stood in line with pails or old

Chapter 11 Growth of the Hong Kong Mission in the 1950s

At Concordia Bible Institute, instruction in the chapel/classroom utilized natural light to read the large written charts. Materials were also reproduced by mimeograph at CBI or the hectograph at Savior mission.

Martha Boss, Herb Hinz, and Gertrude Simon worked closely with adults and children in the refugee camp at Rennie's Mill, training both men and women as evangelists, One major goal was to train workers to return to China if and when the situation there might change.

tin cans waiting for their family's portions, which they would then take back to their huts to share and eat.

Concordia Bible Institute

A $300 donation from students at Concordia Junior College in Ft. Wayne, Indiana, was used to replace the original thatch-roofed chapel in Rennie's Mill camp. A recent typhoon had made near ruins of the old structure, and the dilapidated bamboo matshed was soon replaced with bricks and sheet metal. Dedicated on February 25, 1951, it doubled as St. John's Lutheran Church and Concordia Bible Institute. A small shed behind the chapel became Miss Simon's residence and office.

Gertrude Simon's work at the CBI (also called Tiao Ching Ling Bible School) grew to the point that new students had to wait to enroll until the first class graduated in 1952. Martha Boss, Paul Chang, and Herb Hinz traveled to the camp two days each week to help with teaching. Lorraine Behling usually taught and managed the chapel at Savior Lutheran Mission back in the city at Sham Shui Po. Several men and boys who would later become leaders, teachers, and pastors were part of the earliest classes—Andrew Chiu (age 30), Timothy Lan (age 26), Phillip Ho (age 23), Daniel Lee (age 15). Simon was loving yet strict, trained as a deaconess/nurse. She ran a tight ship, insisting that men and women sit traditionally on opposite sides of the classroom. All teachers and students spoke Mandarin, the language of their home regions.

Simon's curriculum involved two years of study, based on her detailed hand-written syllabus. Her mantra to the students was, "Are you a Galatians 2:20 Christian?" Materials were duplicated by hectograph-stenciled prints, on the machine that Mrs. Holtje had carried to Hong Kong when she arrived in 1950.

On Reformation Day afternoon (also Generalissimo Chiang Kai-shek's birthday) a fire erupted on the camp hillside, destroying over 200 tar paper shacks. Simon's shed was consumed, along with Bibles, library materials, mimeograph machine, kerosene projector and furniture. Downhill, praying students surrounded the new wood and stone chapel. Flames burned right up to that building on two sides, but it was spared. Communist elements, who had declared the Rennie's Mill camp as a public enemy of the PRC, were blamed for the fire.

CBI students occasionally made the long trip into Kowloon to serve at Savior Church. A possible relocation of the school to the nearby village of Sai Kung was explored, but eventually abandoned when the building there was found to need much repair work. Student "personal work" involved doing waitang on the streets of Kowloon, teaching Sunday school, talking with children while the missionaries visited adults, and publishing a small newspaper called the *Weekly Lutheran*.

Field work was also done among refugees in the camp and at a nearby village. Student Silas Chang made friends with several families, including a bean-curd grinder and a wine merchant. Sometimes they met in the village tea shop which was the local gathering place, and sang and prayed in front of the Buddhist temple. Harold Ren was one who would read parts of the Bible and Catechism aloud, show filmstrips using a kerosene projector (there was no electricity), distribute copies of the *Weekly Lutheran*, and end each Saturday visit with prayer. CBI students also served in Lye Muen [Lei Yue Mun] village at the eastern passage into the harbor.

Paul Chang began visiting a group of inmates at Stanley Prison (the same fortress where the Buuck and Ziegler families had been interned ten years earlier). A group of prisoners began taking Lorraine's Bible Reading Correspondence Course as a re-

Chapter 11 — Growth of the Hong Kong Mission in the 1950s

Lutheran Hour broadcasting started in 1951, carried on Redifusion, using locally generated Chinese language programs. Ruth Proft brought a tape recorder with her from the States in 1952, and programs were then taped in the apartment of the women missionaries. Rallies in Hong Kong and Macau attended by Dr. Eugene Berterman celebrated success in the Correspondence course.

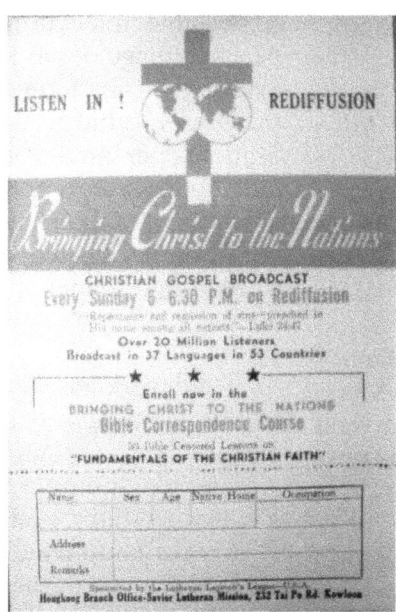

Dr. Walter A Maier, Lutheran Hour speaker (seated) and Dr. Eugene Bertermann on the right.

Cha Kwo Ling chapel

sult of Chang's monthly visits. Several were evangelizing among other inmates. When released, John Wei started his work among refugees in Macau.

Visits were also made regularly to medical patients at two crowded Chinese hospitals, Kwang Hwa and Tung Hwa. Several patients were brought to faith in Christ during their final hours through one-to-one witnessing, Bible reading, and prayer.

One of the last three LCMS missionaries still in China was released when Rev. Frederick Schalow came across the border in May 1951. He was undernourished and in need of rest, yet eager to continue work with the Chinese. He had been tried by the court in Hankow for "disturbing the economic stability of China," and given a suspended sentence of six months. Schalow spent several months in Hong Kong, helping the nascent mission while awaiting travel arrangements to rejoin his family. After a furlough in the U.S., the Schalows returned to serve Taiwan in 1953.

A Working Vacation in 1951

After intense work for 18 months, Boss and Behling took a four-day trip north via freighter in July, to attend the third annual Japan missionary conference in Tokyo. They reunited with several former China missionaries and renewed friendships with nurses Heidi Mueller and Norma Lenschow. BFM director O. H. Schmidt was also present. Focus was on methods of evangelism and issues around schooling, especially seminaries. There was much to share over Bible study, worship, hymn singing, and work seminars, resulting in camaraderie and fellowship.

The Japanese mission had begun in 1948, mostly by displaced missionaries exiting China. Working on Honshu and Hokkaido, they had purchased a four-story former Presbyterian seminary, re-purposing it into the "Tokyo Lutheran Center." There was also a Bible Institute. These developments would eventually foster indigenization and the establishment of local congregations, so that the Japan Lutheran Church grew to become a sister church with the Missouri Synod in 1970.

Coincidently, by just a few days, the Hong Kong women had missed crossing paths with Olive Gruen. The former China missionary deaconess visited Tokyo and several LCMS missionaries, while sailing to Taiwan to begin work with relocated Hong Kong CBI students. Her work would establish the Taiwan Mission (see Chapter 16).

Lorraine and Martha returned to Hong Kong much encouraged by their time with their LCMS co-workers. During their absence, some money had disappeared from their apartment above Savior Church. They were disappointed, but undaunted.

Radio Opportunity - The Lutheran Hour

Rev. Eugene Bertermann visited Hong Kong in September 1951, holding several evangelism services. He represented the LCMS' *Lutheran Hour* radio ministry, initiating HK broadcasts sponsored by the Lutheran Laymen's League (LLL). Herb Hinz coordinated the broadcasts. Translated into Cantonese, sermons were provided by Paul Chang and Isaac Mah, a former professor of education at a Canton university. Rev. Hinz usually wrote the original sermons, and occasionally a special speaker was engaged.

Eventually, tapes for the broadcasts were made in a flat at #227 Tung Tsoi St, residence of three mission women. They used a reel-to-reel Wollensak tape recorder that had been provided by the father of newly arrived missionary Ruth Proft. Blankets and quilts were hung to cover walls and windows in an effort to minimize ambient noises. Music came separately from the local choir at Saviour Church, directed by Lorraine Behling. Within four months, over 700 listeners were en-

Chapter 11 Growth of the Hong Kong Mission in the 1950s

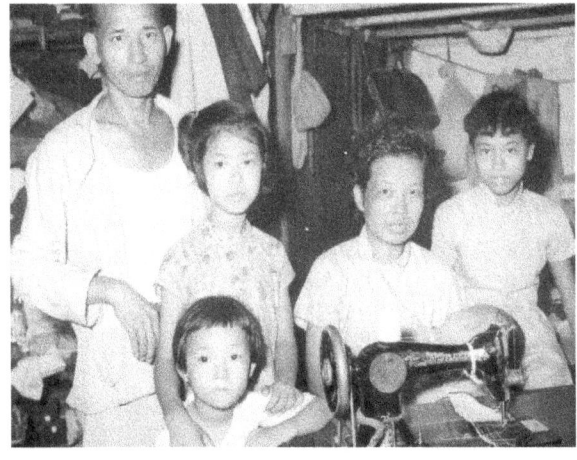

Refugee women found employment doing piecework sewing, which they could finish in their homes. Training through various agencies taught them the skills to use sewing machines so that they could work in factories.

Other employment could be found in noodle and other food factories

Using a flannelboard, missionary Len Galster illustrates Bible stories.

rolled in the Lutheran Hour correspondence course.

A colony-wide Lutheran Hour rally was held on November 10, 1952 to celebrate the completion of the "Fundamentals of Christian Faith" correspondence course by 117 listeners. Over 600 were in attendance at the event, organized by Miss Behling. Also celebrated was the increasing number of broadcasts in Cantonese from Singapore and from Kuala Lumpur and Penang in Malaya. Clement Chen was baptized on November 2, the first convert from the radio broadcasts. He became a member of Savior Lutheran's choir, the English Bible class, and was soon teaching Sunday school.

Broadcasts would continue through 1955, when Government policies towards religious broadcasting were changed.

Lutheran Handicrafts

Employment possibilities were almost non-existent for the newcomers. From its earliest days, Hong Kong had been a trade and entrepôt port, not a manufacturing community. The small industry became endangered under the United Nations embargo. With hillsides chock-a-block with willing laborers, local educated business people with minimal capital began innovating and establishing factories to produce textiles, followed by sewn finish work and embroidery. Toys and plastic flowers (a new American fad at the time) were assembled in huts and shanties from parts stamped or molded in nearby shops. Transistor radios, a recent invention, were assembled in the thousands. A technique was discovered for the mass production of wheat noodles, and a food industry was born. Cheap and abundant labor made it all possible.

Many charities experimented with projects that could help destitute refugees earn their "rice bowl" and maintain a bit of dignity. The LWF, YWCA, Church World Service, and private firms such as Kadoori Farms came up with many schemes. One refugee woman asked Martha Boss to buy some dolls that she had made, so that she could afford food for her family. This soon led to a cottage industry. Simon began encouraging women isolated at Rennie's Mill to produce cross-stitch work. The refugees started making hand-embroidered clothing, table settings, and gloves. Men at the camp fabricated handicraft items from bamboo and wood. Simon and Boss would buy materials, pay the workers from their own funds, and market the goods to overseas customers through church and family.

It was not long before women in stateside LWML chapters and other women's groups began ordering the hand-crafted items. A small paragraph in the *Hong Kong Letter* advertised:

For Sale: Hand-painted stationery, embroidered table cloths and scarves and woolen cross-stitched hand-bags. These are all products made by the refugees at Rennie's Mill Camp. Anyone interested write Miss Simon for further details.

Simon and Boss did this in their free time, only after all official work was done for the day. The effort would morph into the entity called "Lutheran Handicrafts." In January of 1953, Savior Lutheran Mission, the Norwegian Lutheran Mission, and the Swedish Free Mission organized to form the Rennie's Mill Missions Welfare Industry. The groundwork had been laid to provide income for the unemployed that would continue over 40 years. Products were sold from the "Welfare Handicrafts" shop in Kowloon on the Salisbury Road tourist route. In that shop, six handicraft societies sold their products to pedestrians bound for the Star Ferry. Orders for products were received from women's groups in Britain, Canada, and the U.S.

When Miss Simon took furlough in 1954, Martha moved out to Rennie's Mill. She assumed the full time role as teacher/deaconess and combined the doll and handicrafts op-

Chapter 11 — Growth of the Hong Kong Mission in the 1950s

Drama and pageant were popular methods to teach the Easter story. Fully costumed students acted out scenes on a hillside near Savior Church. The multi-purpose storefront faced busy TaiPo Road. Pointed arches were installed to distinguish a religious character.

erations, keeping over 50 people employed. Gertrude also launched a book store near Kai Tak airport. Funding came from friends in the States, mostly Grace Lutheran Church of New York.

Savior Lutheran Mission

Savior Lutheran Chapel (aka Kowloon Chapel, aka Saviour Church) had been established in October 1950, just a short walk from the Shek Kip Mei refugee area. Sunday school classes in Kowloon multiplied—four met in the rear courtyard of Savior Mission; four in the chapel; one on the porch upstairs; one in Gertrude's bedroom; an English- speaking class met in the office; and a Cantonese Bible group used the living room. Flannel board stories held the attention of children despite fussing younger babies sometimes strapped to the backs of older brothers and sisters. Walter, a new Chinese Christian, began teaching English and a Bible class to about 60 children in a nearby wooden hut. Several students returned midweek, hoping for more stories.

Sunday worship services continued at the Zenith Theater, with smaller gatherings at Savior in the small multi-purpose chapel area. A very active youth group met Saturday evenings at Saviour, although there were also grandmothers and babies present. Churchcraft slides (from CPH) of Bible stories and filmstrips from the Walther League were shown, as were movies from Moody Bible Institute of Chicago. LCMS television in America was generating a weekly series called *This is the Life* about Christian living, and although the missionaries tried unsuccessfully to obtain film copies, they did obtain several other LCMS 16mm films. In the summer, many youth attended a week-long camp which greatly reinforced their sense of community and dedication to their new faith.

Friday evenings were designated for younger children's activities, as they also wanted to be included in the various worship and recreational activities at Savior.

Evangelism took place in many forms. Boss and Evangelist Chang made house calls, following up with families who had visited the church. They often got involved in family difficulties over health, employment, severed communication with the mainland, poverty, and Chinese traditions. Free "Bible portions" were handed to interested pedestrians on the street corners. The focus was on inviting people to worship.

One energetic teenager who found Christ at #232 TaiPo Road was a self-described "street urchin." He admits to being a troublemaker and loner when he first saw a sign about a magic-lantern show in the shopfront chapel window. He attended the slide show, found a friendly group of young people and caring adults, and got involved with Saviour Lutheran. When he was baptized a year later by Rev. Hinz in 1951, Miss Boss gave him the Christian name of Daniel, because he had survived the lion's den of life. Daniel Lee was soon telling Bible stories to the Friday night youth gatherings, and helping with translation. Daniel attended the Basel Mission English Secondary School, and Grantham College. He went on to teach and administer in Lutheran schools in both Hong Kong and the U.S. Daniel Lee became a pastor, and continues to serve his Lord in Hong Kong.

Rev. Martin Chiang, previously with a different denomination in China, joined the LCMS mission, and helped open a third station, in 1951. Grace Chapel, was opened on Hong Kong Island in a dingy upper flat at #265 Des Voeux Rd West, in very crowded Sai Wan, near Western Market and the harbormaster's office. His ministry would eventually bring him to Canada.

Relief Work

Overwhelming needs for housing, food, clothing, and medical help of the transient masses were constant in Hong Kong. The undercurrent of survival pervaded daily life. Feeding and housing an estimated two million civilian refugees strained the resources of local government, charitable and religious

Chapter 11 Growth of the Hong Kong Mission in the 1950s

Milk, and nutritious foods, were distributed by Lutheran World Relief and other agencies. Refugees, once stable and prosperous families in China, adapted to the unstable existence as squatters, dealing with hunger and health issues as they occupied concrete resettlement blocks.

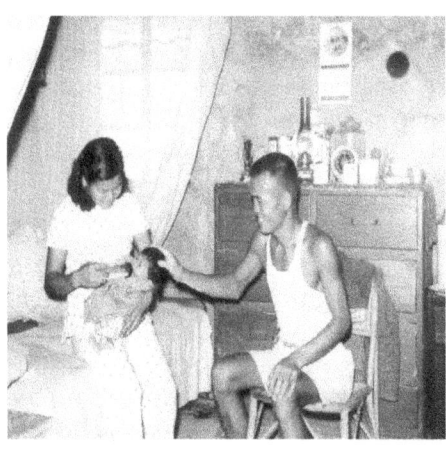

relief agencies, and involved international organizations on a scale never before seen. Food aid and medical services were coordinated between Government, religious, and charitable organizations by the Hong Kong Council of Social Service. The Maryknoll Sisters provided major services, as did CARE (Cooperative for American Remittances to Everywhere) and the World Council of Churches.

Soon, the Lutheran World Federation (LWF) also became a major contributor, supplying food, powdered milk, and health services. The fledgling pan-Lutheran Swiss-based organization had only been formed in 1946, but soon mobilized worldwide resources to provide basic food and medical care in many of the refugee areas. The relief agencies of the new United Nations, and many smaller international groups worked to house and feed the dislocated humanity.

The Korean conflict embargo was lifted in 1953. Shipping slowly returned to normal. In the chaos of refugee-strewn Kowloon, several denominations helped with relief efforts, established hospitals and clinics, and witnessed a social gospel message to potential converts.

Exempt from the embargo, boxes of used clothing and surplus Sunday school materials began arriving at the mission in larger quantities—at one time there were over 200 boxes waiting to be sorted. American congregations, church groups, and individuals donated goods and money. LCMS groups continued sending clothing, and many LWML and Walther League chapters were able to ship new and used clothing (not all of it well-laundered). Several donors were previous missionaries, or families of the missionaries, and in a few cases, individuals who would become missionaries. Donations had to be sorted before distribution both at Saviour and at Rennie's Mill. The room Behling and Boss slept in was often stacked high with boxes of Sunday school leaflets and piles of clothing. Monies were also donated for supplies and furnishings of Savior Chapel.

By September, the Tai Po Road space was busy night and day, and more space was needed for church activities. An adjacent building was rented. The missionaries had relocated to another living space, four blocks away on Tung Tsoi Street. The quarters were renovated, the Lutheran Hour office was set up, and a space with a piano and reading materials was designated as a recreation center. A more dignified facade replaced the old storefront. The new front was shaped into three gothic arches and made of pearly-textured paneling. Large bright red characters in Chinese and English proclaimed that this was a Christian church—Saviour Lutheran Mission!

Back Home

Articles about Hong Kong appeared in the *Lutheran Witness*, although emphasis was still being placed on missionary situations on the mainland. A two-page article by Lorraine Behling about the new Hong Kong mission in April of 1952 included photos. A set of 99 color slides, explaining the Hong Kong mission were made available to church groups upon request. The Board for Foreign Missions eventually had three sets of these slides in circulation. None of those can be located at the time of this writing.

Significant Changes – 1952

New BFM assistant director Rev. H. H. Koppelmann spent four weeks with the missionaries in Hong Kong in March, 1952. He visited locations, surveyed work in progress, and presented a series of lectures to mission workers. Several considerations were discussed after Koppelmann's first two weeks of observations, reinforcing suggestions from Dr. O. H. Schmidt in St. Louis. These included:

1) re-direction and emphasis on the local Cantonese language;

2) focus on establishing an indige-

Chapter 11   Growth of the Hong Kong Mission in the 1950s

Schooling for newly arrived youngsters was not universally available. Government encouraged church and charity organizations to operate schools, which carried out a recommended curriculum. Veteran teacher Gertrude Simon focused on adults while Frieda Thode, recently released with husband Elmer from China, helped in establishing elementary schools.

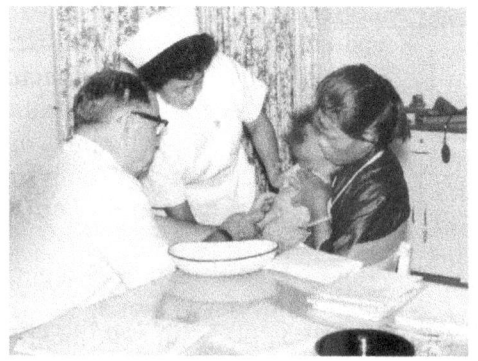

nous Hong Kong church;

    3) refining of the Bible school curriculum;

    4) inclusion of three graduating Norwegian Seminary evangelists;

    5) authorization by the board to open a seminary by September 1953;

    6) extending divine calls to at least two additional men to the mission.

After waiting nearly eight months for visa and travel arrangements, Ruth Proft arrived May 15, 1952, on the *SS President McKinley*. She was the first LCMS worker in Hong Kong without prior experience in China. Her previous five years had been in public health nursing, teaching, and work with the Visiting Nurse Association of St. Louis. She was also an organist, a skill learned from her father. She had once shared an apartment in St. Louis with Lorraine, who had encouraged Ruth to join the Mission. Her HK assignment was initially for six months, since Hong Kong was still unsettled because of Chinese troop movements related to the Korean War.

At Behling's suggestion, Ruth shipped a refrigerator and transformer along with her meager possessions. To make the most of moving allowance funds, the BFM had the shelving removed and filled the fridge with hymnals for the mission. Proft had been told to convince "those determined women" that they should quit Hong Kong and return home. But the Koppelmann visit changed the direction of the mission. No one left, and now there were four determined women and Herb Hintz.

Once on the scene, Ruth realized the work to be done, and got busy. She had been discouraged from learning Cantonese, since so much time was required. But she soon launched full bore into Cantonese language study. She couldn't wait to start working in any way in the Kowloon area. Hours were spent sorting through the boxes of donated clothing, some of which had developed mildew and mold in the humid climate. She began teaching a catechism class through an interpreter. Ruth soon discovered the challenge of teaching Christian spiritual concepts via a non-Christian interpreter. Her enthusiasm and flexibility provided spiritual adrenaline for those around her.

With training from the Lutheran School of Nursing in St. Louis, Proft worked with refugees around Shek Kip Mei. She found that refugees feared the British *dai bye* (big nose) medical clinics with their imposing hospitals, so she often accompanied clients to the clinics. She became known as "Barnabas" (the encourager). Ruth championed the drinking of milk provided by refugee organizations in the diets of children. She put a bit of sugar into the milk to first convince youngsters to sample it. Cheese was frequently distributed by relief organizations, but also alien to the Chinese diet. She taught children how to eat it with crackers. Hand-washing was also demonstrated, using scarce water frugally.

A Hillman station wagon was purchased for the mission, which was used to haul materials to and from Rennie's Mill, and to transport people and supplies at Savior Church. Proft was the only staff who qualified for a driver's license. Driver-chauffeur became part of her job description.

The last two of the LCMS mainland missionaries, Elmer and Frieda Thode, were released after nearly three years of house arrest in Hankow,. Reluctantly applying for an exit visa from the PRC, they had been fined about US $2,700 by the agrarian government movement for supposed damages to the swampy rice-land on which the 1932 Hankow seminary had been built. The Thodes reached Hong Kong on July 10, 1952, then waited three months for passage home.

Not just biding their time, they assisted Hinz and the women with Mandarin-speaking refugees. Rev. Thode spent hours in private instruction, offered his guidance and experience, and began exploring the concept of a seminary. Frieda gave organ lessons, began

Chapter 11   Growth of the Hong Kong Mission in the 1950s

Education soon became a major element in the Lutheran mission, teaching with a minimum of equipment or textbooks. Student desks were more often long narrow tables at which at least two students were seated. In the midst of crowded Tai Kok Tsui, a large cross marked the location of the chapel and classroom.

36

Cantonese instruction, and helped set up living arrangements for the mission's women on Tung Tsoi Street. Quarters for Hinz and the Thodes were at the Basel Home nearby. Simon continued to live in her shed at Rennie's Mill. The Thodes sailed in October for an overdue home leave. Frieda had experienced three evacuations, having been in China with only two furloughs since 1923. They would return in 1953, to serve another twelve years in the Hong Kong mission.

Three Chinese Lutheran men were accepted as evangelists with the LCMS. These were students at the Norwegian Lutheran Synod's relocated Shekow Seminary at Shatin in the New Territories. The Norwegian church had decided not to develop mission work in Hong Kong, and these men—Chang, Jiang, and Lee—wanted to serve Christ locally. They began teaching in the Bible School, worked with new converts, and established local congregations among pockets of new Lutheran Christians.

Education

From the earliest days of the mission, the need for schools was constantly discussed. All four missionaries had taught English in various HK schools, but the value of church schools was in daily reinforcement of the Christian message. Contending forces and philosophies were a constant presence in the colony, especially amongst refugee elements. Rev. Hinz was particularly concerned about the Jehovah's Witnesses, and the teachings of the Seventh-Day Adventists

Several Christian groups were active in operating local schools, especially Roman Catholics, Baptists, and Anglicans. Among Lutherans, the Norwegians had operated a middle school and the Rhenish church ran primary schools. At the time, there was no compulsory education in the British Colony, nor were there enough places for all school-age children. Attendance at middle schools was by tuition, but highly desired, and was the norm for a successful Hong Kong citizen. "Colleges," all private and usually Christian-run, were the equivalent to American high schools.

Sunday school had been the first enterprise of the women at the Basel Mission Home. Reaching children should lead to reaching mothers and, hopefully, the fathers as well. New Christians were enthusiastic in their Bible study. Bibles were usually carried to worship services. Hymn singing quickly gained popularity. Although Christian tunes were alien to native musical ears, few Chinese folk tunes were used because of their association with the mainland regime. With persistence, Lorraine formed and conducted a choir, singing Chinese words to German hymn tunes. A choral tradition was thus established with Chinese Lutherans.

Galatians 2:20

Gertrude Simon had initiated the Bible School at Rennie's Mill, mentioned earlier, as soon as the government-assigned plot was available. She had approval from Rev. Holt but he was unable to provide any financing, materials, or curriculum. Students were teenagers and adults from the camp. Her education and deaconess training convinced her that Christian education in the spirit of Galatians 2:20 was essential for the new converts. Her long range goal was the training of 500 men to be able to return to the mainland as evangelists. Twenty-nine men had graduated from the Institute by mid-1953; 107 had completed the program by 1955. Stateside donations were solicited to support each CBI student. Graduates worked in Hong Kong, or if they could obtain visas, migrated to Taiwan or Malaya to continue as evangelists.

A class was begun at Savior mission on Tai Po Road for illiterate women. Mrs. Isaac Mah led sessions by first reading Bible stories, often reinforced with a filmstrip. Memorization of related Bible passages followed. The story would be written in simple characters on a blackboard, and the women were taught to copy them. Another group of more

Chapter 11　　　　　　　　　　　Growth of the Hong Kong Mission in the 1950s

Wilbert and Geri Holt returned after his 3-year recovery from TB at Wheat Ridge, resuming involvement with schools and congregations. Connections were made with the Lutheran Literature Society and with the U.S. servicemen's center at Fenwick Pier.

During the same period, Paul Chang was ordained and soon accepted a call to True Light Chinese congregation in New York City

38

educated women worked with Behling, who read Bible stories to the group, followed by instructions from Mrs. Yee on how to sew, knit, crochet, and bake.

Mission work in private homes evolved when Lorraine or Ruth visited women who had attended services at Savior. Showing the filmstrips and telling Bible stories soon attracted relatives and neighbors, and another form of outreach was inadvertently created, similar to the methods used by Bible women back in China. Some women there did function as unofficial Bible women with Lutherans, although their work is rarely mentioned in LCMS writings. The term never appears in writings of the LCMS Hong Kong mission.

The need for Lutheran literature was acute. Rapid evangelism required follow-up literature to reinforce new Christians in their faith and biblical knowledge. Most materials were translations of Lutheran writings. Illustrations were taken from Renaissance depictions of Bible stories and characters. It would be a few years before Christian materials specifically addressing Chinese traditions would be printed.

While some materials were available through the Roman Catholic press and other groups, the nine Lutheran mission groups in Hong Kong decided to establish the Lutheran Missions Literature Society (LMLS). Within a year, reprinted and newly-translated books were coming off the press. The largest project completed was a new edition of the Lutheran hymnal, *Hymns of Praise*, a joint project of the LMLS and the Lutheran Seminary faculty at Tao Fung Shan, overlooking Shatin. Several indigenous translators were included as part of a plan to bring local Chinese believers into literature work. Sunday school materials and theological works were also printed.

How much of the LMLS materials were utilized by the LCMS is not recorded. The Missouri Synod had printed 10,000 copies of its own 16-page booklet entitled *Basic Teachings of Christianity*. The topics covered were the Bible, law and gospel, the Ten Commandments, the Apostle's Creed, the Lord's Prayer, the Lord's Supper, Baptism, the Office of Keys, and the end of the world.

Fenwick Pier

Lorraine and Ruth found time to become involved in the local Hong Kong expat community. They practiced and performed in a musical, *Elijah*, with the Hong Kong Singers. Ruth volunteered at Fenwick Pier, the social center for American sailors and other non-British military on shore leave. Fenwick Pier, established in 1953, was not part of the LCMS mission. Director Gordon DePree and local American volunteers aided military men in connecting with missionaries, local American families, and attending English worship services. Seamen often helped with social service projects, such as work with the blind. Co-sponsoring programs at Fenwick were the American Women's Association (AWA) and the social welfare department of the Government. This ministry to sailors was a significant development in chaplaincy work, more so in the 1960s, during the years of the Vietnam conflict.

Wilbert Holtje and wife Geri (a nurse) returned to Hong Kong in November 1953, after nearly three years of TB rehabilitation. Holtje's name had been changed to "Holt" while in the U.S. for family business reasons. This also was a blessing for his work in Asia, as when "Holtje" was pronounced by the Chinese, the sound was like a local word for "drinking liquor." Joe Holt's second term in Hong Kong lasted until 1962, when his wife became seriously ill.

In December, veteran China missionaries Elmer and Frieda Thode returned from home leave. Martha Boss sailed with them, having taken her first furlough since 1945. At this point the Hong Kong team consisted of three Mandarin-speaking men, two with wives, two deaconesses trained in medicine and education, and one teacher. All but Ruth had experience from Mainland China.

Chapter 11　　　　　　　　　　　　　　　　Growth of the Hong Kong Mission in the 1950s

Large flat rooftops were quickly converted into schools, playgrounds, and children's clubs atop the 7-story concrete blocks. Four children's clubs and one school were operated by Lutheran congregations. The government-built walk-ups became ubiquitous in the late 1950s, each housing about 2000 tenants.

The LCMS mission under guidance from Rev. Hinz, had constructed its first permanent building—a two-story residence for missionaries at #32 Oxford Road in Kowloon Tong. (In 2010, the sale of this structure would help finance Concordia International School in Hanoi. See chapter 19).

Serving the Overseas Chinese

In February 1953, Evangelist Paul Chang married Eleanor Ho, an educated young refugee he had met in Macau. The following month, Chang was ordained into LCMS ministry, authorized by the Board of Foreign Missions. In March, they sailed for New York City, where Rev. Chang became assistant pastor at True Light Lutheran Church, the only stateside LCMS Chinese congregation at the time. The congregation originated in 1936 near Wall Street with the energies of former Methodist African missionary Mary Banta who was attracted to Walter A. Maier's Lutheran Hour messages. Chang was the first Chinese-speaking LCMS pastor in America.

Chang was to work with the founding pastor, Dr. Louis Buchheimer, especially in reaching non-English speakers in New York City's Chinatown. For six years his work brought growth to True Light. Additionally, he took on leadership in helping newly arrived Chinese negotiate the immigration process and facilitating almost 500 new arrivals towards citizenship. Beginning with Chang, graduates of CBI began to serve, witness, and be known far beyond Hong Kong, Macau, and Taiwan. Many Chinese from Rennie's Mill and Saviour Church created an extended family in New York. True Light brought Chinese ministry to the attention of the LCMS and modeled outreach to the Chinese population. The Chinatown church was destined to become the "mother church" for 34 LCMS congregations serving Chinese Americans by 2012. These churches now form CLiMB (Chinese Lutherans in Mission-Bulding).

In San Francisco, furloughed China Missionary Herb Hinz had been assigned to be missionary-at-large to the Chinese community in 1950. But before he could actively begin work there, he was re-assigned to Hong Kong to replace tuberculosis-stricken Wilbert Holtje (Holt) as described above.

In 1963, the Northern California District of the LCMS called Rev. Holt back to America as a missionary-at-large to carry the gospel to the Chinese of the Bay area. The result was the founding of the Lutheran Church of the Holy Spirit in a Chinatown storefront on Jackson Street that same year. Evangelist Amy Mui, after serving in Hong Kong and with the Lutheran World Federation, became the deaconess at Holy Spirit in 1966. Her insights into the local Chinese culture and love of Christ helped expand the church. The congregation relocated to larger quarters with financial help from the LWML, and produced ten "sons of the church" who became LCMS pastors, serving throughout the U.S. In 2012, their facilities expanded again (see Chapter 19 about current LCMS Chinese congregations).

Shek Kip Mei - December 24, 1953

Following Christmas Eve services at Savior Chapel, Daniel Lee, Rev. Hinz, and Evangelist Isaac Mah were preparing displays for the next day's events when shouts of "Fire! Fire!" caught their attention. A blaze had begun about two blocks away, on a hillside covered with shanties and refugee shelters. Dry weather and high winds fanned the flames over three square miles of cardboard, wood, and tin lean-tos, reducing the tightly crowded hillside to ashes within six hours. The blaze spared most shop fronts along Tai Po Road, including the mission church, although the men had removed valuable records and put out flare-ups started by flying cinders.

Holocsust read the *South China Morning Post's* Boxing Day headlines. The historic conflagration was to become a watershed event, much like the Great Fire of London in 1666, and the fires of Chicago (1871) and

Chapter 11   Growth of the Hong Kong Mission in the 1950s

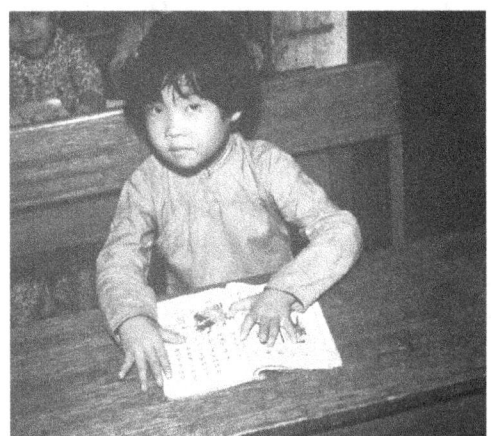

Two new resettlement blocks at Shek Kip Mei were provided to Lutheran congregations for rooftop clubs. Within the buildings, large families were provided with one space, their cooking areas on the backside and a trough drained the grey water. Shops selling every possible need occupied ground floor spaces. Below, students at the Redeemer rooftop club have recreation time between activities in the shelters at each end.

San Francisco (1906). Miraculously, there were few fatalities, but 70,000 refugees faced a new level of homelessness. Streets were filled with milling crowds who had no food or possessions, Members of Saviour Church received donated food, blankets, and clothing. Government social services, although unprepared for the vast needs of so large a helpless group, rallied local and international forces within days to deal with yet another humanitarian tragedy. Barely had the ashes cooled, when the first major Hong Kong public housing scheme materialized. Bulldozers cleared the 45-acre site, leveled the grounds, and the first government-built emergency cottages appeared within 53 days. Another fire erupted within weeks at Tai Hang Tung, rendering another 24,000 refugees homeless.

Rooftop Schools
Meeting Christ on a Rooftop

Construction of large concrete seven-story walk-up housing blocks materialized by 1955 with a new block of 400 rooms completed every week to ten days. The massive resettlement program was run by the Hong Kong Housing Authority, and partially financed by the United Nations. These "resettlement estates" were eventually constructed at 40 different Kowloon sites, including Shep Kip Mei, Wong Tai Sin, Hung Hom, Tsuen Wan, and at Chai Wan on the island. Yet, as late as 1965, an estimated 500,000 refugees still lived in squatter shacks on hillsides too steep for commercial development. Visible from passenger jets over Kowloon on final approach to Kai Tak airport, the multi-block estates became an ubiquitous presence in the Hong Kong landscape for 30 years.

A family of five was allotted a cubicle measuring 10 feet by 12 feet. Smaller families were assigned an 86 square-foot space, or were combined with other families. Semi-open communal toilets and a water spigot were located at each end of the floor. Because of rationing, the water supply was often cut off at 10:00am. An open space at the rear of each cubicle allowed a common trough for grey water and ventilation for cooking, done over small charcoal or gas burners. Average population in each block was 2000.

A level concrete roof topped each of these tenement structures, measuring about 2000 square feet. Surrounded by iron bars, there was also a large open shed at each end. Planners realized that the rooftop space could be used in many ways. One motivation was to make a safe play or recreation area for the resident children of that block. The earliest project may have been proposed by Rev. Verent J. Mills of the Christian Children's Fund. Another advocate of rooftop education was a former POW and missionary, Rev. Charles Reinbrecht of the Rhenish church, who later befriended several LCMS missionaries.

Florence Munroe of the Oriental Mission Society has been credited with initiating the first rooftop Boys' and Girls' Club in August 1955. As a precedent for rooftop usage, she had cited one roof being used by the government as a relief distribution center. Her *amah* had a relative working in the new housing area at Tai Hang Tung, who was also a Christian. With his help, the first formal application for a club was made. Within a month, it was approved.

The HK Social Welfare Department set guidelines. One condition required that these spaces were to be exclusively for children. To be a school, the organization had to register and conform with the Education Department. To accommodate as many youngsters as possible, morning and afternoon three-hour sessions were held. Some rooftops could be Boys and Girls Clubs but not actual schools. Various charitable organizations could sponsor such clubs and each was to have a management committee. Little or no rent was charged. For about $1000, the covered areas could be enclosed and used as classrooms, leaving the central space open for recreation.

Gertrude Simon applied for rooftop usage from the Department of Resettlement

Chapter 11   Growth of the Hong Kong Mission in the 1950s

Roof tops were used by congregations for meetings, worship, schools, children's activities far above the congestion of streets and markets below. Close by were the mountainous spine of Kowloon (Nine Dragons).

in Li Cheng Uk Estate in June, 1956. She was granted a roof atop block "T" in the Shek Kip Mei complex on behalf of Savior Church. Technically a club, adults were soon informally tutoring and teaching English and arithmetic. The adults were mostly educators, well-trained and experienced, but now refugees. Parents were keen for their children to obtain any education possible. Club leaders also had the opportunity to share the "one thing needful" with children, "meeting Christ on a rooftop." Savior Lutheran Church opened a second club atop block "O" at Shek Kip Mei.

Two additional rooftops were opened with the financial support of an American charity. After his visit to the Shek Kip Mei clubs, a representative of the Baker Foundation offered to fund as many new rooftop schools as the LCMS could open within twelve months. The first of these was Salvation Lutheran Boys' and Girls' Club located on the roof of block "Y" in the Wong Tai Sin Resettlement Estate. This rooftop was soon used for congregational activities in the off hours, holding a Sunday school, instruction classes, choir and other groups. This rooftop congregation had no other building.

Another club opened within the year atop block "D" in Hung Hom. Between 350 and 600 children were served at each location. As much as possible, the clubs were to be self-supporting. At each of the four clubs, a fifty-cent monthly tuition fee was charged which financed very meager salaries to staff, often refugees themselves. Monthly teacher pay (about $17.50) was below subsistence level, and some funding also came from Lutheran World Relief. LWF also provided milk, food and clothing.

A fifth rooftop, atop block #26 Chai Wan Estate on Hong Kong Island was certified as a registered school in 1962. Missionary Roy Karner supervised the development of the school with the aid of Mr. Tam Tau. The Chai Wan Lutheran Rooftop School became a government-subsidized primary school the next year, easing tuition fees. With this momentum, a new subsidized school was proposed by the general conference that would cost about $12,000, with start-up funding coming from several private groups in America, including the Southern Wisconsin District LWML.

Support of each club was to come from a sponsoring congregation thus making the operation more indigenous and less dependent on the mission. Pastors Philip Ho and Lee Kwan Rau were especially supportive. By 1963, there were 206 rooftop clubs in the colony, enrolling nearly 14,000 boys and girls. The four Lutheran clubs enrolled 1,931 children, taught by 34 Christian Chinese teachers. By the late 1970s, standardized primary schools were replacing rooftop operations throughout Hong Kong.

Concordia Lutheran School

British Hong Kong ran a unique system of subsidized primary schools, wherein two-thirds of all students in government-supervised schools were benefactors of a Grant-in-Aid scheme. Missionaries of many denominations had played a predominant role in the supervision of rural and urban schools from early on. Curriculum was an amalgam of European influences and cultures, Christian missionary practices, and traditional Chinese Confucianism. Support of the British Empire was an underlying goal. Students were intense and competitive; during the school year they were *ho m tak haan* (very much no leisure time). Education was not compulsory, schools required tuition, and there was a major lack of spaces. Thousands of refugee children had no hope of an education.

The Lutheran tradition of education matched well with British goals of universal primary schooling, with its comprehensive subjects in math, English, science, social studies, the arts, and morality. Out at

Chapter 11 Growth of the Hong Kong Mission in the 1950s

Concordia Lutheran School opened amidst resettlement blocks at the base of Shek Kip Mei hill in 1957. A small local sacred shrine had to be carefully relocated before construction could begin. The Mission's first education director, Mel Kieschnick, posed with student groups and taught Bible lessons using a large illustrated flip chart.

46

Rennie's Mill, a one-room school opened in September 1951, taught by Mr. Li in a space behind the chapel. This was short-lived, because of lack of workers. In January of 1952, the Board of Foreign Missions in St. Louis approved the concept of opening a primary school in Kowloon. That May, Gertrude Simon advocated establishing primary and high schools, where graduates of the Concordia Bible Institute could teach and witness.

Three months before the 1953 Shek Kip Mei fire, the mission initiated its first successful school in the Colony—Concordia Middle School. Mostly through the efforts and research of Lorraine Behling, Concordia School opened at 232 Tai Po Road, inside Savior Church, with 44 students. Establishing a school in Hong Kong was extremely complicated due to government regulations, lack of funding, and scarcity of building sites. Behling took on the education department bureaucracy and used her teacher training to get the school up and running Sham Shui Po by September 16, 1953. Walls at Savior were moved and benches made by local carpenters. Pride and excitement inspired the dedication sermon by Rev. Martin Chiang at the opening day ceremony.

Two brothers attended Concordia School its second year. They were local Hong Kong-born residents, not recent refugees, whose father had been a KMT soldier. He served in the Volunteer Defense Forces, but was killed in the defense of Hong Kong in 1941. The Chu boys became close with the missionary teachers, some of whom ate and slept at the school during the week. Several students also slept nightly on school benches, and a small community and family atmosphere evolved. James and John were destined to become successful leaders of the church.

The co-educational school held classes at Saviour Church for the next three years. With enrollment topping 100 students in 1954, an additional classroom space was rented in an adjoining building at #65 Barwick Street. The founding principal was Isaac Mah, a former professor from Canton. Teachers included Proft, Behling, Holt, and several Chinese Christian staff. As the enrollment grew, Chinese teachers were added, including Lai Oi Man, who would one day become headmaster.

Another primary school opened in 1954, connected with St. Phillips Chapel in the fishing village of Lye Mun, near Rennie's Mill. Some of its students would migrate and become active at True Light congregation in New York. Mr. Li's St. John's School was also re-opened in Rennie's Mill Camp in 1955. Incrementally, the Lutheran education tradition was taking root in Hong Kong.

Mel Kieschnick Arrives

Education had gained such importance in the mission venture by 1956 that Lorraine Behling requested the board to send over a man to direct the various education programs she had started. An experienced young teacher-principal from Glendale, California, was called to be the mission's director of education. At 29 years old, Mel Kieschnick became the youngest person on staff. He started learning Cantonese, and began teaching at Concordia Lutheran School. Two months after his arrival, Kieschnick penned a lengthy report to Lutheran educators in the States. He noted crowded conditions and multiple usage of every room and space at the fledgling school. The chapel space became the classroom—became the lunchroom—became the study hall—became the theater. Some teaching spaces were dirt-floored. Teachers had no space for a desk, there were no pictures on the wall, and no display boards. Young students read their lessons in the traditional loud sing-song rote style used throughout Hong Kong.

Government granted an 80,000 square foot site on Tai Hang Tung Road for construction of a permanent school building in 1955. As the foundation was laid, local villagers protested the takeover of a small sacred

Chapter 11　　　　　　　　　　　　　　　Growth of the Hong Kong Mission in the 1950s

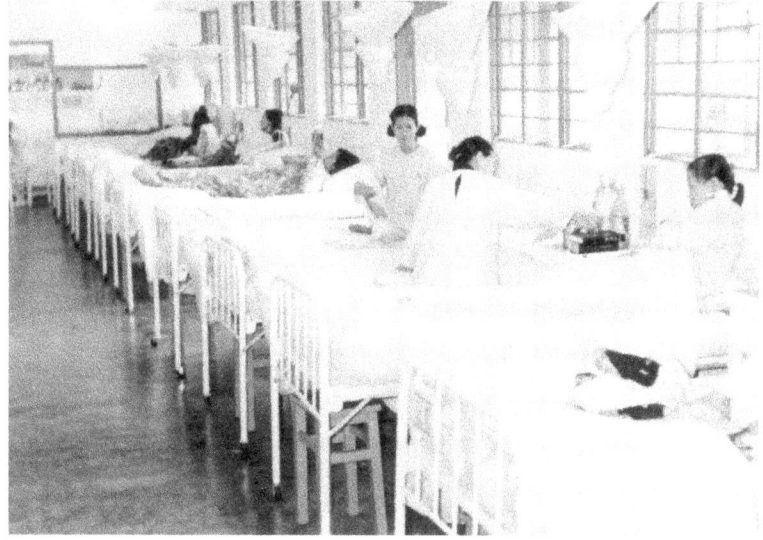

Martha Boss worked with Norwegian nurse Annie Skau in starting Haven of Hope Sanatorium overlooking Junk Bay near Rennie's Mill. The tuberculosis wards were designated for children, men, and women. The attendant nursing school graduated many classes of well-trained women.

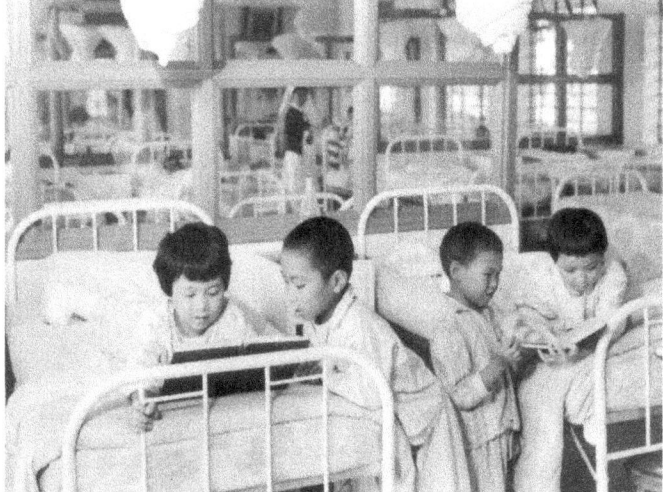

48

shrine at the middle of the site. Kieschnick had workers move the shrine a few inches each night towards the perimeter until it was beyond the fence. Relations improved with local villagers and squatters. Staffing all 38 teaching positions with Lutheran Christians was nearly attained. All teachers had to be certified by the education department. Curriculum aligned with government standards.

So it was that Concordia Lutheran Middle School's own new building, funded with a grant from the LWML, was dedicated in the winter of 1957. That spring, the first graduating class of ten students all passed the education department's "school leaving" exam, an unheard of accomplishment for any local school! At this time, the school also added kindergarten and primary sections. The initial 16 classrooms were expanded to 23 within ten years. In the 1960s, Concordia became a subsidized government school, easing the tuition burden on families. New facilities, doubling capacity, would be added in 2011.

Kieschnick also oversaw the operations of the four rooftop clubs, was the principal at Concordia, and opened six other schools. He did groundwork for Anglo-Chinese middle schools in Kwun Tong and North Point, and was instrumental in establishing the K-12 Hong Kong International School during his ten years. Through his own charisma, motivation, and the blessings of God, Kieschnick established a good working relationship between the LCMS mission and the education department. His philosophy: "When it comes to the essentials, we are all cut from the same fabric by the same Lord."

Haven of Hope

Concurrently, major changes had been taking place near Rennie's Mill. Annie Skau, a nurse from the Covenant Lutheran Church of Norway, having been imprisoned in China until March 1953, was expelled to Hong Kong because of her poor health. She returned to Norway for healing, but was determined to return within months to work with the Chinese refugees. She learned of the small cooperative "window clinic" at Rennie's Mill where tuberculosis patients—up to 600 daily—were treated. Skau met Martha Boss there and the two women worked together, sharing one thermometer, a few antiseptics, dressings, and makeshift furnishings.

Finances were desperate; then in December, ten letters arrived with donations to the clinic. Annie spent the windfall ($200) on food and medicines, distributing them on Christmas morning at the camp, the very day of the Shek Kip Mei fire. Word spread of her venture, and gifts began arriving from local and overseas welfare organizations and individuals. The refugees needed medical and mental help. Many had realized they most likely would not return to the mainland to ever see family again. The despondency, combined with poor housing, food, and sanitation often led to drug abuse and more disease.

Tuberculosis was a major health challenge throughout warm tropical climates. TB is a bacterial condition spread by breathing microscopic particles from saliva and other bodily fluids. Affecting the lungs primarily, nearly all organs are susceptible. It was known as "consumption," since the patient eventually dies from wasting away. TB was rampant in the Rennie's Mill Camp, Hong Kong, and most of South China.

Near Rennie's Mill, Miss Skau spotted a knoll above an inlet on Junk Bay. She knew that God had led her to this spot, where a TB sanatorium and chapel would one day be built. Her vision started to become a reality after Gertrude Simon's 1954 furlough. Simon shared Skau's plan with her Wisconsin family, friends, and supporters in a July newsletter. She reported that 64 TB patients were being served, that they needed housing cottages for each group of 20 patients, and that these would cost about $700 each to build. Annie's vision was for ten cottages.

Haven of Hope Tuberculosis Sanatorium officially opened in Junk Bay on October 22, 1955 with one ward of 15 children and four

Chapter 11 Growth of the Hong Kong Mission in the 1950s

The green-roofed Haven of Hope chapel and cross dominated the Junk Bay headlands, easily seen by boatmen and used for a navigation point. Pajama-clad patients participated in daily worship. The Sanatorium was composed of several buildings facing a commons.

adult patients, all members of the Rennie's Mill congregation. Other members were in training as nurses and orderlies.

About $7500 of start-up costs were donated by the Wheat Ridge Foundation. Financial donations and interest in the project began to circulate in LCMS circles. When Rev. Ed May became director of the Walther League's Denver-based Wheat Ridge Ministries in 1956, one of his tasks was to distribute a large grant designated specifically for sanatorium support. TB treatment methods in the U.S. had modernized with the use of antibiotics, and traditional residential treatment centers were closing. But he found four locations in third world countries, where there was still a need for such institutions. In true LCMS extended-family fashion, his best friend and seminary classmate, Walter Boss, knew about the Rennie's Mill clinic served by his sister Martha. Rev. May visited potential sites in Ambur, India; Ajiro, Japan; Eket, Nigeria; and Hong Kong. One third of the grant money went to the Rennie's Mill facility, enabling construction of five buildings and the chapel of Annie's vision. The rest is history.

Wheat Ridge, with funding from the Walther League's annual Christmas seal campaign, donated $64,200 for ward buildings, beds, medical and nursing care, drugs, X-ray equipment, and sponsored food and supplies for 60 patients. Several other Protestant denominations supplied the other 25% of costs. The five-building facility was completed by 1957, on the site Annie Skau had chosen overlooking Junk bay. Well known to local sailors, the lighted cross above the green-roofed chapel became a point of navigation. Martha Boss became the assistant matron under Skau's direction. Church and medical volunteers have donated countless hours since then, helping with nursing, housekeeping, and evangelism opportunities. Many TB patients have come to faith and become active church leaders through their experiences of kindness and Bible reading and instruction at Haven of Hope.

Missionary wife Clara Seltz visited Haven of Hope ten years later and described worship there in her 1969 News Letter #16:

Having had an early morning ride with my good Norwegian friend Annie Skau, I had an hour before my classes started with the nurses (Since I have been putting in more time with the Blind, I have cut my classes here to one day a week! This morning I took advantage of this hour and when I heard the chapel bell ringing at 8:30, I followed the worshippers to the nearby church on a hill overlooking Junk Bay. It's a large building with a green tiled roof - the only one having this, as it is purely picturesque and not practical. A typhoon will tear off the tiles and it is not rain-proof, but it is beautiful. Inside are high dark beams with altar and pulpit on one end, entrance on the other, and the side walls are all glass doors which were open to the cool sea breezes. This is always cool in the hottest of weather, and scenery is pleasant and peaceful.

Who were the worshippers? I counted 37 patients, some in pajamas and others in day clothes. Seven foreigners were present. Miss Boss played the piano; a couple from England, paid by their mission - she is a nurse supervising the children's ward and he is a "handy-man" able to fix anything. In his spare time he teaches English to those needing help; also an American nurse from another Mission group here who is in charge of a ward. Two male doctors, one from England and the superintendent for many years, and another American supported many years by his Mission, were present. The service was in Mandarin, with an interpreter for the Cantonese-speaking people. The pastor was one of ours (LCMS) but often they rotate from other denominations, always Chinese.

The singing was good and is all broadcast over the loudspeaker system to the wards. During the service, the birds were cheerfully flying back and forth among the rafters and chirping. It sometimes happens that they leave their mementos on the white caps of the nurses! At 9 o'clock everyone was back at their station, having received spiritual strength for the day"

Chapter 11　　　　　　　　　　　　　　Growth of the Hong Kong Mission in the 1950s

As the Mission grew, the staff became a large family. Sad times came with the death of business manager Ralph Gihring. His wife had volunteered at Haven of Hope, and his funeral a major event. The Seltz family rejoined the China mission. Eugene had arrived in 1929, Clara in 1932 and they married in Shihnan in 1933. Staff occasionally celebrated events at the floating restaurant in Aberdeen.

Back row from eft, are Frieda and "Deth"Thode, Florence and George Winkler, Roy Karner, Wilbert Holt and Ruth Proft. Front row are Lorraine Behling, Gertrude Simon, Martha Boss, Betty Karner with daughter, Geri Holt and four of their sons (eventually there were six).

The Missionary Conference

Added to the overseas missionary staff were Rev. Roy and Betty Karner in 1954. Karner's duties would include starting the ministerial training program, supervising work in nearby Macau, and establishing a congregation in North Point. Rev. George and Florence Winkler arrived in 1955 as evangelistic missionaries. Both Karner and Winkler were fresh from the seminary in St. Louis. Mel and Jane Kieschnick arrived in 1956 to direct the education program begun by Behling.

Former China missionary Eugene Seltz joined the seminary faculty in 1959. His wife Clara (Rodenbeck) was also an experienced "China hand" and deaconess-nurse, who would accomplish much in Hong Kong working with the blind.

With additional staffing came a more defined division of responsibilities in the conference. All four of the founding missionaries were present—Behling, Boss, Holt, and Simon. Ruth Proft had arrived in 1952, China veterans Holt (Geri) and Thode (Frieda) had returned in 1953. Rev. Herb Hinz's position became permanent. The Karners, Winklers, and Kieschnicks were acclimating. Chinese pastors Titus Lee and Martin Chiang completed the team. At the time, Chinese evangelists and laymen were not included in decision-making.

Shek Kip Mei (10-10) Riots

The normally uneasy tranquility of 1950s Hong Kong was briefly shattered in the fall of 1956. Local tension between pro-Peking and pro-Taipei sympathizers reflected the uneasy truce between Communist PRC and the nationalist ROC (Republic of China) elements. The anniversary of the founding of the Republic by Sun Yat Sen was October 10. Known as "Double Ten," the date is celebrated just 10 days after the PRC national day, recalling Mao Tse Tung's declaration of the People's Republic of China.

Nationalist factions broke into a melee of lawlessness and looting, agitated by one resettlement officer's order for the removal of nationalist flags at Shek Kip Mei. Disorder and mob rule increased over the next few days, with violent incidents centered in the Tsuen Wan area. Communist-owned factories and businesses were attacked especially.

British troops were brought in to reinforce the Colonial police forces. The wife of the Swiss consulate general was killed in her car in front of Savior Mission. Several bullets entered the second-story classroom. By October 12, the "disturbances" had subsided, leaving 15 people killed by rioters and 44 dead through police actions. It was a sobering experience for both local Chinese and the expatriate community. Just a month after the arrival of the Kieschnicks, the fragility and insecurity of life and work in the teeming enclave became more real. Yet life went on - worship at the Zenith Theater, construction of Concordia Middle School, and work on the Shek Kip Mei rooftop club, all near the scene of the initial riot.

Lorraine Behling resigned Hong Kong in 1959, believing that a man should take her place in order to fully establish the seminary. With her caring determination, commitment, and organization, many of her students became church leaders, businessmen, and even a filmmaker, John Woo. Harold Schmidt arrived as her replacement in 1960. Behling completed deaconess training by colloquy, married a widower with three sons, and together they owned and operated a Christian retreat center, the Oasis, for over 30 years at Desert Hot Springs, California. She prayed daily for Chinese Christians.

The mission's first full-time American business manager arrived in 1959. Ralph Gehring had previously done financial work with the LCMS Japan mission. He worked harmoniously with the Chinese business manager Chow Sing. Mr. Chow's role was as a comprador, a go-between for European firms to obtain the goods and services of the

Chapter 11   Growth of the Hong Kong Mission in the 1950s

Cromwell Chen, shown with his wife, graduated from Concordia Seminary in Springfield, Illinois, becoming pastor of Kwun Tong Lutheran church. Shown are the Board of directors for the church. Mr. Chow Sing served as business manager. Evangelism classes were held in the evenings and on weekends. A typical meeting of the missionary conference dealt with school issues such as, evangelism, congregational concerns, seminary, and building projects.

local business community. Ten months after Ralph's arrival, he contracted polio and died at age 30, leaving a wife and two children.

A former GI and recent Springfield Seminary graduate Leonard Galster would become part of the mission in 1960, accompanied by his wife, Ruth, a nurse and accomplished musician. Galster was to play a significant role in establishing English and international mission efforts in Hong Kong. Imperceptibly, two rather distinct sub-groups were evolving within the mission - recently graduated seminarians (Karner, Winkler, and Galster) and experienced "China hands" (Holt, Hintz, Thodes, Simon, Boss, and Seltz). Behling's work was supplemented by youthful educators Ruth Proft, Mel Kieschnick and Harold Schmidt. A geographic sub-group began emerging as missionaries lived and worked on different sides of the harbor.

Among a long list of goals was the production of literature for use in Sunday schools. Whereas initially Behling had requested used Sunday school materials from the States, she began designing and printing leaflets and tracts herself. A Christian professor, C. S. Hung, translated English material into Chinese. Jane Kieschnick volunteered to produce illustrations. When Behling went on furlough in 1953-54, Proft took over this task as well as producing the *Hong Kong Letter*.

Rev. George Winkler started intense Cantonese language study for a year before becoming totally immersed in the mission, and supervising Concordia Lutheran Congregation, which had offices and held worship at Concordia Middle School.

Training National Pastors and Evangelists

By 1953, Concordia Bible Institute had graduated 105 men from the initial two-year program at Rennie's Mill. Gertrude Simon had impressed on students the need for personal Bible study, prayer, and personal witnessing. Graduates organized hymn-singing, catechism, and Bible instruction in several Kowloon-side locations. Missionary Hinz became the principal of the Bible school. An obvious need for Chinese pastors emerged, and in 1954, under the presidency of Dr. Thode, an in-service training program was begun whereby men from CBI received further instruction in Christian doctrine, church history, the life of Christ, homiletics, and humanities.

The LCMS established a seminary across the Taiwan strait at Chia Yi in 1956, where nineteen former CBI students enrolled. For family and financial reasons, it was impractical for Hong Kong men to attend the Taiwan campus. After two years, the BFM authorized a seminary in Hong Kong, headed by Missionary Thode. Students were designated as "Special Students of Concordia Seminary." Called the "crash program," candidates studied one or two days weekly while working within a local congregation full-time. Missionaries supervised these several locations, and taught various classes at the seminary.

Elmer Thode and Gertrude Simon celebrated 30-year anniversaries in LCMS ministry, both entirely in China, in 1957. A joint celebration service in January drew a record crowd. Thode was acknowledged for his years in the mainland mission, and his current supervision of six chapels in Hong Kong, administering the Bible Institute, and teaching the new training program. Simon was honored for her time on the mainland, her work in Hong Kong at Rennie's Mill, the Concordia Bible Institute, her handicrafts activity, and current work with women and children.

In January 1959, the LCMS confirmed the establishment of Concordia seminary. Wilbert Holt became president. "China hand" Eugene Seltz was called to be professor of church history and other subjects. A building site on a hill adjacent to Concordia Lutheran (Middle) School was excavated, and construction begun. Having met in six different venues, seven men of the first class

Chapter 11   Growth of the Hong Kong Mission in the 1950s

KwunTong Lutheran school was built on excavated land in a then-remote undeveloped area with a distant view of the Kai Tak airstrip. At the dedication in 1961, the associated congregation celebrated a new permanent home. The preacher was missionary Len Galster, co-pastor with Cromwell Chen.

graduated in 1961. Two years later, July 31, 1963, the seminary building was dedicated and more men of the first class received diplomas as well as calls to congregations.

Youth Work

Sunday schools, primary schools, rooftop clubs, and Concordia Middle School educated young people, many of whom were enthusiastic about their new faith. Fellowship activity and Bible study reinforced initial understandings of Christianity. Behling, Boss, and Proft led the work, assisted by Chinese teaching staffs. Winkler and Kieschnick helped out, especially at week-long summer camps, and youth conferences.

Work with the Blind

Geri Holt, a trained nurse and mother to six boys, became aware of the large population of sight-impaired and blind Chinese. An estimated 4000 blind lived in the Colony, including about 500 children. Not wanting the burden of disabled citizens, the PRC had allowed them to immigrate. The social stigma of being blind probably prevented many more from registering. Glaucoma and cataracts disabled many elderly.

From the recently-formed Hong Kong Society for the Blind, Holt obtained a listing of over 400 blind people living on Kowloon side. There were some who eked out a living from fortune-telling and other mystic practices. There were no locally available reading materials in Braille for the Chinese.

Hong Kong government became interested in establishing clubs for teaching Braille and handicrafts, and was also open to allowing religion to be taught to the blind. Several other churches and individuals also took on the challenge. It required repeated visits to tell and explain the gospel to each individual, requiring many hours and patience.

A visitation program was begun. Women and men from Savior Congregation, plus Simon and Holt, met with the blind in their homes, getting to know them and telling them about Jesus. Florence Winkler and a few Chinese women became involved.

A club was started at Savior Church for a half day each week. About fifteen teenagers and children were taught religion, fundamental English, handicrafts, and basic Chinese Braille. An evening religion class was started, attended by 30 blind adults. Large-print Bibles were obtained for those who had some vision. In 1957, a tea party was arranged with cakes and soft drinks donated by a local business. Visiting sailors at Fenwick pier began making contributions for gifts for blind children. A blind boy was among 40 Chinese baptized that year.

In 1959, Clara Seltz, became active with the group. She was a trained nurse and knew Mandarin from her earlier years in the China mission. An annual summertime beach party and a Christmas service and party attracted up to 150 blind each year. From these humble beginnings came the colony-wide growth of services to the blind that would eventually serve hundreds by the mid-1960s. The Shek Kip Mei Lutheran Centre for the Blind still functions as of this writing.

Kwun Tong Lutheran School

A second major LCMS school, Kwun Tong Lutheran School, was proposed for a New Territories location. In the four-year planning stage, the school was to be built on reclaimed land that was under water when the nascent Board of Managers first approached the government in 1958 about a building site for a 12-room school and adjacent church. At the same time, the LCMS Board of Missions provided a $35,000 grant. Hong Kong government granted 20,000 sq ft of land and an interest-free $50,000 loan. Two church members each gave $5000 towards equipment. Student tuition would pay for daily operations.

The cornerstone was laid in June of 1961 and the school opened within 100 days.

Churches and Congregations of the LCMS and LC-HKS

1950 - Rennie's Mill (NT) -St. John's Lutheran Church (moved; Cheung Kwan Ou)
Shek Kip Mei (K) - Savior Lutheran Church @ 232 Tai Po Rd

1951 - Cha Kwo Ling (NT) - St. Marks Lutheran Church
Sai Wan (HK) - Grace Lutheran Church
Wong Tai Sin (NT) - Redemption Luthran Church

1952 - Macau - St. Pauls Lutheran Church

1953 - *Concordia Lutheran School @ Savior*

1954 - Macau - St. Peters Lutheran Church (Taipa)

1955 - Kwun Tong (NT) - St.Phillips Lutheran Church
Ngau Tau Kok (NT) - St. Matthews Lutheran Church
Shau Kee Wan (HK) - Eternal Life Lutheran Church

1956 - Tsim Sha Tsui (K) - Nathan Road Lutheran Church
Tsuen Wan (NT) Holy Cross Lutheran Church
Yau Ma Tei (K) - Sharon Lutheran Church

1957 - Hung Hom (K) - Truth Lutheran Church
North Point (HK) - Zion Lutheran Church
Yau Yat Chen (Kowloon Tong) (NT) - Concordia Lutheran Church

1959 - Riviera Village (?) - St. James Lutheran Church

1961 - Kowloon - Kowloon Deaf Church

1962 - Repulse Bay Lutheran Church (HK) - Church of All Nations (1967)

1974 - Lai Chi Kok (NT) - Resurrection Lutheran Church

1977 - Choi Hung (Kwun Tong)(NT) - ELIM Lutheran Church

1979 - Lui Ming Choi (NT) - Cheung Shan Lutheran Church

1981 - Tuen Mun (NT) - Peace Lutheran Church

1983 - HungHom (K) - Shepherd Lutheran Church
Sham Shui Po (NT) - Savior Christ L. C
Kai Yip Chuen (Kwun Tong)(NT) - Kai Yan (Village Grace) L. C.
Sha Tin (NT) - Loving Heart Lutheran Church
Sha Tin (NT) - Blessed Harvest Lutheran Church

1986 - Kowloon - Deaf Church
Rock of Ages Lutheran Church (NT)

1988 - North Point (HK) - Deaf Lutheran Church @ Zion

1996 - Kwun Tong (NT) - Trinity Lutheran Church

Interest in the school was generated at the construction site with evening showings of Christian movies. Such large crowds were attracted that many watched the films through the construction fence. Over 500 primary students were initially enrolled. At the time, public transportation to the area was scant and under-developed.

The curriculum approximated that of a LCMS parochial school, and also met the requirements of the British educational system. Eighteen teachers, all members of LCMS congregations, formed the first faculty, and also taught Sunday school. In classrooms and daily chapel services, students who had never heard of Christ were introduced to Jesus as their Savior. English was taught, but most instruction was in Cantonese.

Holy Trinity Lutheran Church was founded at the Kwun Tong school by Rev. Cromwell Chen and Missionary Hinz. When the church and school opened, Galster, who had been a classmate of Chen at Concordia Seminary in Illinois, served as the co-equal assistant pastor. The cooperative pair helped establish patterns that would shape the character and components of the mission for its transitional phase into an indigenous sister-church in Hong Kong.

Students in summer uniform filled the new Kwun Tong Lutheran School to capacity within its first year, 1961-2.

Significant Sources:

Behling, Lorraine,	*The Hong Kong Letters 1951-1959*
Brauer, Janice,	*One Cup of Water*, 1997
Gleason, Gene,	*Hong Kong, 1963; Joy to My Heart, 1966*
Lutheran Witness	Articles 1951-1960
LWML Quarterly	Articles 1951-1960
Taege, Marlys,	*Women in God's Service*, 1991

Interviews with Lorraine Behling, Len Galster, Mel Kieschnick, Daniel Lee, Ruth Proft, and Florence Winkler

Chapter 12 — Maturity and Diversification – the 1960s

Arrivals

1962	Hafner	Victor & Adeline (China ('46); Philippines ('49); Taiwan ('56))
1964	Dickhudt	Bob & Doris (education)
	Reinking	William & Sue (deaf work)
1966	Christian	Bob & Arleen (HKIS)
	Dingler	Bill & Evelyn (Lutheran Hour) (from Taiwan since 1959)
	Luedtke	Jim & Audrey Luedtke (North Point)
1967	Boehmke	Karl & LaVerne (CAN)
	Jasper	Louis & Joan (deafwork)
	Trinklein	Michael & Jan (sem (Taiwan before 59)
	Coates	Thomas (sem)
1969	Berndt	Manfred & Ute (sem)
1971	Ranta	Hillard & Hilme (sem?)

Departures

1962	Proft	Ruth
1966	Galster	Len & Ruth - Thailand
	Simon	Gertrude (illness)
	Reinking	William & Sue
1969	Karner	Roy & Betty
1972	Dickhudt	Bob & Doris

Death

1965	Thode	Elmer	(age 63, heart)

But they that wait upon the Lord shall renew their strength; they shall mount up with wings as eagles; they shall run, and not be weary; and they shall walk, and not faint.

Isaiah 40:31 (KJV)

Chapter 12

Maturity and Diversification – the 1960s

A major re-definition of LCMS Asian missions was initiated with the first Missouri Synod All-Asia Conference, held in 1962 in Hong Kong. In addition to India (1894) and the Philippines (1940), five new Pacific Rim mission fields had been opened since the end of WWII—New Guinea (1948), Japan (1949), Hong Kong (1950), Taiwan (1952), and Korea (1957). These newer missions had all been salted with staff from the former China mission.

Each mission field sent one missionary and one national representative to the January conference. Four LCMS men came from the States. Executive Director of the BFM, Herman Koppleman, Victor Bartling of the same board, and William Danker from Concordia Seminary in St. Louis were returning from the India Evangelical Lutheran Church Convention at Ambur. Arthur Nitz joined them in Hong Kong. Tamil, *pidgin*, Japanese, Visayan, Cantonese, Mandarin, and English were all spoken and interpreted. It was a unique gathering over ten days filled with brotherhood and networking opportunities. Mutual issues from the field were verbalized and explored. Several working themes would affect work in for the next two decades:

1. Most significant was agreement that the spirit of paternalism toward the mission field needed to transition to local leadership and strong independent indigenous churches. English should take a back seat to local language and literature. Theological works needed to be translated into regional tongues. The missionaries aimed to work themselves out of a job within 20 years.

2. National church bodies would be sister churches with the LCMS. The young Lutheran churches should concentrate on just being the church in their particular area. The remoteness of St. Louis necessitated the emergence of local church organization along traditional and ethnic lines.

3. The five Asian national seminaries needed to strengthen their faculty to continue producing national pastors (170 men had been trained in those five schools by 1962). Hopes were expressed for an all-Asian graduate seminary "somewhere in Asia."

4. Asia should make its own contributions to Lutheranism, in relation to eastern cultures; Lutheran theology should not be seen as an imported western exclusive. The Lutheran Hour had the assignment of bringing Christ to native areas until missionaries studied and mastered the local languages.

Chapter 12   Maturity and Diversification – the 1960s

The theological education in the Hong Kong mission began with Concordia Bible School, the graduates like Andrew Chiu became instructors, while missionaries like Roy Karner met with representatives from Synod, planned, and taught at the new Seminary, completed in Yau Yat Chen in 1962.

Each person took his turn at leadership roles during the conference. Practical and administrative commonalities were shared and balanced with theological study and devotions based on St. Paul's letter to the Ephesians. Delegates left with a more complete picture of situations and solutions.

Missions who had felt isolated by geography formed into one enthusiastic force, finding common strengths and frustrations. Representatives found several parallels. Racial and national differences faded, as a spirit of unity in Christ dominated. Laymen and missionaries were equals, learning from each other, not shepherds leading or tending the sheep. In a spirit of unity and sharing, mutual respect grew.

Asian churches wanted to sponsor joint outreach to other Asian fields, aiming first at Southeast Asia. The delegates left with new information, ideas, and friendships; energized as leaders, and renewed as members of the body of Christ.

Vision: "Hong Kong - the Formative Years"

A visionary report was commissioned by LCMS missions' director H. H. Koppelmann and presented seven months later in September, 1962. The major author is not identified, but seems to have been Rev. Phillip Ho. The aim was to establish goals and financial estimates through 1970. This period is seen as the adolescent stage of the mission. The paper began:

This awkward age, 1962-1970, will see significant changes in the young church. It is a period which will see:

• the church emerge as an organized church, governed by delegate conferences;

• a period in which the seminary program gets on solid footing and begins training and graduating students from a full-time regular program;

• a period in which congregations not only have adequate physical plants for their program of outreach and deepening, but also have learned to stand more steadily on their own feet;

• a period by the end of which financial aid from the U.S. will probably be approaching the peak and leveling off stage.

Budget projections included an increase from 15 missionaries to 20 by 1970, two of these as faculty for the seminary, and others for expanded evangelism and education efforts. A full-time worker with the handicapped was proposed and it was hoped that Lutheran Hour could be restored. Estimated increased costs of each new missionary were calculated at a salary of $300 per month, plus housing and benefits.

Summarizing developing and future projects, the report itemized:

1. Finishing the new school in Kwun Tong, with a supporting congregation;
2. Completion of Savior School and Church (regarded as the "mother church");
3. Construction of Redemption Church and parsonage in Wong Tai Sin;
4. Church, parsonage, and middle school construction at Cha Kwo Ling;
5. Expansion of Zion (North Point) into an Anglo-Chinese middle school;
6. Building more permanent facilities for Lye Mun congregation and school;
7. Exploring the possibilities of a church and school in Tsuen Wan;
8. Exploring building a 12-classroom school connected to Grace, West Point;
9. Exploring starting a school similar to Kwun Tong in Lai Chi Kok;
10. Expanding work at TaiKokTsui, ShauKiWan, HungHom, and NgauTauKok;
11. Transitioning English work in Repulse Bay (begun 1962) to self-support.

Two Worlds or None

Coincidently, 1962 was the year of "Vatican II", the first of the four councils of the world-wide Roman Catholic Church. Initiat-

Chapter 12 — Maturity and Diversification – the 1960s

Profiles of several Christians in the HK Lutheran Mission

Paul Chang (張學宏, 又名張保羅) was a Seminarian from the Basel Mission in HK. He was key in helping the transplanted mainland missionaries (Holt, Behling, Boss, Simon) establish their work and make contacts in Hongkong. Equally as significant in the founding of the mission as any of the expats. Talented young pastor, and did much for True Light (NYC) with Louis Bucheimer. After he left True Light, he attended Seminary; stayed in the mid-west; changed his profession, operating a gas station. He remarried, and went on to do real estate, and later moved to Florida.

Too Heung Lee - Born 1932 in Macau, came to HK after Pacific War to study. Met Martha Boss at Heung Kong College, learned about Christ, became diligent student and asked to learn more about Jesus. Drowned one week later at "Children's Festival", May 1950.

Nelson Wong - Born in China of well-to-do Buddhist family; met Martha Boss at St. Peter's Evenong Shool, overcame family pressures and converted, overcame fears thru Matt 10:29 and Gen 28:15, accepted Christ, and was baptized by Rev Holtje, 1950.

Chan Teen Kase - Born 1931 self-confessed lazy naughty boy, hurting family & friends till age 17; Baptised at age 8. First came to funeral parlor class of Martha Boss, attended young people's meetings on rooftop of Tropic Island Hotel, then took Bible Reading Correspondence Course. Experienced "miracle" healing of his tooth, accepted Christ; was known to all as "Skillful Chan."

Luke Chau - Young student baptised by Rv Holtje in June, 1950, returned to China to study dentistry at Kwong-Wah Medical College in Canton.

Mr. Chen - principal of Heung Kong College, Buddhist, not interested in Christianity but provided a classroom for missionaries to use for worship; 6 months later asked to receive "tutoring" in Christianiay. Many family pressures held him back many years. Patience prevailed and requested baptism 4 years later.

Russell Yau (丘世儀, Yau Sai-yee) - Born HK 1932, family walked 14 days to return to Kwantung village during Japanese occupation, Took refuge in mountains and witnessed the evil man can do. Dad was KMT, fled to HK in 1949. A friend at Heung Kong college invited him to Rev Holtje's class, also Simon, Boss & Behling, who recognized his talent in singing;. Baptised July 26, 1950, became Sunday School teacher.

Yeung P'ing Shan (Peter) - born 1940 in China of christian mother, dad was Canton police, fled in 1950; lived on roof top. First came to mission when he heard music. Visited by Martha & Chang, began attending every activity, determined to be baptised with other 10-year olds on March 18, 1951.

Andrew Chiu (丘美仲, 又名丘恩處) - Born in China, was newsman, middle school teacher, KMT operative, Fled to HK in 1950. Given gospel tract (Luke) by Holtje and Simon, read, identified with prodigal son, accepted Christ, baptized in first of Holtje's groups June 11, 1950; attended Bible Institute, with wife; ministered in Macau 1 year; became evangelist, then pastor, studied at Concordia Seminary in St. Louis, eventually became President of Hong Kong Synod. Founded seminary for Chinese in New York and on-line, has written and translated many books.

Phillip Ho (何萬泉, 又名何腓力, Ho Wan Chien) - Born Peiping, 1923; graduated from Central Military Academy, worked with KMT, fled to HK 1950; read a Lutheran tract while in hospital for TB; baptized, confirmed, attended Bible Institute, became evangelist, replaced Chiu in Macau then became Pastor in Hong Kong and Macau, worked with the deaf.

Harold Ren - born 1925 in Nanking; family worshipped idols, rejected all "foreign religion"; fled to HK alone and friendless in 1950 ; first experienced God's love that April; baptised in same group as Andrew Chiu; turned life over to Christ, attended Concordia bible School in Rennie's Mill and soon was evangelizing at Cha Kwo Ling.

ed by Pope John XXIII and completed under Pope John Paul VI in 1965, the progressive decisions were the first to significantly re-align church practices since the Council of Trent (1545-63). Changes were made that were to have influence on both Catholic and Protestant practices, such as the changeover to vernacular language, social ministries, re-definitions of the roles played by the laity, dialogue with other denominations, and hopeful first steps to a more unified and collegial worldwide Christian communion. The spirit of change in Rome would influence even distant Hong Kong.

Former Japan missionary William J. Danker toured Synod's Asian installations as part of the India and Hong Kong mission conferences in 1962. His resulting book *Two Worlds or None* anticipated the emergence of the LCMS from denominational isolation and gave encouragement for the Synod to engage in the common task of spreading the gospel without losing its distinctiveness. University of Chicago Divinity School professor Pierce Beaver's forward to the book identifies the major challenge of combining confessional loyalty and obedience to Christ in one universal mission, so that a skeptical world will be convinced by unity in the church while Christians still safeguard a full understanding of the gospel.

Ground Breaking for Concordia Seminary

Concordia Theological Seminary was the outgrowth of Gertrude Simon's original Concordia Bible Institute. Saviour Church housed the earliest seminary classes, later moving into space at Concordia Middle School in Yau Yat Chen. The first class graduated in 1961. Among the new ministers was Andrew Chiu, originally a teacher in China. With his educational background, he had become an early assistant to the women at Rennie's Mill and accepted the Lord Jesus Christ as his Redeemer. He married Sharon, another Bible Institute student, and they had begun ministry together, assigned to Macau as evangelists. That same month construction began atop the hill adjacent to Concordia School for the longed-for permanent Concordia Theological Seminary.

The Great Hunger

Without warning, large masses of refugees began inundating the China - Hong Kong barrier in 1961. Across the border, Mao's "Great Leap Forward" of 1955-58 had fizzled; a social disaster. Citizens were uprooted, re-assigned to different jobs and geography, and an emphasis placed on basic manufacturing to catch up with the West. Agricultural production slowed radically, with millions starving to death in China while peasants tried to manufacture the most basic of commodities. Sporadic information about this situation trickled out of the PRC. The "Great Hunger" ensued, and in 1962, China briefly relaxed the border. Seventy thousand dispirited Chinese crossed the frontier at Lo Wu and Man Kam To.

Hong Kong authorities were swamped, turning back as much of the human flotsam as they could round up. Len Galster wrote to *Lutheran Witness* in July that members of LCMS churches were bringing food, clothing, friendship, and the gospel message to detainees on the other side of the perimeter fence, before they were deported. Repatriated Chinese at least had heard about the good news of Jesus Christ, and some took tracts and Bibles from the Hong Kong church members back to the provinces. Fourteen LCMS missionaries and about 7,500 Lutheran Christians participated in this program over several weeks. The mission's four rooftop clubs absorbed many new children into their program of reading, writing, handicrafts, and basic nutrition.

A non-anniversary

The 50th anniversary of Edward Arndt's 1913 arrival and pioneer mission in Hankow was barely noted by either the missionary conference or the Missouri Synod. China, mysteriously behind a bamboo curtain, had

Chapter 12　　　　　　　　　　　　　　　　　　　Maturity and Diversification – the 1960s

Profiles of several Christians in the HK Lutheran Mission

Wei Yun-nan (John) Refugee at Rennie's Mill, began going to chapel; imprisoned at Stanley for 6 months, visited and baptized by Hintz; began Bible Reading Correspondence Course; released and deported to Macau; began visiting and evangelizing at refugee camp there; immigrated to Taiwan, began work with Olive and Jen Chih P'ing (Harold) 1951

Daniel W. Lee (李永禎, LEE Wing Ching) - Born 1937 of idol-worshipping parents; attracted to Bible story/Filmstrip youth group at Saviour Mission; knew he was guided by Holy Spirit, baptized 3 months later on Palm Sunday, March 1951; joined confirmation class, told Bible stories at Children's nights; became pastor, served in Seattle many years, returned to HK and still active with LCHKS.

Daniel Li Yat Shing, younger than Daniel W Lee, 1st Vice President of LCHKS.

Daniel Chow (周星) - Attended English Classes; baptized and confirmed, brought wife and children to faith; worked for the mission full time.

Joseph Yeh (葉龍) - Born in Chekiang Province, 1931, orphaned at 17, worked as secretary, journalist, teacher, and in a soy sauce factory; endured "thought reconstruction" 1950; fled PRC; lived in hut, wrote humor for SCMP, studied at YMCA, found Saviour Mission wandering the streets for stories, found new life, baptised April 1950; attended Summer Camp, then Concordia Bible School at Rennie's Mill.

Walter Jiang (姜永文) - Student in Lorraine Behling's English Bible Class at Heung Kong College, Although not baptised yet, he established a Sunday School (1951) in a small 9 x 11 hillside hut with 50 children, using materials from Lorraine. Overcrowded, they soon used a nearby soy sauce factory. whose owner, Mr. Shih, was a Catholic.

Paul Chen (陳特, 又名陳保羅) - studied under Gertrude; requested baptism in 1951, then confirmed. Participant then president of young people's activities.

Chen Tzen Keh - Refugee and Bible Institute student at Rennie's Mill; emigrated to Taiwan, worked alone witnessing against Japanese-influenced religions, sent requests (Dec 1950) to Rev Hinz & Gertrude to send CBI grads to Taiwan & Mission Board to send missionaries.

Timothy Lan (藍光熙) - Born 1923 in Wuhan; translated for US forces in China and CNRRA; fled Canton 1945; baptized in HK by Holtje, wanted to become a preacher. Served as translator, interpreter, secretary in 1950; led singing; visited hospitals with Hinz; did translations for the *Hong Kong Letter*; attended Concordia Seminary in Tokyo 1 year; moved to USA in 1972 & became volunteer lay preacher and Bible Study leader in California.

Bible women, as such, are barely mentioned in the literature:

Mrs Yee - leads group of women teaches sewing, kitting, crochet & baking
Mrs Shau – spoke 4 dialects, interprets for Lorraine
Esther Sue - attended Lorraine's class at Heung Kong college, joined baptism class and brough her brother too; confirmed, joined choir
Ellie Woo (吳慧麗) - formerly attended Catholic school; joined Lorraine's Sunday classes 1952.

been tucked away into distant Synodical consciousness, and everyone seemed engaged in new programs in the emerging economies of East Asia. In 1963, missionary Eugene Seltz did write an eight-installment history of the mission, in German for **Der Lutheraner**.

Rumblings in Southeast Asia

As the nearest major urban center between Singapore and the Philippines, Hong Kong became the "R & R" (Rest and Relaxation) port of choice for U.S. military personnel in the region. As the Indo-Chinese war intensified, confrontation between Communist-backed national forces in Vietnam, Cambodia, and Laos led to the armed build-up that would dominate East Asia for the next ten years. This would permanently alter the face of Hong Kong and the lives of Hong Kong Chinese, the expatriate community, Southeast Asia, America, and its military.

The British navy had long-established recreational facilities at the China Fleet Club in the Wan Chai area for their garrison. Americans operated an adjacent service center at Fenwick Pier, mentioned in Chapter 11. Sailors and soldiers on leave could get out of the war zone and off their ships for a few days in Hong Kong. In addition to feasting, drinking, shopping, and meeting women, many men were also looking for spiritual experiences, and yearned for Christian friendships and worship.

Ruth Proft continued to take a few hours each week from her mission-related duties to help at Fenwick Pier, and thus formed a link between the navy operation and the LCMS Lutherans. American families hosted the sailors for meals in their homes, a memorable Thanksgiving or Christmas holiday was enriched with new friendships and a home-cooked meal. The American expatriate community at the time numbered under 3,000, primarily in the Colony to conduct business, work at the U.S. Consulate, or serve with Christian missions. Work with soldiers and sailors was the Lutheran's first tangible outreach to the non-Chinese community in Hong Kong. More on this in Chapters 13 and 14.

Growth of Primary and Middle Schools

Educator Mel Kieschnick continued to work with the Hong Kong government on the location and establishment of several schools. This entailed coordinating a local congregation's need for a worship sanctuary with a proposed primary school, promoting site selection with the government land office, fulfilling education department requirements, and procuring furnishings and a qualified teaching staff. Meanwhile he supervised all rooftop clubs, taught at Concordia Middle School, and served on the missionary council.

The results of this work were several nurseries, kindergartens, and primary schools. The Hong Kong education department held strict guidelines regarding capacity, teacher-student ratio, furnishings, as well as equipment for sanitation and recreation. Salaries and staff qualifications were also stipulated. The government encouraged schooling for all, and supported those organized by church and private groups, with grants, lands, and low-interest loans.

The second full-time LCMS educator to be called from the U.S. was Harold Schmidt in 1959, a principal and teacher from Waterloo, Iowa. In Hong Kong, he worked with Kieschnick to develop and supervise the Lutheran school system. He helped with teacher training, and functioned as liaison between the LCMS and the Education Department. Several more schools were established under his guidance.

Over 100 Chinese Lutheran school teachers representing the mission's eight schools and four rooftop clubs, gathered for a retreat at the Castle Peak Hotel in the New Territories. This seaside conference of 1962 was chaired by Schmidt, the assistant education coordinator. Away from the noise and masses of urban Hong Kong, participants studied the

Chapter 12　　　　　　　　　　　　　　　　　　　Maturity and Diversification – the 1960s

Education became a major component of the Hong Kong mission. Concordia Lutheran School initiated the concept of parent-teacher conferences. Ruth Proft taught religion and Bible courses. "Blackie" Schmidt took charge of faculty retreats and in-service. Board members held multiple roles as supervisors of various schools as well as assignment to congregations and committee work.

teaching methods of Jesus, and prepared for the coming school year.

Robert Dickhudt, fresh from the University of Minnesota with a Masters degree in school administration, accepted his call to Hong Kong in September of 1964. He studied Cantonese full time, and after just one year, took over for Kieschnick, who unexpectedly returned to the U.S. for family health reasons. Dickhudt became principal of Kwun Tong School, which enrolled 2,000 primary students, and an evening English school of 300 high school-age pupils. He also took over supervision of the rooftops.

Deaf Ministries

The church's awareness of the need for services to the deaf of Hong Kong came about when Rev. William Reinking of the LCMS surveyed Far East missions in 1960. The plight of the deaf had first became a concern of the LCMS following the American Civil War, and by 1883, a school and orphanage for the deaf opened in Detroit, Michigan. Rev. August Reinke preached and had his sign choir perform at the 1896 LCMS convention in Ft. Wayne, Indiana. The LCMS then established a Board of Deaf Ministry. By Synod's 1947 centennial, there were 59 full-time pastors to the deaf who convened annually in the Ephphatha conference. Over 4000 deaf communicant members were served in 42 states. Concordia Publishing House produced the monthly *Deaf Lutheran Magazine*. A second major school, Mill Neck Manor School for the Deaf, opened in New York in 1951.

In China, having deemed disabled citizens as "undesirable," the People's Republic was amenable to the emigration of such people since they were perceived as unproductive and a burden to the new state. As a result, a disproportional number of deaf Chinese arrived with each refugee surge. From early on, evangelists at Rennie's Mill and in Macau became aware of the deaf population and their needs. Titus Lee Fu Sheng worked with deaf individuals at Rennie's Mill camp in the late 1950s, and seminary student Phillip Ho ministered to them in Macau.

Rev. Reinking, executive secretary of Synod's Board for Missions to the Deaf, visited Hong Kong and Taiwan in February 1960, as part of a three-month fact-finding tour of LCMS Asian missions. He found that only in Japan did the government provide any education for the deaf. More than 200 deaf persons were tallied in Hong Kong in 1960, with about 80 more in Macau.

At Reinking's encouragement, Phillip Ho began reaching out to the deaf community and to several deaf individuals in Rennie's Mill. Through the efforts of Miss Yip Wai Ying, a teacher of the deaf at a private school, a party for the deaf was first held at Chatham Road Lutheran Church in 1961. In spite of inclement weather, 70 individuals attended the event, singing psalms, praying, lip reading some preaching and having tea.

Miss Yip began a successful Sunday school that same month. Three groups of deaf were enrolled: those deaf from birth, those deaf thru disease or accident, and the deaf-blind. Within a month, a center for the deaf was up-and-running at Chatham Road, with a committed enrollment of 28. Within eight months, there were 49 baptisms and six deaf students were confirmed. Missionary mother and wife Florence Winkler provided significant leadership and dedicated work from the onset. Another evangelist with sign language experience was Titus Lee Wei Tao who also began ministering to the deaf in the North Point area on Hong Kong Island.

Reinking's background with the deaf had begun during his seminary years. His first pastoral call was to Holy Cross Lutheran Church for the Deaf in St. Louis. He was appointed as executive secretary of deaf missions for the LCMS. After his Asian visit, he recommended the calling of a full-time missionary to the deaf in Hong Kong. No one accepted the opportunity, so the board called

Chapter 12 Maturity and Diversification – the 1960s

Savior Lutheran became the home of Deaf education, utilizing sign language and forming a congregation. At Concordia, science education and science fairs became a hallmark, as did music. The first graduating class of ten, in 1957, all passed the School Leaving Examination.

Reinking himself in 1963, who arrived the next year with his family.

Working in Hong Kong, Rev. Reinking advised pastors Titus Lee Wei Tao and Phillip Ho in developing worship and educational programs. Lee conducted Sunday afternoon worship at Zion Church in North Point. Phillip Ho also conducted Sunday evening worship and Bible class at his congregation on Nathan Road.

Forty miles east in Macau, an initial survey in 1964 revealed no private or government work with the deaf there. Reinking, Ho, and Lee coordinated an evening class, first meeting only one evening per week. Growing quickly to 40 students, classes were soon held five nights a week. Mr. Ip, deaf himself, was one of the two teachers. Religion was an important part of the curriculum, and on Christmas Day 1965, twenty-seven deaf students were baptized at St. Paul Lutheran Church. Sunday school for the Deaf also became part of St. Paul's program. Additional Macau developments are covered in Chapter 15.

At the time, there was only one government school and two private schools for the deaf in Hong Kong. Reinking started the Lutheran Deaf Evening School in 1965, meeting in rooms at Concordia Middle School. Reinking instructed the staff on teaching methods, Chinese sign language, and lip-reading. Three hearing and one deaf teacher held sessions five nights a week.

Recognizing the need for a full time expert in deaf education, Reinking recommended a fellow seminarian who had also worked at Mill Neck Manor. Rev. Louis Jasper was then called by the LCMS Board for Deaf Missions, to replace Reinking. Jasper had been working in deaf education since 1959 in New York, having earned an MA degree from Columbia University in education for the deaf. With his wife Joan and three daughters, he located in Hong Kong in 1967 with the expectation that schools for the deaf would be established in Hong Kong and Macau. Only funding and locations were lacking.

No space was available in the Hong Kong mission for a deaf day school. Night classes were begun in 1968 in a shared classroom at the Saviour Lutheran primary school. The deaf school doubled its enrollment within a year. More classrooms were rented on the top floor of nearby Ming Kei College, a school operated by the Church of Christ in China. With the construction of nearby Sharon Lutheran Primary School in Mong Kok, it was determined that an additional floor could be incorporated into Sharon's building design specifically for the deaf school. This was financed with $15,000 donated by a single Lutheran congregation in Michigan. Thus the Mong Kok Lutheran School for the Deaf (MLSD) opened in 1970.

This facility was rapidly outgrown, but served while a new school building was under construction. Darien Curtis and John Rae, trained teachers of the deaf, were recruited and assisted in the training of teachers. Charles Tang became the school's principal when MLSD moved into its own premises on Cherry Street. Enrollment grew to 160 students. With the move to the new premises, worship services for the deaf were initiated on Sunday mornings and Rev. Hui Ming Kin served as the school chaplain.

During this period, Rev. Jasper also coordinated with Martha Boss and her school nursing program. These nurses specifically served the students of the LCMS schools. Jasper increased the visibility of Lutheran deaf work as one of the founding members of the Hong Kong Society for the Deaf. Joan Jasper, in addition to work with congregations and family, was also a founding member of the Hong Kong Oratorio Society, creating another link between mission personnel and the expat community.

The deaf school continued to grow while Jasper took furlough to earn a doctorate in special education in 1975. Upon his 1981 return, plans began for yet another new larger

Chapter 12   Maturity and Diversification – the 1960s

Supervisor Mel Kieschnick posed with the student body of St. Mark's Lutheran school in Cha Kwo Ling with teachers James Jung (l) and Walter Wu (r).

Handicraft production and sales increased in the 1960s. The office in Tsim Tsa Shui became the overcrowded venue for packaging shipments, later loaded onto sampans destined for shipping to America.

school building, this one in the Kwai Chung area. In February 1990, the school moved into its new building and was renamed the Lutheran School for the Deaf, where it exists to this day. Dr. Jasper also organized the first Asian-Pacific Regional Conference on Deafness in 1986, taught courses in English, psychology, and education at Concordia Seminary, gave lectures on special education at Macau University and in Beijing, and became an advisor to the Hong Kong Special Schools Council. The Jaspers repatriated to New York in 1996.

Missions to the Blind

Missionary wife Geraldine Holt first began work with blind refugees in April 1957. Inspired by the exuberance of a blind boy named Lo Wan Sing at his baptism, Geri contacted the Social Welfare Office. She found that there were an estimated 4,000 blind people in the colony. Only 1,100 of them were registered with the government. At the time, there were only two schools in Hong Kong for the blind, each limited to 60 children. The Hong Kong Society for the Blind had been established in 1955. Their program grew to include prevention, rehabilitation, recreation, education and vocational training. The blind were taught sewing, brush-making, and rattan work.

With help from Florence Winkler, Clara Seltz, and other women of the mission, Geri Holt made about 400 home visits within a period of two months. The blind were invited to the church and to a party that August. American sailors at Fenwick Pier heard about the event through Ruth Proft, and sent money for gifts. A local bakery sent cakes; another firm supplied Coca-Cola. Working with Bible Institute graduate John Tuan, a Monday evening Bible class for the blind was begun at Savior Lutheran. Mr. Tuan also initiated a weekly lunch-time Bible class at Savior's rooftop club, where he was principal. A group of teenagers formed a club that met each week at Savior. Pastor Martin Chiang soon baptized three blind adults and confirmed one blind boy.

Mary Burtt, a retired American from Massachusetts, worked independently among the aged and refugees in squatter shacks and in the lower class tea-houses. Her heart-wrenching and pitiful stories told of dislocated blind people living in dire straits and appalling conditions. She coordinated medical, spiritual, mental, and nutritional needs of the blind in Wong Tai Sin. She was responsible for several baptisms in Lutheran churches. Her work was well known to Ruth Proft.

Two women began teaching wickerwork and knitting to the blind at Savior's rooftop club. Philip Ho, having worked with the deaf in Macau, started teaching a Bible class at the Sacred Music School, and opened a music center for blind children. Private citizens paid the room rent. From Charter Oak, Iowa, Mrs. Leo Bruhn and her volunteer transcribers sent Sunday school lessons in English Braille. Other available Lutheran Braille literature included *The Lutheran Messenger, Portals of Prayer,* and *Teen Times.* Clara Seltz, became immersed in expanding Cantonese Braille to include religious materials.

Social outings were organized for the youngsters twice a year. Parties included lawn games, candy and cookie treats, and scavenger hunts organized by Mrs. Holt's six sons. Christmas parties attracted about 200 children, and the annual picnic usually drew up to 90. Going to the beach was especially popular. Eventually, the Social Welfare Department established more clubs for the blind.

The Lutheran Fellowship for the Blind was also organized. This group met monthly for worship, singing, and social activity. Usually around 40 teenagers attended, about ten of whom were members at Saviour. By 1965, the local radio station broadcast announcements of a Braille Lutheran correspondence class. Materials for the class had been developed for a course in Mandarin in Taiwan. Volunteers helped put parts of the catechism into Cantonese Braille, as well as

Chapter 12   Maturity and Diversification – the 1960s

Handicraft workers produced original paintings, learned new skills of production and accounting, and enjoyed the occasional outing. Salesrooms within the Colony were opened in connection with Welfare Handicrafts, marketing to tourists and local expatriates, at a time when such products made in China were not available for export.

some hymns and liturgy. Seven other classes in various congregations, with a total of about 50 students, were meeting weekly. Hopes were also high for the establishment of a community center and library in the Wong Tai Sin area, where the majority of the blind resided.

Lutheran Handicrafts

Continuing activity from the earliest days at Rennie's Mill, Gertrude Simon's handicraft venture grew into a substantial operation in the 1960s. Organization and marketing went through several changes. The venture, which began with a single request for handmade items in 1953, eventually provided income for 150 families, and required a full time accountant, Benjamin Lee Ming. Gertrude and Martha, working on their own time and with their own funds, financed the purchase of a flat on the sixth floor at #21 Hankow Road in May, 1960. The space became showroom, warehouse, office, shipping department, and sometimes sleeping quarters. Export certificates, certificates of origin, customs forms, and Royal Mail shipping complicated overseas sales. When confronted with a major problem or minor issue, Miss Boss would say, "Let's see how the Lord leads us."

Items for sale grew to include woolens; plastic thread animals and toys; plastic handbags and totes; bamboo plates and wickerwork; beaded purses, gloves, and slippers; brocade items; hand painted scrolls, greeting cards, and book marks; aprons; household items; and even silver jewelry and items of brass, wood, and ivory. Shipments went to Canada, Germany, England, Switzerland, Australia, Iceland, with the majority to the United States. In Hong Kong, products were sold through four Welfare Handicrafts shops, located in strategic shopping areas, especially the Salisbury Road location between the Star Ferry and Peninsula Hotel.

For fifteen years, volunteers helped Simon and Boss run the shoestring operation. They mimeographed price lists, order forms, and piles of individual correspondence. Ladies Aid societies and LWML chapters in the U.S., Canada, and several European countries provided the market for goods made by hundreds of refugees. The handicrafts project officially incorporated on August 8, 1969, as The Hong Kong Lutheran Handicrafts Society. Martha Boss assumed supervision after Miss Simon's death in 1966. Founding Board of Governors included missionary wives Clara Seltz and Arleen Christian, volunteer Beatrice Richards ("Aunt Bea"), Rev. Roy Karner, Benjamin Lee, and mission business manager Chow Sing.

The Hong Kong government recognized the society as a welfare agency. The society became involved in many local self-help projects. The workers were never employees, but considered "suppliers" of the items they made. Some used raw materials supplied by the society, and were paid for them as piece work. Working in individual homes or small shops, this was truly a cottage industry. After her untimely accidental death on furlough in 1973, Martha's role was assumed by "Aunt Bea," the matronly full time volunteer who relocated from Ohio specifically to work with Miss Boss and her projects. She did so for the reminder of her long life.

Kowloon Walled City

When the British leased the New Territories in 1898, one rural brick-walled village was not included. It was, in theory, to remain under the administration of the Kwangtung magistrate. As Kowloon's population swelled, the village near Boundary Street became surrounded with a warren of streets and alleys. During the Japanese occupation of 1941-45 the walls were torn down so the masonry could be used to extend the nearby Kai Tak airstrip. Under the control of no government, the eight acres of tightly packed humanity, still called the walled city, became a teeming mecca of illegal activity.

Technically not under colonial jurisdiction, there were no taxes, no restrictions of any kind, no police protection, but there was

Chapter 12   Maturity and Diversification – the 1960s

Funeral processions were common in both urban and rural areas as traditional ancestral duties were performed by family survivors. Incense and paper models of gifts were burned, often in the street. White is the color of death.

In the tourist area of Tsim Sha Tsui, Nathan Road Lutheran Church opened near Kowloon Park, a 5-minute walk to the Star Ferry Terminal and the Kowloon-Canton Railway station.

delivery of the Royal Mail! It was ill-advised for a non-resident to enter the village unless accompanied by a local dweller. Organized crime syndicates, called Triads, controlled most businesses, gambling parlors, and drug dens. Opium divans and brothels opened onto the twisted alleys. Little daylight reached the cobbled walkways and crooked lanes. A 4-by-6 foot room might be both a factory and a family's living space. Most cooking was done on open charcoal fires. There was no sanitation—troughs and open sewers supplemented chamber pots. The entire zone had but three water taps. A few ancient deep wells supplied a trickle of brown water.

In the summer of 1960, the Colonial government decided to clean up the city. The goal was to at least rout out robbers and murderers who had long used it as a hiding place. No individual or small group of constables had a chance in the lawless area. Teams of 200 policemen conducted periodic raids. Opium dens eventually closed, illicit services went underground, and a basic arrangement began for hauling away piles of accumulated refuse.

Nurse Maureen Clark volunteered to provide needed daily injections, to a bed-ridden child in the now un-walled city. She was appalled at what she saw in the streets. She befriended some of the children and began treating some of their boils, skin ailments, fevers, and runny eyes right on the street with only the equipment in her nurse's kit. Soon children would line up, awaiting her arrival. Church World Service helped her rent a small room, and other nurses and interpreters volunteered two days each week. Catholic Relief started supplying milk powder, syrup, and biscuits, serving about 100 children visiting the clinic per day. Two classes teaching basic reading and writing were started by an interpreter. A Child Care Centre Committee explored ways to improve nutrition, health, and education. By November 1960, a group called Project Concern was coordinating additional trained staff —nurses, a laboratory technician, and teachers.

Manfred Berndt was the only LCMS missionary to enter the city, which he did on a regular basis to visit one of his members who lived there. On his Vespa, he was able to negotiate the narrow streets and more-or-less blend in. With his fluent Cantonese, he was able to pass as a neutral local, not related to the authorities. It was out of the question for the LCMS to attempt any more significant mission work there, however. Residents of the walled city were evicted in 1993, and the site was razed in 1995. It is now an open park in the midst of Kowloon City adjacent to the former Kai Tak airport.

Nathan Road Lutheran Church

Kowloon's major tourist district is located at the southern tip of the peninsula, where the *Star Ferry* piers are located—an area called Tsim Sha Tsui. (TST). Nathan Road, the main north-south boulevard bisecting the peninsula, runs nearby, from the KCR station to Boundary Street and the New Territories. The Missionary Conference determined that locating a congregation in this area would be strategic. There would be worship services in both Cantonese and English, attracting residents and travelers.

Construction costs for a building in the area were prohibitive, so a 2,000 sq. ft. space was purchased on the second floor of a building on Nathan Road, five blocks from the waterfront. It opened in October, 1963 as Nathan Road Chapel.

The first pastors were Phillip Ho and missionary Len Galster. Chinese attendees numbered about 100 communicants at the time of dedication. Ruth Galster played the portable electronic organ and the interior was decorated by Betty Karner.

School Expansion

Mel Kieschnick proposed a major new Anglo-Chinese middle school on Hong Kong Island at North Point in 1962. The school

Chapter 12   Maturity and Diversification – the 1960s

Ten English-speaking expatriate families first met with Rev. Len Galster for worship on the "back-side" of Hong Kong Island at the Repulse Bay Hotel in March, 1962. Attendance at Sunday school and worship increased so that a congregation formed. Desiring their own church building, they eventually planned and opened Hong Kong International School.

would be adjacent to Zion Lutheran Church where a concentration of Chinese Christians was living. Students would receive English and Chinese instruction. Missionary Karner was in charge of the project, which opened its hillside campus as Concordia Middle School, North Point in 1969. Rev. Titus Lee Way Tao's congregation (Zion) also made the new facility their home.

Repulse Bay

In late 1961, Missionary Len Galster was directed to explore the possibilities of a church for English-speaking expatriates on the south side of Hong Kong Island. Galster organized the opening worship service and Sunday school class on March 4, 1962, in the reading room of the elegant Repulse Bay Hotel, near the residences of many expatriates. This was the inauspicious beginning of an entirely new direction for the LCMS overseas, leading to the future establishment of three international schools in as many countries. See chapter 14 for the details.

Confrontations of 1966-1967

Local turmoil and riots in the mid-60s had a major effect on the Hong Kong mission in three areas: staffing, growth, and indigination. Hong Kong occupied a unique piece of historic geography. Jammed into its 400 square miles were now an estimated four million people. Displaced persons of nearly every class, and philosophy comprised 90% of the population, overlain with the cloak of a neutral and beneficent colonial administration. Loyalties crossed language, ethnic, political, and financial lines. The majority of the displaced were regional Cantonese or transplanted Mandarin speakers. This human stew could easily be stirred by local or international events, especially in nearby PRC or across the Straits of Taiwan.

China's Cultural Revolution was initiated in 1966 under Chairman Mao as a program to eliminate alien influences in the PRC, with the goal of restoring a pure Communist society. Drastic changes were initiated in leadership, labor, culture, and family structure. Significant was the involvement of student and youth elements, and the emergence of the Red Guards, militant young enforcers of this zealous reform program that targeted nearly anything old, foreign or threatening to the regime. That spring, a week-long fracas was triggered over a fare increase on the much-used and vital *Star Ferry* linking Kowloon and Hong Kong. A hunger strike led to confrontations, riots, and one death. Fourteen hundred youths were arrested. An inquiry commission determined that the "Star Ferry Riots" were neither financially generated, nor anti-colonial in nature. More likely, the unrest was a symptom of the overcrowded and insecure living conditions.

Worldwide student unrest and rebellion, international geo-political conditions, and the emerging Southeast Asian war contributed to simmering tensions within local groups of under-employed or directionless youth. January of 1967 saw violent riots against the Portuguese authorities in Macau over wages and working hours. Orchestrated by the Communist party, left-wing activists confronted local troops. After much dialogue, the Portuguese agreed to several conditions set by Beijing, which in effect removed most European control.

On May Day in 1967, three labor strikes began in Hong Kong. Workers, led by left-wing activists, protested wages and working conditions. The confrontation began in a dilapidated area of San Po Kong, crowded with residents and workers in a maze of dirty featureless walk-ups. For over six months, car bombings, explosions and riots fueled unrest and insecurity. Real and fake bombs were left along roadsides in innocuous paper pags, designed to detonate and maim. Ordinary residents, both Chinese and expatriate, feared for their safety. Relations between the Hong Kong government and PRC reached an historic ebb.

Chapter 12 — Maturity and Diversification – the 1960s

The Star Ferry provided the main transportation link between Hong Kong Island and Kowloon Peninsula, where the KCR station was the terminus of fair service through the New Territories to the China border. When a proposed fare increase was announced in May, 1967, protests soon led to sit-ins and riots that disturbed much of the Colony for nearly six months.

Rickshaws declined in usage and became tourist attractions. Next to the twin piers on the Kowloon side was the clocktower and terminus of the Kowloon-Canton railroad.

Neither authority sought a showdown. Quietly, the PRC began downplaying its influence on the activist Red Guard. The Hong Kong government held firm and consistently cracked down on illegal activity. No one lost face. The brink was avoided. Since nearly all of Hong Kong's potable water came via pipeline from the PRC, the threat of a water shortage was acute. Rationing was implemented; taps were turned on for just four hours every fourth day, but industry was not affected. The PRC never completely shut off the supply, and as part of October First National Day celebrations, renewed its water agreement with the colony.

By January, 1968, the confrontation had mostly run its course. Locally, the events rallied Chinese and expatriate support of Government, strengthened credibility, and created near-legendary status for many local policemen, and foreshadowed a peaceful co-existence that continued through the handover in 1997. Post-riots Hong Kong resumed an energized life, a mildly euphoric peaceful co-existence of ambitious citizens. The influx of refugees eased, housing and social service challenges were met, and a surge of local pride and cultural awareness pervaded the colony.

Long-term China missionary Frieda Thode, widowed in 1965, stayed on to continue teaching at Concordia School and reading to young kids of missionary families.

Significant Sources:

Behling, Lorraine,	*The Hong Kong Letters, 1950-59*
Carroll, John,	*A Concise History of Hong Kong*
Koyama, Kosuke,	*Waterbuffalo Theology, 1974*
Lutheran Witness	*articles, 1952-60*
Royal Observatory,	*Typhoon, Hong Kong, 1971*

Interviews with Andrew Chiu, Len & Ruth Galster, Roy & Betty Karner, and Ruth Proft

Chapter 13 — Transitions and Partnerships

Arrived
- 1971   Geisler   Herb
- 1976   Wangerin   Walter & Louise
- 1981   Halter   Carol

Departed
- 1966   Kieschnick   Mel & Jane
- 1966   Galster   Len & Ruth
- 1972   Hafner   Victor & Adeline
-          Berndt   Manfred & Ute
- 1973   Boehmke   Karl & LaVern
- 1977   Dingler   Bill & Evelyn

Deaths
- 1979   Coates   Thomas
- 1981   Hinz   Herb

Mel and Jane Kieschnick are surrounded by the staff of Concordia Lutheran School upon a farewell for the Kieschnick home leave. The comings and goings of expatriates was usually an occasion to honor foreigners.

Repent and be baptized, every one of you in the name of Jesus Christ for the forgiveness of your sins, and you will receive the gift of the Holy Spirit. For the promise is for you and for your children and for all who are far off.

Acts 2:38-39

Chapter 13

Transitions and Partnership
The Lutheran Church Hong Kong Synod

Local and international forces and events aligned in the late 1960s to culminate in the formation in 1976 of the Lutheran Church-Hong Kong Synod, as a sister church and partner with the LCMS. One goal of the Missionary Conference had always been to "put themselves out of a job" as foreign missionaries; they desired to establish a self-sustaining local or indigenous church that would depend minimally on the LCMS. Missionaries could then move on to begin work in new fields. They did not expect this to happen as rapidly as it did.

The two partnering synods have developed cooperative programs, services, and activities in Hong Kong, China, and with overseas Chinese Christians, expanding the scope of educational and social services, and providing opportunities for local and overseas participation and support. New volunteer programs include short-term (under six months) and long term (up to two years) with lay people who witness, support, and serve in the name of Christ.

Desire for a National Church

In the mid-1960s, change, modernization, and independence influences were appearing everywhere - the American civil rights movement, the escalating Vietnam War, and the impact of Vatican II on the Roman Catholic church as well as Protestant denominations. Centuries-old traditions, organizational structures, and liturgical practices were being challenged, upgraded, or revolutionized. Within Missouri Synod leadership, a battle of contested interpretations and practices lay ahead. Chinese interest in a self-propagating and self-governing Hong Kong Lutheran church had surfaced at the 1962 all-Asia conference of the seven LCMS mission fields (referred to in the previous chapter).

The initial growth of the LCMS mission in Hong Kong had been sparked by the Concordia Bible School in Rennie's Mill (1952-58) and its successor Concordia Bible Institute (1958-67). Men and women, schooled at CBI embraced a high level of involvement and commitment to congregational growth, to schooling at all levels, and to leadership inspired by Gertrude Simon's commitment to Galatians 2:20. *Lutheran Hour* radio broadcasts (1952-56) and its Bible correspondence courses involved thousands of listeners, many of whom became baptized Christians. The year 1961 brought the last major wave of about 100,000 mostly Cantonese refu-

Chapter 13 — Transitions and Partnerships

Locations of LCMS and LC-HKS enterprise

(Repulse Bay)	1.	Church of All Nations & Hong Kong International School
(Tai Hang Tung)	2.	Concordia Books
(Tai Hang Tung)	3.	Concordia Lutheran Church & Middle School, Kowloon
(North Point)	4.	Concordia Lutheran School, North Point & Abiding Grace Lutheran Church
(Yau Yat Chuen)	5.	Concordia Seminary, SYNOD HEADQUARTERS, Hong Kong Lutheran Social Service's Headquarter & Lutheran School Social Work Programme
(Choi Hung)	6.	Elim Lutheran Church & Center for the Elderly
(Shaukiwan)	7.	Eternal Life Lutheran Church
(Cheung Sha Wan)	8.	Gertrude Simon Lutheran College, Savior Lutheran Church & Youth Center
(West Point)	9.	Grace Lutheran Church & Youth Center
(Tsuen Wan)	10.	Holy Cross Lutheran Church, School & Evening English School
(Kwun Tong)	11.	Holy Trinity Lutheran Church, Youth Center, Day School & Evening English School
(Tuen Mun)	12.	Lui Cheung Kwong Lutheran Schol
(Tuen Mun)	13.	Lui Cheung Kwong Lutheran Primary School & Euon Mission Station
(Tuen Mun)	14.	Lui Cheung Kwong Lutheran Kindergarten
(Cheung Shan)	15.	Lui Ming Choi Lutheran College & Cheung Shan Lutheran Church
(Pak Tin)	16.	Lutheran Center for the Blind
(Pak Tin)	17.	Lutheran Children and Youth Center
(Wo Che)	18.	Lutheran Children and Youth Center
(Tsz On)	19.	Lutheran Centre for the Elderly
(Shek Lei)	20.	Lutheran Cantre for the Elderly
(Mongkok)	21.	Lutheran Centre for the Deaf
(Pak Tin)	22.	Lutheran School Health Nursing Programme
(Homantin)	23.	Martha Boss Community Center & Mission Station (planning)
(Wan Chai)	24.	Morning Star Lutheran Church
(Tsim Sha Tsui)	25.	Nathan Road Lutheran Church
(Wong Tai Sin)	26.	Redemption Lutheran Church & Kindergarten
(Shumshuipo)	27.	Savior Lutheran Congregation & Savior Lutheran School
(Mongkok)	28.	Sharon Lutheran Church, School, Mongkok Lutheran School for the Deaf & Kowloon Cong. for the Deaf
(Rennie's Mill)	29.	St. John's Lutheran Church, School & Haven of Hope TB Sanatorium
(Chakwoling)	30.	St. Mark's Lutheran Church & Kindergarten
(Ngau Tau Kok)	31.	St. Matthew's Lutheran Church, Day School & Evening English School
(Macao)	32.	St. Paul's Mission Station, School & Deaf School
(Macao)	33.	St. Peter's Lutheran Church
(Lyemun)	34.	St. Philip's Lutheran Church, Day School, Evening English School & Kindergarten
(Hungham)	35.	True Word Lutheran Church, Kindergarten & Youth Center
(North Point)	36.	Zion Lutheran Church, Hong Kong Cong. for the Deaf, Youth Center & Kindergarten

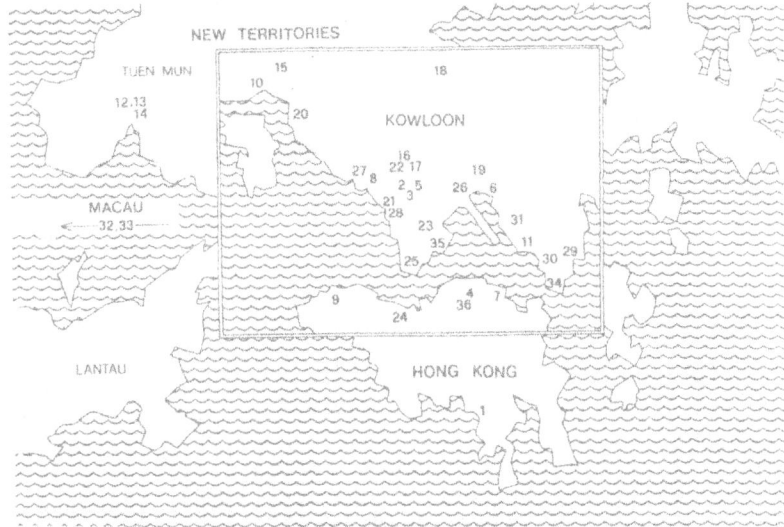

gees to Hong Kong's border. Half of them were turned back by barbed-wire fences and overwhelmed British guardians. The greatest number of members in mission congregations (about 8,000) was reached in the early 1960s, but by the time of the political and economic crisis of 1966 in Macau and Hong Kong, Sunday school and Bible class attendance had decreased nearly 40%. Correspondence course participation evaporated by 1965.

Several unrelated factors surely contributed to the decline. Most early refugees had secured semi-permanent residence in resettlement estates. Many converts had received visas to relocate in Taiwan, Canada, and the United States. The population of idle refugees, still traumatized from relocation, had stabilized somewhat. Job opportunities, and a semblance of economic stability, albeit at poverty levels, were developing in new factories and home industries. The energizing and renewing influences of the Bible school and *Lutheran Hour* broadcasts were gone. Concordia Seminary produced a smaller select group of men committed to careers in the church than CBI.

Another factor was a perception of abandonment. Two of the most energetic LCMS missionaries had returned to the States—Lorraine Behling in 1959 and Ruth Proft in 1962. Veteran Wilbert Holt left for family medical reasons in March 1962 and legendary "China hand" Elmer Thode died of a heart attack in 1965. The dynamic Gertrude Simon died in 1966. Mel Kieschnick left in 1966 for family health reasons. These senior missionaries were highly respected. They were loved by the Chinese for bringing them the Gospel, and for modeling the care of a Christian community.

Transition to a younger generation of missionaries brought out subtle differences in leadership styles. Martha Boss, Herb Hinz, Roy Karner, and George Winkler provided stability and continuity. The esteemed system of the Lutheran schools remained stable and doubled in enrollment, from 5,000 in 1965 to 10,000 in 1970, partially subsidized by the Hong Kong Department of Education. A successful education program was to become the most enduring hallmark of the church, typified by the thriving schools at Concordia and KwunTong Lutheran Primary School, opened in 1961. Government-subsidized schools, including LCMS, increased in number and enrollment.

In a separate development, Hong Kong International School began serving the expatriate English-speaking community in 1966 (detailed in Chapter 14). HKIS enriched Hong Kong as a more desirable community for many American and international expatriate families. Many previously churched families of various denominations joined the Repulse Bay congregation of LCMS staff members, in the school's 7-story building. The expatriate ministry on Hong Kong Island evolved to serve a different demographic. The congregation called its own pastor after founder Rev. Len Galster moved to Thailand in 1966. Karl Boehmke, formerly a chaplain, continued a tradition of welcoming openness for the next seven years.

With the return of relative tranquility after the 1967 confrontations came a period of re-evaluation. The colony-wide water supply crisis seemed to be over. Nationalist and Communist Chinese were co-existing, and confidence in the prospects for Hong Kong was restored. The exodus of Chinese and ex-pats slowed. The uncertainty of 1997, when the 99-year British lease on the New Territories was to expire, was still 30 years in the future. In 1968, the Hong Kong labor unions agreed to a six-day work week. Suddenly, workers had more than two days off per year.

The war in Vietnam was intensifying, strongly affecting the Hong Kong economy. The colony became a base for military R & R bringing a financial boost from British and American servicemen on shore leave.

Chapter 13 — Transitions and Partnerships

Secondary Schools

- Concordia International School (協同國際學校)
- Concordia Lutheran School, Kowloon (路德會協同中學)
- Concordia Lutheran School – North Point (北角協同中學)
- Gertrude Simon Lutheran College (路德會西門英才中學)
- Lui Ming Choi Lutheran College (路德會呂明才中學)
- Lui Cheung Kwong Lutheran College (路德會呂祥光中學)
- Ma Chan Duen Hey Memorial College (馬錦明慈善基金馬陳端喜紀念中學)
- Lutheran School for the Deaf (路德會啟聾學校)
- Saviour Lutheran School (路德會救主學校)

Primary Schools

- St. Matthew's Lutheran School (路德會聖馬太學校(秀茂坪))
- Holy Cross Lutheran School (路德會聖十架學校)
- Sharon Lutheran School (路德會沙崙學校)
- Lui Cheung Kwong Lutheran Primary School (路德會呂祥光小學)
- Leung Kiu Kau Lutheran Primary School (路德會梁鉅鏐小學)
- Lutheran Tsang Shing Siu Leun School (香港路德會增城兆霖學校)

Kindergartens

- Chan Mung Yan Lutheran Kindergarten (路德會陳蒙恩幼稚園)
- Kin Sang Lutheran Kindergarten (路德會建生幼稚園)
- HK Lutheran Church Kwun Tong Kindergarten (香港路德會官塘幼稚園)
- Loving Heart Lutheran Kindergarten (路德會愛心幼稚園)
- Lui Cheung Kwong Lutheran Kindergarten (路德會呂祥光幼稚園)
- Rock of Ages Lutheran Kindergarten (路德會恩石幼稚園)
- Redemption Lutheran Kindergarten (路德會救恩幼稚園)
- Sharon Lutheran Church Kindergarten (路德會沙崙堂幼稚園(正校))
- Sharon " " " (Tsz Oi Branch) (路德會沙崙堂幼稚園(慈愛分校))
- St. James Lutheran Kindergarten (路德會聖雅各幼稚園)
- St. Philip Lutheran Kindergarten (路德會聖腓力堂幼稚園)
- Zion Lutheran Kindergarten (路德會錫安堂幼稚園)

Indigenous Thinking

Within the Hong Kong Lutheran community, awareness of a conundrum emerged. The LCMS Chinese were neither a mission, nor a church, in limbo between receiving support and leadership from abroad yet desiring self-determination.

Trends amongst world missions to localize and nationalize indigenous churches inspired thoughts about separation. The movement to solidify non-aligned Asian and African nations at a conference in Bandung, Indonesia in 1965 had generated the concept of the "Third World." Some Third World cultures tied the concept of nationhood with an indigenous (self-governing, self-promoting, self-supporting) church, independent of overseas control. A distinction was essential to preserve the undiluted message of Jesus Christ, and the realization that the church, young or old, will be what the Lord intends it to be. Mission effort should not deal with symptoms, but with the basic core of the Christian enterprise.

Timing was always a question in terms of how ready the Hong Kong church was to become independent. A 1961 report on this readiness by Delwin B. Schneider pointed out that missionaries often perceived that a young church cannot really know and feel the responsibility and duty and privilege and sacrifice for a Savior who has redeemed it. Schneider observed that the mission enterprise may expect more from a young church than the Lord himself expects. When imported theory and structure is imposed upon a non-western cultural group, a young church may not be capable of taking on responsibility for a vast and complex organization. Well-intentioned but paternalistic programs generated by overseas mission boards, often don't fit the local situation. The Hong Kong congregations had each generated their own constitutions, often an amalgam of LCMS and Chinese culture.

Many staff members of the 1913-1952 China mainland mission, had made recommendations for procedural improvements, but were given short shrift and rarely put into practice. After 1952 in Hong Kong, similar recommendations came from the missionary council, composed of overseas staff and ordained Chinese pastors.

Providentially, the Hong Kong Education Department initiated plans to integrate Chinese and English education for promising young citizens by creating 28 "Anglo-Chinese" schools. All teaching was to be done in English so that students could practice their listening and oral skills. Only Chinese history was to be taught in the local Cantonese. Application was made by the LCMS to start such a school, and permission was granted to construct a middle school in the North Point area, near Zion Lutheran congregation. The school opened in 1967 under educational missionary Jim Luedtke, headmaster. Most construction expenses and faculty salaries were subsidized by the Government.

Several young American teachers bridged the gap between the local and home church. Concordia Teachers College students David Zurey, Dave Hoeppner, Roger Rohrbach and Andy Russell taught for two-year terms at Kowloon or North Point. Herb Geisler, an LCMS pastor's son, did a two-year post-baccalaureate internship teaching music and English. Supervised by missionaries Robert Dickhudt and Manfred Berndt, Geisler was able to immerse himself in the culture of his Chinese students at a grass roots level, working with seminary professor Herb Hinz. He was impressed by the work of the dedicated all-Chinese staff, and network of supportive churches and pastors.

Typical of many expatriates, Geisler became involved in the local community, singing with the Bach Choir, playing viola with the Hong Kong Philharmonic, directing choir and playing organ at Nathan Road, learning Cantonese on his own. He renewed for

Chapter 13 Transitions and Partnerships

Missionary George Winkler piloted a group on Ap Lei Chau island, near Aberdeen celebrating the anniversary of Luther's Catechism. In the Lutheran schools, assemblies featuring drama groups and choral presentations grew in popularity. Administrators met regularly with Mel Kieschnick, coordinating schools with the Education Department.

two additional years, leaving in 1975. Several teachers at HKIS also became involved in local Chinese youth work on the Kowloon side, and at the Timothy Paul study center in Aberdeen.

Concordia Theological Seminary had graduated two classes, a total of 13 men, eleven of whom were ordained. They provided a Chinese voice and vote at conference. By 1965, the Missionary Conference included lay delegates from eleven congregations. Some were disgruntled that there was resistance to their plans and needs. Many members were accustomed to having the Americans solve their problems and disputes with parent-like decisions. Clergy and members expected subsidy for the construction of worship spaces, whether a chapel or a school containing a church space. Attendance and tithing diminished.

New buildings, financial infusion, mass media, and newly-trained pastors were not able to staunch the decline in membership after 1961. A milestone was reached when the third seminary class graduated in 1969 with four members—Richard Law, Mark Lai, David Chiang, and Luke Mak. Two were born in China and two in Hong Kong. Two had been students at Concordia Kowloon. One had been a Christian since childhood; the others had come to Christ during Lutheran schooling.

The clergy-centric nature of local congregations failed to engage the majority of new converts. Pastors were both humble servants and esteemed leaders. The ancient Chinese model of leadership from above and far away did not mesh with American LCMS congregational models, involving lay leadership; individual volunteerism; and service groups like the Walther League, Lutheran Laymen's League (LLL), or Lutheran Women's Missionary League (LWML). It appears that church involvement for some members revolved more around financial benefits, control, and influence than Christian living.

Turf conflicts between pastors vying both for leadership position and for neighborhood exclusivity led to the splintering of a few congregations. The result was a diminished unity of mission outreach. Vitality for the gospel was tempered by political and monetary interests. Elements of ego and ambition were present - factors not unique to Chinese culture. The church had the most trained pastors, teachers, and lay leaders in its 20-year history, but there was no growth in membership.

The conference in 1972 recommended a program of consolidation, mandating that no new congregations be started near another already established church. Opportunities were sought to maximize the use of space, forcing congregations to explore community outreach through nurseries, pre-schools and other social services. To ease financial dependence on the LCMS, steps were taken to develop a worker-priest model, whereby pastors would take on part-time secular employment to subsidize their salaries. While some pastors began looking for outside employment, several balked at the notion.

Discussion - Debate - Division

"When God is working, so is the devil," noted one Chinese pastor.

Several issues stymied an independence movement. Differences between first-wave mainland immigrants and second-generation Hong Kong-born communicants fostered a generation gap. Communist, nationalist, and colonial loyalties remained a shallow undercurrent. Language divisions remained significant. First-wave refugees were mostly Mandarin speakers, many with professional and academic backgrounds. Cantonese was the *lingua franca* of Hong Kong, and most of the younger members spoke the English they heard and learned in the Colony. Hakka people, tracing their heritage to the hills of Fukien [Fujian] and Kwangtung [Guangdong], tended to retain their own singular language. Translators were usually dedicated

Chapter 13　　　　　　　　　　　　　　　　　　　　　　　　　Transitions and Partnerships

School graduations and assemblies for worship filled the auditoriums at Concordia and Kwun Tong schools. Local pastors, like Titus Lee Wei Tao, and missionaries would usually be the featured speakers. Music, as in all Lutheran schools, was essential, sometimes provided on piano by missionary wives such as Ruth Galster.

young seminarians or teachers. They were essential, but sometimes even they were stretched with unfamiliar concepts and vocabulary.

British colonial government, trying to manage the unexpected millions of residents, had encouraged the development of many social programs. Low profile services grew into major programs with support from many sources, including the beneficent Hong Kong Jockey Club. Health care for the destitute and elderly, and programs for the deaf and blind, were among government concerns. Colony-wide uniformity became essential in the effort to marshal local and international, secular and religious, agencies and volunteer groups. Beneficial government support of welfare and education meant grants and subsidy, but also conformity to regulations and bureaucracy. Schools and welfare programs multiplied. Multitudes were served, educated, and employed.

Hong Kong government school curriculum had a Bible history requirement, but LCMS schools placed additional emphasis on evangelism and Christian activities. The issue of who could teach religion courses was debated. Should only missionaries and evangelists (pastors-in-training) be allowed to teach doctrine? Mel Kieschnick came up with a controversial solution. Following a weekly training class, he provided to all teachers detailed lesson plans for religion instruction

Salaries were quite low, but with higher positions came higher pay and more government benefits. The temptation of more money became significant as the prosperity of the colony grew. Lutheran church workers' pay was sub-standard, especially in the early days. A well-educated teacher or pastor was qualified for many higher paying positions in the private sector. Some men did leave for other careers, but most continued their involvement with church school programs.

The Chinese Lutherans had plenty of their own issues to resolve. Theology was not high on the list, until stateside LCMS leadership became seriously interested in influencing local Hong Kong church politics. At home, the LCMS was entangled in its own internal struggles between conservative, moderate, and liberal factions. Among other things, this resulted in the loss of the majority of the St. Louis Seminary faculty, together with much of the student body, who together formed Concordia Seminary in Exile (Seminex), with its own program of curriculum and certification. *Lutheran News*, a conservative monthly tabloid, took up and continues the debate, with journalism that keeps alive a liberal-conservative polarity. These divisive developments remain a sub-current within the LCMS, leaving the question, "can a church divided be a church in mission?"

Many Disagreements, misunderstandings, and questionable communications with the Board of Foreign Missions raised tensions on both sides of the Pacific. Meetings in St. Louis and Hong Kong only furthered misunderstandings and accusations. Theology became a smoke screen masking other divisive issues. In Hong Kong, the majority group chaired by Andrew Chiu, chose to be identified as Lutheran Church-Hong Kong Synod in its first Memorandum of Articles of Association. A minority faction headed by Rev. Martin Chiang and Rev. Dante Yang did not want the name change and identified themselves as the Hong Kong and Macau Lutheran Church. Many other substantive issues were involved.

As the Hong Kong mission approached independence, American LCMS leaders came to visit individual Hong Kong church leaders with a declared intent to heal. The results instead were distrust, confusion, and division. Both missionary Manfred Berndt and Rev. Andrew Chiu were challenged and confronted over their recent doctoral dissertations at the St. Louis seminary. Someone would find fault, and fingers were pointed in every direction. Doctrine, liturgical practices, financial matters, and church power politics were all part of tangled arguments and accusations along a liberal-conservative axis.

Chapter 13 — Transitions and Partnerships

The Prodigal Son

Christ and the Children

The Tenth Leper

The Good Shepherd

Bible history and parables were the main subject of a unique group of painters, following in the style of a Buddhist-Christian convert C.C. Wang. Wang and his assistants lived at Shatin in the New Territories atop the East Wind Mountain. Their monastery, Tao Fung Shan, had been founded by German Lutheran Karl Reichelt of the *Hsin I Wei* denomination Lutheran church in the 1930s. The setting provided a welcome day retreat for many Christian groups in Hong Kong, and the painted ceramic plates, cups, and communion ware were sold to support the mission of Christians to Buddhists.

It was not an era of good feelings.

Although separate from the Chinese congregations, and independent by its constitution, Church of All Nations was courted by Hong Kong and U.S. churchmen to make a commitment to either the local or international church body. In 1974, CAN members voted by a narrow margin to stand beyond the fracas, remaining with the LCMS. Ten years later, the expatriate congregation requested full membership in a LCMS geographic district and in 1987 joined the Northwest District (Oregon, Washington, Idaho, and Alaska). That seemingly insignificant choice precipitated major involvement of the NOW district in the future re-activation of LCMS interest in China.

The Lutheran Church - Hong Kong Synod (LCHKS)

The Lutheran Church-Hong Kong Synod came into official existence on April 10, 1976 as a sister church with the LCMS. The pastor of Sharon Lutheran Church, Dr. Andrew Chiu (once a refugee who first came to Christ through Gertrude Simon in 1950) was elected president. The charter congregations of the new LCHKS were:

Concordia	Yauyatchuen
Holy Trinity	Kwuntong
Nathan Road	Tsimshatsui
Redemption	Laichikok
Saviour	Shamshuipo
Sharon	Yaumatei
St. Matthew's	Ngautaukok
St. Philip's	Kwuntong
True Word	HungHom
Eternal Life	Shaukeewan
Holy Cross	Tsuenwan

Papers filed with the HK government transferred ownership of properties to the new church. LCMS financial subsidy was reduced between 1977 and 1980, primarily due to setbacks in the American economy. At least three pastors resigned. Some took another church-related position in Hong Kong, and some left the Colony for pastorates abroad. In the tradition of the 1920s Term Controversy, lives were changed, but most moved on to do the Lord's work elsewhere

Continuing Programs

The LCMS maintains work in Hong Kong and Asia in partnership with the local Synod (LCHKS). The school for the deaf continued to succeed and grow. At the seminary, Dr. Thomas Coates continued his work until his death in 1979. The sole remaining active missionary from the mainland period, Herb Hinz, continued teaching at the seminary, and also filled vacancies for Chinese pastors until 1981. Rev. Richard Law, on leave to complete graduate studies, was called to teach in the seminary and expanded the Lutheran Social Service Department, leading to the establishment of the Martha Boss Center on Kowloon side.

The LCHKS hoped to open a Lutheran college in Hong Kong, and in October 1976 engaged Walter Wangerin to help with research and implementation. He became Executive Director of the Southeast Asia Lutheran Association for Higher Education and expanded the reach of the proposed school to include Singapore and Manila. LCHKS men Paul Chan and brothers James and John Chu (the boys who once slept under the Concordia school stairs in Chapter 11) were board members. However, after five years of work on the project, there was not enough support by the congregations of the LCHKS and the dream of higher education remains on a drawing board.

Rev. Louis Jasper continued his work as advisor to the Hong Kong Synod in the area of special ministry, with focus on the Mongkok Lutheran School for the Deaf and the Hong Kong Society for the Deaf. Endorsement and full subvention by the Hong Kong Education Department made a free-standing building dedicated to deaf education a reality. In 1990, the Lutheran School for the Deaf opened in Kwai Chung.

Chapter 13 Transitions and Partnerships

Concordia School North Point was the next large school constructed by the Mission, in a dominant location on Hong Kong Island overlooking the harbor from a hilltop.

Long-term missionary Herb Hinz taught at Concordia Seminary and led evangelism workshops with fellow missionary Manfred Berndt. Hinz served in China and Hong Kong from 1943 until his death in 1981.

Chapels opened throughout the Kowloon region, at Chatham Road and at Lye Chi Kok, where a school was operated in the upper floor. Very few church resembled congregational buildings in America. Most were store fronts, apartments ("flats") or were the shared auditoriums and classrooms of schools.

A number of shared positions were created between the various Missouri-related Lutheran entities. Missionaries Hillard Ranta and Jay Frazell taught religion courses at both HKIS and Concordia Theological Seminary. Rev. Paul Tuchardt, pastor since 1973 at CAN, was also on the seminary faculty and worked with programs of the LCHKS. Rev. David Chiang resigned his pastorate of True Word congregation at Hunghom to assume Rev. William Dingler's leadership of the Lutheran Hour office.

Evangelism

The first order of business for the LCHKS was to heal emotional wounds inflicted during the three years of transition. Many instances of pride, unkind words, judgment, lack of love and forgiveness that marked the internal struggle were acknowledged with sadness. All parties accepted their role in succumbing to unchristian behaviors. Forgiveness came first; reconciliation followed in due time. Hong Kong Lutherans restored normalcy and nurtured members who had been lost or ignored in the struggles from 1974 to1976. When the LCHKS was formed, total membership numbered 5,325 baptized members in the eleven congregations. Additionally there were 26 primary or secondary schools with a total enrollment of nearly 17,000 students and about 600 teachers.

Congregational life had been diminished for three years by the internecine disputes among several pastors. St. James congregation ceased activity and their rooftop on block #26 at Chaiwan Estate was returned to Government. Redeemer congregation failed when no new pastor was called. In Macau, neither St. Paul's nor St. Peter's on Taipa Island had a pastor, and the situation was turned over to the young Synod's Evangelism Committee.

Pastors Benjamin Chung and Eddy Wong spent a week in Taiwan where they trained for a new LCMS evangelism plan called Project Timothy. The program encouraged a several week exchange of pastors from different countries as a way to grow and learn about different ministry situations and opportunities. Exchanges waned by the late 1970s. The "Project Timothy" name and concept was picked up by the Wisconsin Synod in 1993, exposing college students to cross-cultural mission work and outreach for individuals and congregations.

The Hong Kong Synod has had the leadership of five presidents since its founding:

Rev. Dr. Andrew Chiu,	1970-1982
Rev. Titus Lee,	1982-1988
Rev. Dr. Benjamin Chung,	1988-1994
Rev. Dante Yang,	1994-1997
Rev. Dr. Allan Yung,	1997-present

Six volunteer American LCMS workers spent several months in Hong Kong in late 1976. They were "Ambassadors for Christ," introducing a fledgling program to train the local youth in evangelism and church life. The enterprise was not as successful as expected, and did not continue in Hong Kong. A similar non-clergy program, the "Prince of Peace Corps" later named Voluntary Youth Ministry (VYM), had been effective in Japan in the earlier 1970s. And in Taiwan over 200 volunteers in its VYM, and successor programs, would provide essential educational help over the next 20 years in Taipei and Chia Yi beginning in 1980 (see Chapter 18).

Education

At its creation, the LCHKS inherited the strong educational system developed by the leadership of Missionaries Behling, Kieschnick, Galster, Schmidt, and Dickhudt. LCHKS' three Anglo-Chinese secondary schools included Concordia Kowloon (1953), Concordia North Point (1969) and the Gertrude Simon College (1977).

Named to honor the missionary/deaconess, Gertrude Simon College in Yuen Long was built with $75,000 granted by the LWML in 1971-73. The first classes entered in 1977.

Martha Boss, last of the founding four, seemed to be involved everywhere - is social work, medical work, handicrafts, personal evangelism, and teaching. The people with whom she worked reported feeling a personal connection and caring they had not experienced previously. Several large gatherings were held in her honor, on her birthday, at the time of taking home leave. Her sudden death near Chicago in a head-on automobile accident during furlough in 1973 startled all she knew. "Aunt Bea" Richards assumed leadership of the Handicrafts project.

A "college" is the Hong Kong equivalent to an American high school. Many planners of the school had been Simon's students and friends from days at Rennie's Mill and the CBI. The school song begins; "To learn to be decent and remember the sages of the past with respect."

Two significant LCMS educational missionary leaders left Hong Kong in 1977, each at the end of his second terms. Robert Christian, since 1966 the first headmaster at HKIS, accepted the call to found Seattle Lutheran High School in 1977. Mr. Christian was succeeded by HKIS high school Principal David Rittmann. It was under his watch that HKIS mushroomed into an institution of four schools (Lower Primary, Upper Primary, Middle School and High School) and expanded onto a second campus five miles away at Tai Tam. After a long tenure, Rittmann went on to serve as head-of-school at Concordia International School in Shanghai in 1998 (see chapter 19).

James Luedtke, founding headmaster at Concordia School in North Point, took a two-year call in Venezuela to advise missionaries in nationalizing K-12 schools. His administrative position was filled by North Point's academic dean, Yeung Yok Wah.

As schools transitioned to LCHKS ownership, several pastors contended for prestigious principalship positions. Long term educator James Chu piloted the transition through times of ambition and disappointment.

The LCHKS youth- and evangelism committees launched renewed evangelism programs. School evangelism work had been neglected, so that a new emphasis was placed on the spiritual nurturing of faculty, students and alumni. Herb Geisler's work was significant in this process. Closer contact with student's families was encouraged.

By 2006, the LCHKS was operating five evening schools, six primary schools, seven kindergartens, and two schools for special education. Hong Kong International School and its staff operate independently. Once including about 30 educational missionaries, HKIS remains linked with the LCMS and continues to operate with a much larger and diverse international staff for 2700 students, with far fewer LCMS personnel.

Hong Kong Lutheran Social Service

Hong Kong Lutheran Social Service (HKLSS) was organized to meet human needs through action. The LCMS had long been meeting social ministry goals, dating back to coordinated refugee programs and work with the deaf and blind. In 1977, the former social welfare, youth, and special service committees of the LCMS were consolidated into the HKLSS.

Martha Boss
Lutheran Community Center

Plans for the Martha Boss Lutheran Community Center (MBLCC), originated in the early 1970s, under leadership from Richard Law, an early convert of Martha Boss. Until the center's opening in 1986, HKLSS offices first operated at Concordia Seminary in Yau Yat Chuen. Under the leadership of executive director Paul S. K. Chan, the MBLCC grew to include 44 satelite locations spread throughout the territory. Today, more than 600 staff carry out their duties in the spirit of Christian service, seeking out "relational witnessing" opportunites the occasion provides.

While the Martha Boss Center is the headquarters for HKLSS offices and meetings, this eight-story building is the home for a multitude of services for the people of Kowloon City and Homantin, approximately 120,000 residents. Facilities include a canteen, covered playground, basketball court, computer room, multi-purpose hall, library, study, and classrooms. Funding from the government supplied much financial aid, subsidies and grants for buildings and oper-

Chapter 13 Transitions and Partnerships

Lutheran women serving the church may be trained as a deaconess, dedicating their lives to service. Both Martha Boss and Clara Seltz were nurses. Clara had initially come to China in 1931; Martha came fro Cleveland in 1944. Mrs. Seltz and missionary wives Geri Holt and Florence Winkler took keen interest in working with the blind, and training in Braille.

ations. Since 1997, in harmony with HKSAR government services, nearly two-thirds of the HKLSS budget comes from subvention and grants, nearly $15 million in 2006.

Elderly Services

Services for the aged at the Martha Boss Center include a senior center for the neighborhood, a drop-in elderly day care center, day-time services for nursing care, independent living, quality of life, rehabilitation, health education, career support, meals, and transportation. Limited permanent housing is also available for the aged. Social activities for these residents encourage family visits, educational and developmental programs, and indoor and outdoor activities. Five units for the elderly serve over 550 men and women, about 250 as full-time residents.

Elderly Centers

Seven neighborhood elderly centers are operated by the HKLSS. These daytime gathering venues provide services to enable the elderly to remain in the community, to lead a healthy and dignified life, to enhance positive attitudes and practices, and to develop elderly volunteerism activities. Two major centers for the aging are located at Sun Chui (in Tuenmun) and Yau On (in Shatin). Lutheran Centers for the Elderly have been open since 1985, serving a total of about 320 people. The Hong Kong Red Cross has partnered with a uniformed corps of volunteers to care for the frail, sick, and disabled. They also operate a mobile library.

"Fitness for Wholesome Health" is an effort for the well-being of the elderly. FWH coaches introduce a plan of physical and psychological practices at elderly day centers. One event, in March 2005, drew over a thousand elderly participants.

Marshaling a three-point program, the "Happy Angels" project uses "Happy Tools" to maintain positive attitudes among older citizens, who may live independently or in residential centers. Stressing practices of good health maintenance, regular gatherings for "Thanks and Praise," and performing acts of charity have helped over 500 participants.

Services for the Blind

Three HKLSS-related social service units were established in 1968 in the Wong Tai Sin area—a blind center, a youth center, and the elderly center. Two social and recreational centers are available to blind, deaf, and physically disabled people. Goals, in addition to providing personal attention to clients, are to foster community barrier-free facilities and policies within the HKSAR.

As mentioned above, help for the blind dates from the 1950s, primarily the work of missionary wives Clara Seltz, Geraldine Holt, and Florence Winkler. While a product of the LCMS and LCHKS sponsorship, the institution is now an independent entity, a model school for the Hong Kong Society for the Blind. Organizing community and civil educational programs, HKLSS provides public transportation, removal of infrastructural impediments such as street obstacles, and clothing with colored warning stripes. Braille materials are produced locally and by Lutheran Braille workers in California.

The LCMS Lutheran Blind Mission Society, based in St. Louis, provides English Braille magazines, large-type publications and cassettes monthly. The society, founded in 1994, encourages, trains, and supports blind people as they share Jesus. The Christian Blind Institute began training blind leaders and missionaries in 1999.

Rehabilitation Service

Training and daily living skills are needed by disabled persons unable to benefit from vocational training or sheltered employment. HKLSS operates three centers to train such people to become more independent in their daily lives, for integration into the community, and for other forms of care. For severe cases, two hostels provide home living for

Chapter 13 — Transitions and Partnerships

Dwelling near the water, or in the harbors and typhoon shelters a large population, in Hong Kong, were known as "boat people." Traditionally, they spent little time on land, and several Christian groups launched special ministry to them.

School activity formed the primary connection with both urban and rural families.

those with a moderate mental handicap and who lack self-care skills.

Two social and recreational centers organize social projects and activities to enhance self-potential and social skills of over 9000 blind and physically handicapped individuals. Home services are also provided by a home-based training and support team for about 100 clients annually.

Community Development Programs

The HKLSS aspires to provide advocacy and education to protect the rights of citizens. Mobilization of residents in specific geographic locations has helped local people organize and approach authorities with concerns over land usage, transportation, and social services. One particular example given in a 2006 LCHKS report highlighted the dilemma of several hundred families living in "squatter" housing near Fanling. They faced certain relocation in 2005 when their village area was to be re-zoned as a residential area. A team from HKLSS worked with the residents, developers, and the HKSAR to delay development pending further study.

Family Care Service

In Shatin, the Family Life Education Centre opened in 1993, providing services to enhance family harmony. Eleven programs include relationship counseling, preparation for marriage and parenthood; activities for youth and family groups; and organized day camps, carnivals and competitions.

Foster Care Service also began in 1993, providing temporary care and matching suitable foster homes for an average of 40 needy children under age 18. The HKLSS Foster Care Unit does not set up care arrangements, but focuses on supervision, liaising with professionals, providing pastoral care, and encouraging healthy parent-child relationships. The foster parents undertake full care and nurture of these children until they can reunite with their natural parents or lead an independent adult life. Through family field trips, celebrations of holidays, and family day activities, about 300 persons are served annually.

Nursery Services

Nurseries to provide day-care and preschool education for children aged two to six have been in operation since 1986. Half-day, full day, and extended hours services are available. Children with Down Syndrome and autism have also been helped since 1992. These have been highly successful self-supporting centers, and in 2006 the ten nurseries had spaces for 1132 children.

HKLSS day nurseries serve needy children who are eligible for fee remission in kindergarten and child care. Children are coached in learning community resources in their neighborhoods; visiting police and fire stations, and using public transportation. Thus youngsters experience cooperation and community in addition to motivating their skill and thinking development.

Youth Services

Children and youth centers first formed in 1980. Four core programs include guidance and counseling; supportive services; socialization development; and social responsibility promotion. Substance abuse centers that link with local hospitals and government probation units, the outreach unit, and family service unit, were first established in 1998.

Several aspects of youth culture are the concern of HKLSS. Serving 14 schools HKLSS provided school social workers, supplies, and casework services to help students overcome problems with school, family, behavior, relationship, or academic challenges. They also work with student groups to better their self-understanding, develop potential, and build positive life attitudes. School social workers consult with students, parents, and school personnel, and also coordinate and mobilize non-school based community resources. A total of 1039 cases produced over 9,800 consultations in 2006.

Chapter 13   Transitions and Partnerships

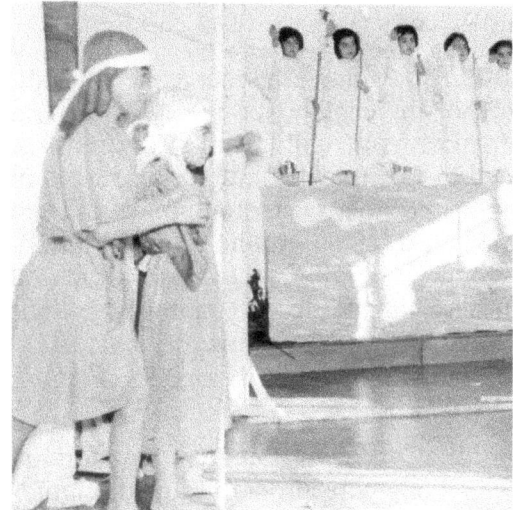

Childhood in Hong Kong created resiliancy, each child growing in knowledge and experience within a crowded community, offered hope and promise to families determined to give their offspring a better future.

The work with students includes personal counseling, academic casework, and modeling inter-generational communication through parent-teacher associations, mobilizing and coordinating school and community. In addition, the Lutheran Social Service Operation Authority fosters programs such as skill training, expedition courses, neighborhood service projects, work with the elderly, physical fitness, and service to children in China.

Seventeen schools participated in the Student Guidance Service Project in 2005-2006. Integrated services provided counseling and venues for activities at eight other schools designed to aid in socialization, responsibility, and competency. The "Future Schooling/Career Plan" facilitates a joint program for 11 schools that participate in coordinated training and activity. Aimed at secondary students choosing career paths, skills of independent and responsible thinking are encouraged thru role-playing, games, practicing job interviews, and visitation of potential venues for employment. Popular targets include the police and fire departments, broadcast and computer positions, hospitality and food service industries, insurance and investment work, and careers in tourism.

Community Chest connections produced a grant to launch the "youngster internet addiction prevention and counseling service." Youth and their family members are targeted to use internet communication in positive ways. Through school-and community-based education, appropriate use of electronic media is modeled.

Two centers aimed at illegal drug abuse prevention, early identification, education, and intervention are jointly funded with the Hong Kong Jockey Club. Multi-disciplinary professionals use intervention strategies to address psychotropic drug usage.

Several programs are also available to college-level students through the HKLSS' Student Counseling Service at the Open University of Hong Kong. Goals incorporate comprehensive individual counseling and facilitation of individual student growth and success.

The Lutheran Church Hong Kong Synod has diversified to reinforce and share the gospel, and serve the people of Lutheran congregations, the Hong Kong community at large, and those beyond the borders of the Special Administrative Region.

Significant Sources:

Board of Control, Concordia Seminary — *Exodus from Concordia, 1977*
Hong Kong Lutheran Social Services — *Annual Report, 2005-2006*
Lutheran Church Hong Kong Synod — *Fiftieth Anniversary Book, 1999*
Lutheran School for the Deaf — *Journal Dedication Issue 22nd May, 1991*
Mueller, Richard — *Mission Made Impossible, 1977*

Interviews with Manfred & Ute Berndt, Karl & LaVerne Boehmke, Jay Frazell, Jim Luedtke, Paul Strege, Virginia Wangerin, and Dante Yeong.

Chapter 14 — English and International Developments 1962-2012

Arrivals

Year	Name	First Name(s)	Location
1966	Christian	Bob & Arleen	(HKIS)
	Luedtke,	Jim & Audrey	(North Point)
	Halter	Carol	(deaconess)
1967	Boehmke	Karl & LaVerne	(CAN)
1969	Rohrbach	Roger	(North Point)
	Russell	Andy	(North Point)
1973	Tuchardt,	Paul & Caroline	(CAN)
1987	Betker	Bruce	(CAN)
1991	Temme	Hugh	(CAN)
1997	Dull	Chuck & Joanne	(HKIS)
1997	Koehneke	Dale & Donna	(CAN)
2001	Wahrenberg	Bill	(HKIS)
2005	Mueller	Richard & Claire	(HKIS)
2011	Dunning	Kevin & Mary	(HKIS)

Hong Kong International School Called Faculty - no official listing available
LCMS Called staff; some couples were both called; many wives worked
Many supplemental teaching staff were classified as "overseas hire;"
Hundreds of teachers and para-professionals are "local hires"

1966
- Duval — Elizabeth
- Witt — Susan

1967
- Brackmann — Edward & "Pete"
- Feil — Dorothea
- Lense — Mariellen
- Mahlke — William
- Rupprecht — Robert & Anne
- Schroeder — Melvin & Karen
- Von Behren — Werner & Marie
- Zimmerman — Lester & Lillian

1968
- Arnett, — Beverly
- Bartz — Dennis [& Connie]
- Dollase — Edward & Vera
- Hollar — Melvin
- Kaufman — Joan
- Prellwitz — Thelma
- Wingfield — Albert & Marge

1969
- Anchor — William
- Berndt — Norlean
- Maxner — David & Marilyn
- Salecker — Rich & Bonnie

1970
- Graef — Ron & Sue
- Holliday — Robert & Sally
- Meyer — Rodger & Elizabeth
- Prout — Rob & Julie
- Rausch — Hank & Sue
- Rogalski — Robert & Mirka
- Schmidt — Walt & Lois
- Siegert — Rich & Kathy

1971
- Carlton — Paul [& Becky]
- Harnisch — Del [& Pat]
- Pfaff — Fred
- Ranta — Hillard & Helmi
- Rutherford — William & Nancy
- Tieman — Ernie & Evelyn
- Wallis — Darell & Eileen
- Westrick — Earl & Marj

1972
- Elmshaueser — Dale & Carolyn
- Feddersen — Alan & Carole
- Himmler — Art & Corky
- Landdeck — David & Kathi
- Silzer — Mark & Barbara

1973
- Barnes — Gary [& Anne]
- Bloomenberg — Paula
- Kohl — Dave & Katy
- Kolb — Barry & Nancy
- Rittmann — David & Doris
- Voeltz — Bruce "Fritz" & Lois

1974
- Frazell — Jay
- Heissler — Mary Kaye [Soderlind]
- Knisely — Jay & Dusty
- Schroeder — Norma [Moore]

1975
- Dieckhoff — Bill & Jo
- Driskill — Bill & Lynne
- Lindner — John & Cheri
- Meyer — David & Shirley
- Neumann — Larry & Darlene
- Schiefer — Carl & Virginia

1976
- Anderson — Bill & Terri
- Reimer — Chris & Diane
- Talbott — Jim

1977
- Schalk — Jan [Westrick]

1979
- Van Andel — Roger & Judy
- Smith — Bob & Alice

1980
- Kuhn — Bill [& Kris]
- Oetting — Dennis & Donna
- VanLuchene — Darrell & Sue
- Denow — Dennis

1981
- Erhardt — Walt & Gretchen

1982
- Weber — Mike & Louise

1983
- Englebrecht — Ted & Jacqueline
- Handrich — Jim
- Yung — Jan

1988
- Eichert — Larry
- Renken — John & Gayle
- Wirgau — Otto & Delores

1990
- Eichert — Carol
- Hoeppner — Dave & Beth
- Schmidt — Marty [& Zella]

1994
- Frerking — Patrick & Susan

1996
- Markin — Gerry & Karen

2003
- Leese — Bill & JJ

2006
- Klekamp — Patricia

Departures - data not available

Deaths

Year	Name	First Name	Age	Cause
1968	VonBehren	Timothy Paul	age 10	(carbon monoxide asphyxiation)
1978	Kohl	Aaron Michael	infant	(hyline membraine disease)
2011	Sawyer	Cyndi	teacher	(heart)

For as many of you as were baptized into Christ have put on Christ. There is neither Jew nor Greek, there is neither slave nor free, there is no male and female, for you are all one in Christ Jesus.

Galatians 3:27-28 (ESV)

Chapter 14

English and International Developments 1962-2012

Language groups are a fundamental underlayment of the Hong Kong tapestry. Mandarin had been the initial language that originally linked evacuated missionaries with Nationalist refugees. Living in Cantonese-speaking Hong Kong, LCMS workers soon recognized their need to know the common dialect of the Colony. As the scope of the mission expanded, it encompassed mainland refugees and Hong Kong natives.

Several other minority Chinese dialects were spoken, especially Hakka, but Cantonese was dominant. China coastal pidgin, a spoken English patois commonly used between foreigners and workers, combines Chinese grammar, word order, and tense with English vocabulary. Also called "Chinglish" by locals, it is most often associated with stereotypical depictions of China in Hollywood movies, and is less common today.

Missionaries and their wives who arrived after 1954 (Karners, Winklers, Kieschnicks, Schmidts, Dickhudts, Galsters, and Berndts) immersed themselves in a minimum of one year of intense Cantonese study. They made extensive use of young men from CBI to interpret or deliver messages and sermons until they became proficient with the vernacular Cantonese. Evangelist Paul Chang had been the essential translator for the original four - Boss, Behling, Simon, and Holt. Several other Christian converts helped as Cantonese translators for the Americans, both in preaching and in official situations. Among them were Andrew Chiu, Isaac Mah, Daniel Lee, and brothers James and John Chu.

Conversely, many resident Chinese spoke an adequate level of English, and some better-educated locals used very proper British English. Many had attended schools in the UK. A few of these young men were eventually sent to the States for LCMS seminary programs in St. Louis or Springfield, or for education courses near Chicago, at Concordia College in River Forest, Illinois.

This chapter details English language enterprises of the LCMS among the bi-lingual Chinese and international expatriates in Hong Kong.

Kwun Tong Lutheran School

There seems to have been scant thought of a local English-speaking LCMS ministry before about 1960. Following the success of Concordia Middle School, the mission's ear-

Chapter 14　　　　　　　　　　　English and International Developments 1962-2012

Concordia Lutheran School on Tai Po Road was the home of Concordia Congregation. In the school auditorium, worshippers held services in Cantonese and Mandarin languages, and in the afternoons, missionaries held their own community services in English. Some expat worshipers made the 2-hour trip from distant Repulse Bay, traveling by car on the vehicular ferry, or via trams on HK Island, the Star Ferry to cross the harbor, then riding in 14-passenger Public Light Busses.

liest Anglo-Chinese school was planned and built with the leadership of Mel Kieschnick. "Anglo-Chinese" implies that some classes were taught in English, and some in Cantonese. Kwun Tong Lutheran School, an elementary school for 525 students, opened in 1963 on reclaimed land near Kai Tak airport. The government also permitted Holy Trinity Lutheran Church to operate within the building. Missionary Len Galster and Rev. Cromwell Chen used the school's auditorium and classrooms on weekends and evenings.

Rev. Chen, the third Hong Kong man to study in America at the seminary level, graduated from Concordia Springfield seminary in 1960, alongside Len Galster. Len and Ruth Gastler devised innovative programs and events which created neighborhood interest. In the school courtyard on warm summer evenings, Galster screened black and white movies in English about the life of Christ, using a kerosene projector. Many of the neighborhood youngsters who watched the films returned to attend Sunday school in Holy Trinity's classrooms.

With a background in publication and graphics, Galster was also assigned to chair the HK Lutheran Publicity Committee. In this capacity, he assumed editorship of the *Hong Kong Letter* from Ruth Proft, and wrote articles for LCMS home publications. In 1963, it was determined that the expenses of printing could be reduced by simply including Hong Kong articles in the more widely circulated *Lutheran Witness*, Synod's major bi-weekly newsmagazine. This altered an important link with supporters and LWML groups accustomed to the familiarity of the old newsletter. Galster re-focused on public relations, and became well acquainted with journalism and printing contacts in Hong Kong. These contacts would be of future benefit to the mission, in the international context.

Nathan Road Lutheran Church

Tsim Sha Tsui (TST), on the Kowloon peninsula, is the heart of the tourist zone, just a seven-minute ferry ride within sight of Hong Kong Island. Nathan Road connects Kowloon hotels and night spots with the Star Ferry terminal, KCR railroad station, and Kowloon piers. Boundary Street, a few miles north, marks the beginning of the New Territories. Travelers usually lodged there in the less expensive hotels set among a warren of shops and emporiums. Rev. Holt believed the TST area to be an opportune location for a new outreach and chapel.

An upstairs space was found and purchased in Majestic House, a new commercial building on Nathan Road near Kowloon Park. Finished in 1963, the worship space, with pews that face a pedimented chancel, can hold 200 people. Missionary wives Betty Karner and Jane Kieschnick sewed curtains and alter paraments to create a sacred space. Evangelist Phillip Ho, a graduate of CBI, was in charge of the sanctuary and later started a deaf ministry.

Initial numbers were disappointing. Missionaries and occasional tourists attended, but there were few resident English speakers in TST, nor was this an area much frequented by European residents. However, the Chinese congregation that met there grew under the leadership of Evangelist Ho. Meanwhile seeds were being sown for a more established English language congregation on Hong Kong Island.

Repulse Bay Lutheran Church

Until Nathan Road opened, English-speaking LCMS worshipers gathered on Sundays in the Concordia school gymnasium, where missionary George Winkler was in charge of afternoon services. Anglican worship in English was also available in Kowloon at historic St. Andrew's Church on Nathan Road, and on Hong Kong side at St. Johns Church on Garden Road. But Lutherans like to worship with their own.

One Missouri Synod business family regularly drove from Repulse Bay over winding Wong Nei Chong Gap Road and crossed the

Chapter 14 — English and International Developments 1962-2012

The historic Repulse Bay Hotel offered space to meet. The congregation simply tipped the staff to set up chairs. Sunday school proved popular and Rev Len Galster worked with a council to set up a congregation based on the LCMS model. Christmas pageants. Bible class, and worship grew from the initial service on March 4, 1962 of Repulse Bay Lutheran Church.

harbor on the vehicular ferry to reach those English worship services in Kowloon. This American couple, Joe and Dotty Mache, proposed that the mission consider holding English services in distant Repulse Bay, where over 1500 English-speaking expatriates lived in villas or tall apartment blocks. Most of the missionaries felt that they were in Hong Kong to work in the Chinese language, and that expanding into English work would drain their limited resources. No efforts were begun.

On a business trip in 1961, Mr. Mache visited with Rev. Herman Koppelmann, the LCMS Secretary for Missions in St. Louis. Koppelmann considered the idea of an expatriate ministry, and investigated the situation when he visited Hong Kong in early 1962. Len Galster, already living on Hong Kong side, was appointed to survey and explore Repulse Bay as a potential area for serving an expatriate population.

Galster knocked on about 400 doors to discuss the possibility of holding a Sunday school in Repulse Bay, and garnered strong interest from about 100 families. In a gathering at Mache's flat, it was suggested to approach the dignified Repulse Bay Hotel for a space in which to hold a Sunday school. Mr. Ostramoff, the manager, offered the use of the elegantly paneled colonial reading room, a large well-lit high-ceilinged space off the main library. Ostramoff felt the group was proposing a good social service and there would be no rental fee as long as the hotel set-up boys were tipped. With these details in place, formal invitations announced March 4, 1962, as the first service of what would become Repulse Bay Lutheran Church (RBLC). It was the same week that American astronaut John Glenn completed the first orbital space flight around the earth aboard *Friendship 7*.

Twenty-seven children attended the first Sunday school session; eighteen adults also worshipped that Sunday, and momentum was begun. By the end of the year, weekly worship attendance numbered 33 committed adults and 128 Sunday school children. Modeled on traditional Lutheran churches, the group developed into a congregation. Worship and social committees soon formed, complimenting the Sunday school. Pageants, parties, and a cycle of church festivals added variety to regular worship. Pastor Galster held confirmation classes. Ruth Galster played a small pump organ for services, a choir formed, and soprano Nancy Li (Zi) sang memorable professional solos. Pan American Airways flew in a fresh Christmas tree for holiday services at the historic hotel.

The American-style congregation grew in numbers and programs. English-speaking Christians of many denominations were drawn to the program of worship and education at the hotel. Missionary Eugene Seltz from Concordia Seminary provided history and perspective about the Chinese church from his experiences in China. Seltz had just written, in German, a serialized history of the mainland mission effort before 1949. C. S. Hung, a RBLC member and a Hong Kong University professor, helped with understanding how to work with and appreciate Chinese culture.

In January 1963, plans for a permanent worship building were proposed, and a committee formed - Galster, Mache, Professor Hung, and chaired by Mel Kieschnick. When approached with the concept, the Hong Kong Lands Department informed the committee that Government could not provide land (which all belonged to the Crown) for a church, but it could do so for a school building even though that building might contain a church space. There were already several of these church-schools of various denominations in Hong Kong. A few were Anglo-Chinese mixed language operations. The committee returned to the drawing board to investigate building a parochial school!

Rumblings about starting an American-style school on Hong Kong Island came from several sources—the Maches, busi-

Chapter 14 — English and International Developments 1962-2012

As the congregation grew, the need for it's own facility became desirable. Building lots were unavailable. Investigations led to the conclusion that by building a school, the congregation could designate space within that building for congregational activities. It was the origin of Hong Kong International School, initially designed for 600 students in grades K-12.

ness man Hooitberg, missionaries Seltz and Galster, and language professor Hung. Toward the end of 1962, the idea of a community Lutheran school on the American model was discussed with Mel Kieschnick, who happened to be the education director of the Missionary Conference. The RBLC youth group printed invitations for services, and delivered them door-to-door to area expatriate families, recruiting by word of mouth.

Students in the Repulse Bay school would be fluent English speakers, on a track to harmonize with American education curriculum, philosophy, and testing for college admission. Such a situation was not currently available at the Colony's only English language British upper school, named after Queen Elizabeth's grandfather, King George V. Most British families sent their secondary students to the U.K. for boarding school, a practice which did not appeal to Americans.

The LCMS had established a respected reputation with the education department, because of its four successful rooftop clubs, and Kwun Tong and Concordia Middle Schools. One hundred percent of the first graduating class from Concordia had passed the rigorous school-leaving exams in 1957. Lorraine Behling's 1953 efforts at Saviour/Concordia now paid off, and Kieschnick's near decade of good relationships with the Hong Kong Education department portended future success.

Hong Kong International School

Four years of development of a very innovative concept lay ahead for the six person steering committee: An American-style international school (similar to those already operating in Singapore, Tokyo, and Taipei), designed for English speaking K-12 students of many nationalities in a British colony, with a staff and curriculum based on Lutheran Christian educational philosophy, to be initially financed jointly by HK Government, the Lutheran Church Missouri Synod, international business firms, and individual tuition. Unknowingly, groundwork was being laid for large schools in Hong Kong ,and, 30 years into the future, at Shanghai, ShenZhen, and Hanoi.

With the concept of a school in mind, a survey was conducted in July 1963 among ex-pat families in Hong Kong which revealed overwhelming support for such a school. Galster researched the Lutheran High School movement in the U.S. regarding funding, physical plant, administration, faculty and curriculum. Community Lutheran High Schools, supported by associations of local congregation, were successful in St. Louis, Chicago, Detroit, Cleveland, Los Angeles, and another dozen larger cities during the 1960s. They would slowly replace Synod's traditional, mostly male, residential prep schools.

William Wong, a local American-trained architect, offered to draw building plans *pro bono*, with the understanding that if and when approval was received for the Repulse Bay Lutheran School, his firm (Wong and Threadgill) would be engaged. He designed a 26-classroom school with additional rooms for laboratories, art, music, typing, library, gymnasium and offices.

In these early stages close coordination was established with the American Chamber of Commerce (AmCham) and the United States Consulate. The Consul General, Mr. Green, gave encouragement at every point, since such a school in Hong Kong would solve the significant challenge of educating expat students in an American format. The uniqueness of overseas students, *Third Culture Kids*, was later identified by author David Pollack.

A hillside in Repulse Bay, just off South Bay Road, was identified by Galster, Kieschnick, and Education Director W. D. Gregg as a school site. The Hong Kong Education Department approved a grant for a 43,000 square foot plot on February 25, 1965. The Hong Kong government promised

Chapter 14　　　　　　　　　　　　English and International Developments 1962-2012

Eugene Seltz (pictured in his early days as a China missionary) assumed leadership of the Board of Managers when Mel Kieschnick returned to America in 1966. Familiar with Chinese ways and language, he led the committee and congregation through the vicissitudes of construction and the calling of a Headmaster. Len Galster coordinated with architect William Wong in designing the 28-room school. Construction began shortly after final approval was received from the LCMS Detroit convention in the summer of 1965.

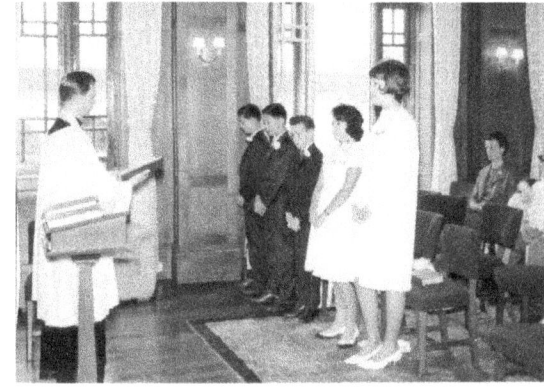

an interest-free loan towards the erection of the school.

The LCMS Board for World Missions gave its blessing to the unprecedented project. Dr. Koppelmann had taken great interest in a school shortly after Repulse Bay Lutheran Church had formed, and under his leadership the board set several operational conditions. The school was:

    1) to finance daily operations without subsidy from the Lutheran Church;
    2) to have a complete (Lutheran) Christian educational program;
    3) to be planned under the supervision of the Mission Education coordinator;
    4) to be administered by a called experienced LCMS educator.

Questions centered on the proposed curriculum. Could a fully American curriculum be taught in Hong Kong, staffed primarily by Lutheran teachers? Should the school combine British and American curriculum so students could prepare for university entrance exams in either country? The proposed American International School would prepare and keep students in the mainstream of U.S. curriculum, with a clear religious philosophy and activities; distinctly Christian yet not coercive. Lutherans would focus on the nature of man, his needs, and salvation through Jesus Christ. The resulting message to students (and parents) is left to the power of the Spirit through the word. Coercion and legalism should not be involved in the teaching process of a truly Lutheran school.

Proposed staffing would draw from the heritage of synodically-trained educators, salaried on the same scale as all LCMS missionaries. Suggested monthly salary for a male teacher with three children would be about $415, with travel, housing, and leave benefits of another $400. Qualified teachers already living in Hong Kong (Local Hire) would be employed for specialty areas and needs, but would not be provided with housing or travel benefits. Foreign language and strong college preparatory offerings would receive emphasis over traditional vocational courses. Music and art programs were essential.

Construction

All these planning pieces came together at the 1965 Synodical Convention in Dallas. With a complete set of Wong's drawings in-hand, Galster made a convincing presentation that the Hong Kong project was serious, well thought out, and ready for approval. Major funding came from Synod's recent "Faith Forward" national thank-offering. The school was approved. A grant and a low interest loan from the Synod filled in the financial pieces, incorporating the Hong Kong government's beneficence.

Site work commenced even before Rev. Galster's return to Hong Kong. Due to an emergency family illness, Kieschnick, a driving force and link with the Education Department was forced to leave HK permanently that same November. Dr. Eugene Seltz, veteran of the mainland mission, assumed leadership, and piloted the project through the next three years. Another veteran China missionary, Victor Hafner, also joined the board. Kieschnick's role was assumed by educator Harold "Blackie" Schmidt, just two years after his arrival.

Ground breaking ceremonies on April 28, 1966 initiated a rapid construction phase. The hillside was excavated foundations were poured, steel was bent, brick was laid. But nothing happens in a vacuum in Hong Kong.

Three weeks before groundbreaking, on April 4, a young Chinese man protesting the fare increase on the cross-harbor Star Ferry declared a hunger strike at the Hong Kong pier. Within a day, the *Star Ferry* terminal in Tsim Sha Tsui was also occupied by protesters. About 1400 youths were arrested during four days of riots. Later, a government commission concluded that the incident was the

Enthusiasm among American expatriates led to the opening of the school a full year before construction was to be completed. A complete apartment block on Chung Hong Kok became the Provisional school for grades K-8, and Dow Chemical Corp. operated a high school there for one year.

1967 was a year of water rationing, the year the Cultural Revolution went into full swing, yet a year tourists could still experience the eclecticity of Tiger Balm Gardens.

result of local frustration over-crowding, insecurity, under-employment, and living conditions.

As political unrest simmered, construction moved ahead at the school site. Robert Christian, 36-year old teacher and principal of Our Savior Lutheran School in the Bronx, NY, had accepted the call in February 1966 to be the first headmaster (a British title combining principal and superintendent). He arrived in August, 1966, with a year to prepare for opening of the school in September 1967.

However, this was not to be. Man's plans are not always God's plans.

Provisional School

Rapid growth of the American expatriate community during the mid-60s was the outcome of several factors. In 1966, Dow Chemical Corporation moved its regional Asian headquarters to Hong Kong, bringing a large number of new staff and their families. More significantly, Pan American Airways received the contract to fly U.S. military personnel to the Colony for R&R. American military involvement in the escalating Southeast Asian war meant increased usage of Hong Kong as a port for weary troops. Basing Pan-Am's staff in the colony meant that about one hundred new families, many raising school-age children, would take up residence.

Looking for suitable schools for staff families, Pan Am and Dow learned of the Repulse Bay project. Intense and urgent proposals in May to the Board of Managers to open a provisional school that same autumn were agreed upon. By early summer 1966, Seltz and Galster had found a newly-built apartment building just past Repulse Bay on the Chung Hom Kok peninsula. The entire three-level building, with two three-bedroom flats on each level, was leased for a year.

Bob Christian was informed of this development prior to his August 8 departure from New York. He revised his focus, ordered textbooks, and had two Lutheran teachers called by the LCMS, Liz Duval and Suzanne Witt. They and several locally-hired teachers would open the serendipitous school on September 26 with 170 pupils. Community learning happened in closets, kitchens, bedrooms, hallways, and verandahs overlooking the East Lamma Channel.

As that first school year was nearing completion and families were making furlough and summer plans, a new and more disruptive political situation erupted in Hong Kong, the riots explained in chapter 12. By mid-May, the unrest had spread to Hong Kong Island. Most students ceased riding on public transportation, all were taught to be wary of suspicious bags and containers, and non-essential shopping or pleasure outings were curtailed. HKIS students living on the Kowloon side were especially affected as they ventured through crowded narrow streets toward the ferries and the #6 bus. Taxi cabs and unregistered private-hire cars (*pak-pai*) took many extra trips to Chung Hom Kok.

Opening the new school

Throughout spring, workers continued constructing the eight-floor "American" school. Building materials were scarce, yet brick was somehow procured from across the bamboo border. As the provisional school was closing, Bob Christian was heavily engaged in managing the recruitment of a permanent overseas teaching staff for the new building's September opening. An experienced staff was desired, but most teacher candidates had school-age families and were reluctant to move them to unstable Hong Kong. A mostly Lutheran-trained American faculty was expected, setting high standards in the experimental school. The assurance of a consistent and stable American faculty was the appeal of HKIS to potential parents and their hesitant U.S.-based firms.

Chapter 14   English and International Developments 1962-2012

The seven-story walk-up school opened in 1967, staffed by four principals - Bob Ruprecht, Werner Von Behren, Mel Schroeder, and Les Zimmermann. The school opened a second building in 1975, complete with regulation-size swimming pool. Swim team and track were the largest athletic groups at the time.

The fears that a China-Britain stand-off could escalate were daunting. After receiving six candidate rejections, Bob enlisted Werner and Marie VonBehren, onetime classmates at Concordia Teachers College, River Forest. When the VonBehrens accepted, that seemed to reassure other stateside candidates, and a full complement of overseas and local staff assembled to open the 1967-68 school year on schedule in the barely-completed building at 6 South Bay Close.

Two guiding lights of the HKIS project departed the Colony permanently just as completion of the building neared. The Kieschnicks left to handle a family medical emergency and the Galsters seized an opportunity to open ministry in Thailand, their initial goal in coming to Asia. Dr. Eugene Seltz, an experienced LCMS China missionary and U.S. Navy chaplain, became chairman of the board of managers.

Galster's unexpected departure left RBLC without an ordained pastor. In true church-worker fashion, Bob Christian took on leadership of the hotel-based congregation, in addition to managing HKIS. It was a year until Rev. Karl Boehmke arrived as the first pastor to serve at the nearly completed sanctuary. The pastor's job description also included membership on the Board of Managers - a constant and continuing church-school link.

Expansion

In 1971, HKIS received full accreditation from the Western Association of Schools and Colleges (WASC). A four-month self-study was followed by a week-long visitation of educators from Taiwan, Thailand, and the United States. The June report gave HKIS academic validity with the American education system. HKIS was WASC-accredited for the second time in June, 1976.

K-12 enrollment increased far beyond original projections. A second building, designed as a primary school, was constructed between 1973-75, on a site carved into an adjacent hillside. The school had an open-classroom format of moveable walls for student groupings. A competition-length swimming pool, rooftop activity areas, and a 13-story residential tower for faculty were notable features envisioned by architect Tao Ho.

Junior and senior high schools occupied the original building, expanding art, science, library, and classroom facilities. No longer did kindergartners and high school seniors share the cafeteria and the lunchtime catering of the Repulse Bay Hotel and Ping Shan restaurants, nor the innovative limited pre-order menu from the recently-opened McDonald's at nearby Repulse Bay Beach. Mrs. Cheng Chan, the cafetorium manageress, continued to sell ice lollies, nutty nibbles, joy sticks, and the occasional piece of jade from her window.

Momentum in academic, athletic, and cultural programs raised the school's local profile. An increasing expatriate population and the desirability of an American school diploma for local Chinese students so overcrowded the two-building campus that a third complex was needed. Land was granted about five miles beyond Repulse Bay and Stanley on then-remote Red Hill, overlooking Tai Tam Bay. Construction of the new high school was completed in 1988, and linked with an extensive middle school building and office complex in 1992. The original Repulse Bay buildings became, and remain, the upper and lower primary buildings. As of this writing, student enrollment is 2700 students, 70% from North America, complimented with students from 34 nations. Half of the faculty comes from the United States, the balance representing Canada, Australia, England, Hong Kong, China, and more.

One of the most noteworthy elements contributing to the success of the school is adherence to the six-point system of school-wide goals, called the Student Learning Results (SLRs). When HKIS administration developed mission statements and educational

Chapter 14   English and International Developments 1962-2012

 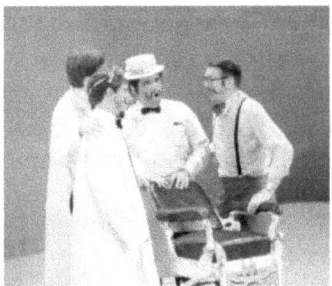 

HKIS rapidly became a community center, especially for American and other expatriate families. The US Navy visited. Faculty and students participated at American Fortnight and Dragonboat festivals. Founding headmaster Bob Christian passed the baton to Dave Rittmann in 1977. Construction of the Repulse Bay complex finished in 1975.

policies in 1998, community service was identified as one of six SLRs which continue to define the HKIS program. The other five SLRs include academic excellence, spirituality, character development, self-motivated learning, and appreciation of Chinese culture. The concepts were formulated under headmaster David Rittmann (1977-1996) and refined under headmaster Chuck Dull with implementation from assistant administrator, Jan Westrick.

Church of All Nations

Repulse Bay Lutheran Church was renamed "Church of All Nations - Lutheran" (CAN) in 1967 when the congregation moved to its permanent worship space on the 5th level of the HKIS building. The name implied a welcoming inclusivity, and may have been inspired by the Church of All Nations on the Mount of Olives in Jerusalem, or the Methodist church of the same name from which True Light congregation grew in New York.

Pastor Boehmke came with a chaplaincy background, and some experience with Chinese people dating back to his Bronxville college days. There, he volunteered often at True Light Lutheran Church in New York City's Chinatown. This was the congregation served in 1953-59 by Paul Chang, the evangelist who had worked so energetically with pioneer Hong Kong missionaries Martha Boss, Lorraine Behling, and Gertrude Simon (chapters 10 and 11). New traditions similar to those of an American congregation, emerged under the leadership of long-term worshippers from the Repulse Bay Hotel days, intermingling lay people with called HKIS staff. CAN and HKIS are two separate entities.

The Order of Worship came from the *Lutheran Hymnal* (TLH) of 1941, yet worship innovations utilizing newer music and instrumentation gained popularity. There was never a shortage of organists for the newly donated instrument and vocal soloists such as Nancy Li (Zi) and Carol Yamashita, augmented the small but robust choir directed by Werner VonBehren. Chancel dramas and children's pageants were frequent. At Christmastime, a large crèche was set up in the chancel. Dependably, a child would show up with a doll to be placed in the empty manger.

LaVerne Boehmke brought experience in establishing altar guild practices - decorating the sanctuary, furnishing altar flowers, organizing pot luck meals. Betty Karner, Dottie Mache, Marge Ottley and Trudi Hooijberg designed and embroidered paraments. At Easter, palm fronds were harvested from the Protestant cemetery in Happy Valley. Communion supplies were purchased at the Roman Catholic Center or Charitas House. HKIS classrooms and the cafetorium became Sunday school facilities. There was always coffee, and much more tea than at most Lutheran churches. Sunday school continued to grow with new families and students at HKIS. Boehmke's first confirmation class of three included teenagers from business and staff families.

Links with the LCMS remained strong through the work of area counselor Paul Strege, a veteran of the Japan mission. While involved in some work with the Hong Kong Mission Conference on the Kowloon side, CAN did not formally affiliate, maintaining closer ties with the Board of Missions and stateside connections. Lutheran Hour was headquartered in Hong Kong, directed by former Taiwan missionary Bill Dingler, but did not broadcast locally. Many LCMS leaders visiting Asia, included CAN and HKIS in their itinerary, notably Lutheran Hour speaker Oswald Hoffman, theologian Norman Habel, LCMS president Jack Preus and several district presidents. In later years, this list would grow to include Professor Martin Marty, hymnologist Carl Schalk, and others.

Membership

The English-speaking congregation with its own facilities within HKIS welcomed wor-

Chapter 14　　　　　　　　　　　　　　English and International Developments 1962-2012

Repulse Bay Lutheran became Church of All Nations when the school opened and sanctuary were dedicated in 1967.

The Timothy Paul Center was supported by congregation volunteers to honor the life of a 4th grade boy tragically died from fumes of a faulty water heater.

shippers from around the Colony as well as international visitors. The 145-foot tower and cross were easily visible from the Repulse Bay bus stop. Welcoming other denominational affiliations, the dominant LCMS faculty brought rich experience in Lutheran congregational tradition and worship from strong Walther League and LCMS college backgrounds.

Attendees from other denominations and many cultures came, looking for worship and social involvement. The status of "associate member" enabled parishioners to remain members of their home overseas congregations while being a full member of CAN. With fond humor, members could be called "CAN Lutherans" while in Hong Kong. At other times it was the 'Church of All Notions," a reference to more flexible worship practices. Fr. Harold Naylor, SJ, an Irish priest, was especially helpful in Christian networking within the Colony. The Anglican cathedral of St John, supported CAN's programs. Fred Staubach brought expertise in balancing policies and practices as the congregation created a new model as the first expatriate church in the LCMS. "Our" Father takes on special meaning in the fellowship of an overseas setting.

A board of elders was established, with ministries of worship, education, stewardship, evangelism, fellowship, and youth. The first CAN president was teacher Mel Schroeder. Trustees had other responsibilities, including the properties and seemingly constant roof repairs. Women took leadership roles in the altar guild and library, and were worship assistants, voters, and office holders. HKIS teacher Bill Mahlke took charge of all publicity for CAN and HKIS, writing press releases to the South China Morning Post and Hong Kong Standard newspapers. Most were published, often with accompanying photos.

Timothy Paul Center

The third-grade son of Werner and Marie VonBehren was asphyxiated in their home by a faulty water heater during a typhoon. The bright, cheerful, and inquisitive boy was well-known to the church members, and they were stunned by the accident. As memorials and gifts came in, the family decided that it would be fitting to use donated funds to establish a study center for Chinese students to honor Tim's memory. In a resettlement estate near Aberdeen, about a 20-minute bus ride from Repulse Bay, a welcoming atmosphere was created so that children could come from the crowded tenements to do their studies. David Chan was employed as the first director of the center. On a regular schedule, volunteer adults and secondary students from CAN tutored. Vacation Bible School (VBS) was offered and well-attended in the summer.

CAN remains a case study of a church keeping pace with its setting in time and place, incorporating a respectful mixture of people, heritage, and culture. No major disputes have challenged the relationship of CAN and HKIS. The church serves as a worship home for Christians in and beyond the HKIS community. Facilities have always been shared - the CAN worship space used for school chapel services, graduation ceremonies, drama events, and concerts (despite a chronic leaky roof). The congregation has an active on-going outreach to several groups in Hong Kong and is a hub for programs in greater China.

Youth programs

Sunday school had been the initial attraction in 1962. Once CAN was affiliated with a K-12 school, many group activities were available for youngsters, and a youth group seemed redundant. Around 1975, HKIS teacher Walt Schmidt organized a youth group on the Walther League model, when his own children were of high school age. Both he and his wife, Lois, had experience from Lutheran Service Volunteer (LSV) training and leading Walther League groups in Baltimore, Maryland. In addition to social and worship events, the group began work

Chapter 14　　　　　　　　　　　　English and International Developments 1962-2012

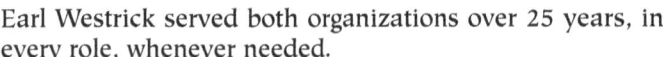

HKIS and CAN activities were intertwined, many faculty families being part of the congregation, and school events happening in the shared chapel and cafetorium.

Earl Westrick served both organizations over 25 years, in every role, whenever needed.

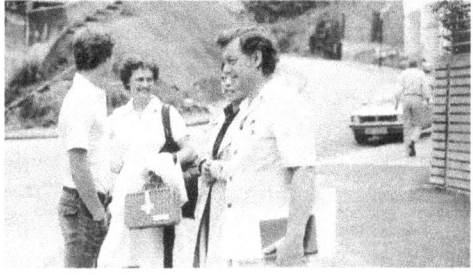

with refugee children, whose families had fled Vietnam. Busloads of these young people were bussed to the Repulse Bay campus for organized games and swimming in the school pool.

As the situation in the crowded camps became publicized, Schmidt began volunteering his own time in 1978. He became a full time supervisor of the Shamshuipo camp in 1979, and its director until returning to the U.S. in 1981. Schmidt provided a strong link between the government, church, the United Nations High Commission on Refugees, and social services agencies.

The needs of one small English-speaking LCMS congregation for its own worship building has thus grown into the jewel of the Synod's education system and one of the most highly regarded of international schools. Its format and success have been the inspiration for Lutheran schools throughout East Asia. (See chapter 19).

Celebrations took many forms - the joy of graduation and the exuberance of a backyard birthday party for faculty kids about 1980.

Significant sources:

Carroll, John,	*A Concise History of Hong Kong*
Kohl, David,	*DragonTales, 2007*
Lee, Daniel	*Lorraine Behling – Handmaid of the Lord*
Lee, Jean,	*Bringing Christ to the Chinese, 2011*

　　Interviews with Karl & LaVerne Boehmke, Robert & Arleen Christian, Jay Frazell, Len & Ruth Galster, Dotty Mache, Walt & Lois Schmidt, Barbara Schwerdtmann, Natalie Seltz, Paul & Caroline Tuchardt, and Earl Westrick.

Arrivals – Until 1988, missionaries from Hong Kong supervised Macau enterprises. This is not an official listing. Detailed information is unavailable.

Year	Surname	Given name
1988	Hu	Patrick & Edna
	Fox	Chip [& Hannah]
1994	Dunseth	Tom
1996	Wilch	Anastasia
	Paul	Michael & Irene
1998	Holste	Herman & Barbara
1999	Chiu	James
2001	Lesemann	Bruce
2002	Kan	Sunny
	Owens	Sharon
	Rohnke	Ruth
	Blau	Carrie
2003	Martens	Emily
2004	Scheiwe	Joel & Iantha
	Fiess	Julie
2005	Schmalcs	John
	Eddy	Mary Elizabeth
2006	Schmalcs	John Juris
2007	Moore	Anna Louise (GEO)
	Beske	Carol Avis (GEO)
	Bowerman	Lloyd John (GEO)
	Bowerman	Doris Arlene (GEO)
	Williams	Kali Anne (GEO)
	Latimer	family
2008	Foytek	Janet Ielaine (GEO)
	Pfeifer	David (GEO)
	Horkey,	Anna (GEO)
	Ulrich	Michael John (1 yr)
	Luebbe	Jessica Katharina (1 yr)
	Welcenbach	Bryn Erin (1 yr)
2009	Mills	Elaine Evelyn (GEO)
	Dell'Immagine	Cecilia Anita (GEO)
2010	Myers	Matt & Kim

Macau (Macao) holds the distinction of being the first site of European activity on the China coast, Japanese Catholics feeing persecution from the Shogun settled here in the 1600s, constructing a monumental hilltop cathedral.

The kingdom of heaven is like a mustard seed that a man took and sowed in his field. It is the smallest of all seeds, but when it has grown it is larger than all the garden plants and becomes a tree, so that the birds of the air come and make nests in its branches.

Matthew 13:13 (ESV)

Chapter 15

Macau - Not the Least of These

Between 1842 and 1999, scant western interest has been focused on tiny Macau (Macao), six square miles of islands, inlets, and bays, 40 miles from Hong Kong on the western mouth of the Pearl River (Chu Kiang). Yet for over 300 years, this Portuguese territory was the great Asian emporium where all of Europe traded with all of China. European sailors led by Jorge Alvare first stepped onto Chinese soil here in 1513, four years before Martin Luther nailed his 95 theses to the castle door in Wittenberg. Unless it was transported across the central Asian Silk Road, every piece of porcelain, every ounce of tea, and every yard of silk bound for the west was transshipped from Kwangchow [Guangzhou] through Macau from 1557 until the 1840s—even the infamous shipload of 342 crates of Bohea tea destined to flavor the waters of Boston Harbor in 1773.

This Iberian enclave lies just a 3-hour ferry ride across the Pearl estuary from Hong Kong, 90 miles downriver from Canton (Kwangchow). The historic bastion of capitalism and Catholicism once rivaled Goa, Malacca, Batavia, Nagasaki and Manila as a baroque European jewel set in maritime Asia during the centuries before their economic eclipse. Those ports of Empire were replaced by Bombay, Penang, Hong Kong, Singapore and Shanghai in the nineteenth century. Macau's small inner harbor is well protected, while the outer harbor faces the South China Sea. Lush rocky terrain underlies the peninsula and islands.

But Macau became a backwater, eclipsed by the rise of Hong Kong as a superior free enterprise emporium and deep water port. The territory languished, almost frozen in time for 100 years. The harbor filled with silt. During the Cultural Revolution of the 1960s Macau, located on the China border, experienced riots and strikes, linked with those in Hong Kong. The People's Republic of China reclaimed Macau as a SAR in 1999, rejuvenating the territory into a gambling and entertainment mecca.

If Hong Kong island is about the comparable size of New York's Manhattan, Macau is about the size of Central Park. And for the church in 2013, Macau has become a fount of new opportunities.

About Macau

The name Macao derives from the fifteenth century A-Ma Buddhist temple on the shoreline honoring Tin Hau, the sea goddess

Macau Peninsula LCMS Locations

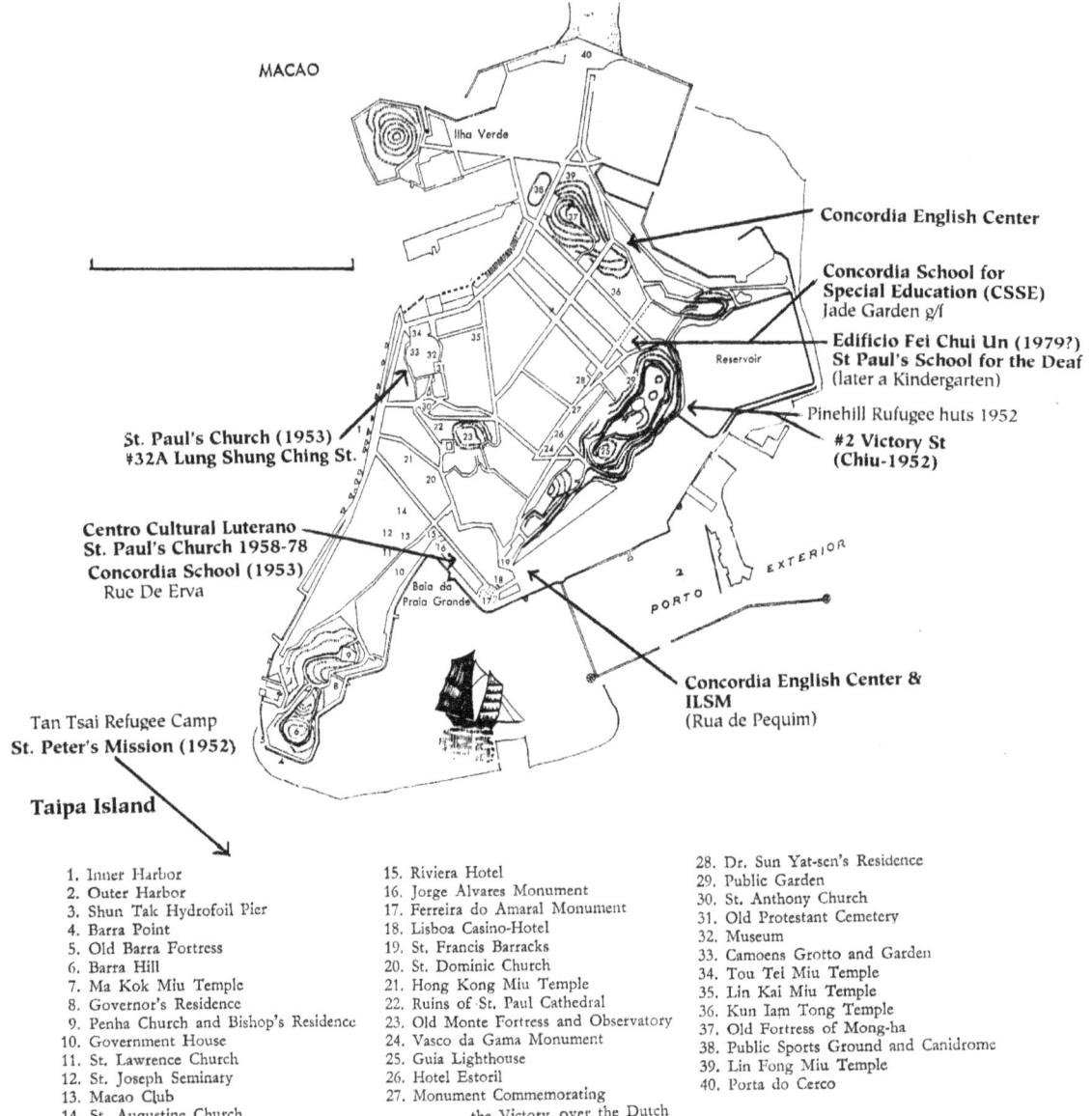

1. Inner Harbor
2. Outer Harbor
3. Shun Tak Hydrofoil Pier
4. Barra Point
5. Old Barra Fortress
6. Barra Hill
7. Ma Kok Miu Temple
8. Governor's Residence
9. Penha Church and Bishop's Residence
10. Government House
11. St. Lawrence Church
12. St. Joseph Seminary
13. Macao Club
14. St. Augustine Church
15. Riviera Hotel
16. Jorge Alvares Monument
17. Ferreira do Amaral Monument
18. Lisboa Casino-Hotel
19. St. Francis Barracks
20. St. Dominic Church
21. Hong Kong Miu Temple
22. Ruins of St. Paul Cathedral
23. Old Monte Fortress and Observatory
24. Vasco da Gama Monument
25. Guia Lighthouse
26. Hotel Estoril
27. Monument Commemorating the Victory over the Dutch
28. Dr. Sun Yat-sen's Residence
29. Public Garden
30. St. Anthony Church
31. Old Protestant Cemetery
32. Museum
33. Camoens Grotto and Garden
34. Tou Tei Miu Temple
35. Lin Kai Miu Temple
36. Kun Iam Tong Temple
37. Old Fortress of Mong-ha
38. Public Sports Ground and Canidrome
39. Lin Fong Miu Temple
40. Porta do Cerco

Macau is a hilly peninsula two-miles long facing the Pearl estuary, 40 miles west of Hong Kong. Pastel Mediterranean-style houses and shop-fronts line cobblestone streets with arches and columns, built centuries ago by Chinese craftsmen. As a Portuguese territory, Macau was neutral during World War II. The map shows Macau of the 1950s, with the outline of expansions since 1998. The islands of Taipa and Coloane are close by, connected with causeways and bridges.

form of Kuan Yin (Goddess of Mercy). Macau is a peninsula plus Taipa and Coloane Islands, which were allowed to Portugal as a territory in 1557 by Ming dynasty Chinese officials in exchange for military favors during a local pirate rebellion. It was a key post in the Portuguese trade empire, linking Mozambique, Goa (India), the Spice Islands (Indonesia), and Deshima (Nagasaki, Japan). In 1611, the Portuguese maritime empire in Asia collapsed under conquest by the Dutch East India Company (VOC), but Macau defenders repelled both Dutch and Spanish attacks to remain a piece of Portugal. It maintained its unique role in trade and religion, until the mid-1800s, as the only toehold that foreigners had in China.

At its prime in the later 1700s, Macau's outer and inner harbors provided safe anchorage for the sailing ships of 13 nations awaiting the annual six-month trading season at Canton. For Americans, passage to Boston required another six months at sea, until the age of the great China Clippers in the 1850s reduced the voyage around Cape Horn to a record 89 days. But by that time, Macau was no longer the China port of choice.

When Hong Kong Island was ceded in 1842 to Great Britain by the Treaty of Nanking, Macau began a decline into a minor trading and transshipment point in the lucrative coastal China trade. The voyage west to England was routed past Singapore, Malacca, Goa, the Cape of Good Hope and the Cape Verde islands. Ships bound for America and the Spanish Main sailed via Manila, Monterey, Acapulco, an overland portage to Vera Cruz, and through the Caribbean and Atlantic to Seville.

Pelts, furs, ginseng, cotton and some manufactured goods from 11 European countries, Japan, and America, were no match for silk, tea, rhubarb, and porcelain from China. All the tea, porcelain and *chinoiserie* of royal Europeans and American plantation owners (and the presidential White House!) were first warehoused in godowns at Canton and shipped from Macau. All transactions in the *Canton System* were made by Chinese *hong* compradors and Tai-pans representing foreign trade companies.

Silver was the only mode of exchange accepted by the Chinese. To obtain enough silver, the British East India Company and others began trading India-grown opium illicitly along the South China coast for bullion and coin. The Chinese called the drug "foreign mud." The habit would taint diplomacy, induce warfare, ruin lives, and plague western (and Christian) credibility for centuries.

The Macau harbor silted up about the same time that foreign traders relocated to Hong Kong. Macau's commercial importance was soon eclipsed by its new British neighbor. The enclave became a backwater relic of the Portuguese empire. Gambling was introduced by the 1860s, making Macau a lucrative financial destination. Many a freshly-paid laborer from Hong Kong played the fan tan tables and slot machines in hopes of quick fortune—a rare occurrence.

A number of Hong Kong's wealthier families maintained holdings in Macau. There were several daily sailings of the Macau ferry. Amphibious air service with Hong Kong was introduced in the 1930s (missionary Daniel Nelson and family died on one ill-fated crossing). Macau took on renewed significance during WWII, where many Chinese and Europeans took refuge there since Japan did not occupy Macau, because of Portuguese neutrality.

Macau itself is one of the most picturesque communities on earth, known as the "Garden City of the Orient." Banyan and other large trees line the *Praya Grande* esplanade along the outer harbor. Pastel-framed louvered windows and Mediterranean arcades distinguish tiled shop houses, elegant mansions, and public buildings.

Dominating the small territory are seven hills, the highest being a rocky massif topped

Chapter 15 — Macau - Not the Least of These

Strong religious traditions exist side-by-side in Macau. Ancestral worship is part of the daiy ritual - offerings and smoldering incense. Carved images of Confucian, Taoist, and Buddhist figures adorn temples. Roman Catholic churches in the style of the counter-reformation, came with the Portuguese Jesuit tradition, dominating the cityscape with white-washed facades and bell towers.

with the Monte fort. On the slope of the outcrop sit the stone ruins of the Church of Mater Dei. Known as St. Paul's (Sao Paulo), it was built by exiled Japanese Christians from 1583-1602. The mostly wood edifice burned during a spectacular typhoon in 1835. Miraculously, the flaming sanctuary provided flickering light for the storm-ravaged populace to find higher ground. Only the ruined stone facade with its twisting columns was left to acquire a patina of time. Viewing the crumbling monolith, Hong Kong governor Sir John Bowring was inspired to pen the hymn *In the Cross of Christ I Glory*.

Macau's population after WWII totaled about 300,000, about 3% Portuguese and 97% Chinese of either Cantonese or mixed Macanese stock. The Portuguese language remained official, but Chinese dialects and a Cantonese patois are most commonly heard. After the 1949 rise of the PRC and resultant exodus, Macau became a safe haven for thousands of refugees from neighboring Kwantung province. They were in similar straits as the Hong Kong homeless, albeit in smaller numbers. Many were boat-people, living, working, even schooling their children on small sampans or larger junks anchored in the bays. Livelihoods were eked out on shore by coolie labor and in the home manufacture of fireworks, transistor radios, or handicraft items.

Early Lutheran Contact

Unlike other Chinese areas within the LCMS mission enterprise, Macau has a historic Christian component. Europeans worshipped in large Iberian-style Roman Catholic churches built and decorated as part of the Counter Reformation. An abundance of beautiful classical and baroque churches line the esplanades and hills of the city. Macau became the beachhead for Jesuit mission efforts to China and Japan. Matteo Ricci, the influential Jesuit educator, lived there after 1583, and a strong Franciscan and Dominican presence grew in later years. Fleeing persecution and expulsion under Tokugawa shoguns in the early 1600s, Japanese Christians flocked to Macau, and built the hilltop Sao Paulo church.

Hong Kong evangelist Paul Chang first visited Macau in June 1950 to investigate the status of refugees at the resettlement camps. During the same period, Chang also visited "John" Wen Yun Nan, serving a six-month term in Stanley prison. After John's baptism and release in July 1951, he followed Gertrude Simon's suggestion to visit refugee camps in the Portuguese enclave. Hong Kong government deported John Wen to Macau, and he began full time work with refugees encamped near the Barrier Gate.

At the Tan Tsai refugee camp, Wen handed out the mimeographed Lutheran Weekly and read the Bible regularly to groups. Soon he established a Bible class, and enrolled about 50 interested individuals in the Bible Reading Correspondence Course from Hong Kong. At the camp, an overturned rotting junk provided shelter for a start-up school where John taught the children lessons from the New Testament. When the boat's hull disintegrated, space was found on Rua da Erva, which would one day become St. Paul's school.

Missionary Herb Hinz started visiting the Macau camp once a month to conduct services. By the time Wen received a visa to emigrate to Taiwan, about 40 worshipers were attending the services at St. Paul's Lutheran congregation. He would later become a leader in the Taiwan Lutheran church. Supported initially by Gertrude Simon, Evangelist Andrew and Sharon Chiu—fellow students of the Concordia Bible Institute—moved to Macau after their wedding and served this group for 18 months. By April 1952, attendance at services numbered 70 souls.

Paul Chang married Eleanor Ho, a student from China whom he met in Macau, before taking a call to New York's Chinatown to work at True Light Lutheran Church with Mary Banta and Rev. Louis Buchheimer. Rev.

Chapter 15　　　　　　　　　　　　　　　　　　　　　Macau - Not the Least of These

On Taipa island, where refugees assembled fire crackers for meager income, St. Peters mission was established in the early 1950s. The congregation utilized local musicians in worship and welcomed guest from Hong Kong and abroad.

Paul Ho then pastored St. Paul's congregation, and Silas Chang handled Lutheran Hour connections. Worship was held in an old garage building on an ancient cobblestone street. The electric lights often failed during services, so a spare candle was always kept handy.

The one-year anniversary of official LCMS Macau ministry was celebrated in December 1953 with a service conducted by Rev. Hinz. The keynote message was delivered by Isaac Mah, who was also the regular speaker for Hong Kong Lutheran Hour broadcasts. Visiting director of the International Lutheran Hour, Eugene Bertermann, spoke at the Macau rally. Recognized at the event were Macau graduates of the Lutheran Hour correspondence course.

In July of 1954, Redifusion, the Hong Kong broadcasting service, did not renew the license for the Lutheran programs. Transmissions from Hong Kong ceased, but the correspondence course continued serving enrollees who had begun the program. In that year, *The Lutheran Hour* (aka *Bringing Christ to the Nations*) was aired worldwide in 56 languages over about 1100 stations in 58 countries. St. Paul's congregation, located at #32A Lung Shung Ching Street, continued to receive help from the LCMS as part of the Hong Kong mission. Sunday school at St. Paul's was so crowded that children had to bring the previous Sunday's lesson sheet as a "ticket" to gain admission. Andrew Chiu began work on Taipa Island, where a second worship group formed St. Peter's Church.

Elmer Thode accompanied Hinz several days per month in Macau, instructing, baptizing, advising, and accounting. Four teachers from Macau congregations attended an all-day Sunday School Institute in July 1954, at Grace Chapel in Hong Kong. With 65 other teachers from Rennie's Mill, Kowloon, and Hong Kong Island, they held sessions on teaching demonstrations, Bible study, and leadership in hymn singing.

Like the refugees in Hong Kong, the displaced Chinese in Macau found a means of earning their "rice bowl" by making handicraft items. These were sent to Hong Kong and distributed with other handicrafts being made at Rennie's Mill.

St. Paul Lutheran School

During the summer of 1953, Concordia Lutheran School opened on Rue De Erva. Under the supervision of the education chairman of the Hong Kong mission the school grew rapidly. There was a shortage of primary schools in Macau due to a nearly constant flow of refugees during China's "great hunger."

By 1957, St. Paul's congregation numbered 400 baptized members, 85 of whom had been confirmed. Evangelist Titus Lee Fu Sheng, isolated from his wife and children in China, began 18 years of ministry with the congregation. Two Bible school graduates and Vicar Cheung also aided the efforts, supervised by Roy Karner, who visited monthly to conduct communion services. In addition, St. Peters Chapel on Taipa Island drew a regular attendance of about 40. Four Sunday schools were scattered around the territory. Karner and Kieschnick recommended that a permanent building replace the dingy garage and unsuitable rental spaces.

The Mission Board allocated $45,000 for the construction of a church and school. At Karner's suggestion, Rev. Lee selected a corner lot on reclaimed land at the end of the main street. The site on Rua Dr. Pedro Jose Lobo could not be purchased, but it was available to rent at a very low rate. Plans were drawn and construction began on the leased site, with the oversight of a resident on-site building supervisor. St. Paul's congregation raised funds to match the LCMS grant.

Since by Macau law the church's main office would have to be in Macau, the LCMS could not be registered as a legal entity in the Portuguese territory. Ownership of the build-

The Centro Cultural Luterano was completed in 1958 near the Praya Grande, housing classrooms and an auditorium-sanctuary. Much of the construction cost was borne by St Pauls congregtion and school.

Specialist LCMS missionary William Reinking and family arrived in 1964 to begin work with the deaf population of Macau and Hong Kong. Schools for the deaf were eventually established in each location.

ing was therefore recorded in the name of Rev. Titus Lee Fu Sheng, who registered with the government as a "merchant." Clear title to the building would later prove problematic.

Centro Cultural Luterano was dedicated with much fanfare in September 1958 during the mid-autumn festival. Missionary George Winkler needed police help to restrain crowds during a week of nightly services in the new church and school. On the street level was the assembly hall seating 500, also useable as a worship space for the congregation. Six classrooms occupied the upper two floors, above which were also staff quarters. Concordia School was re-named St. Paul Lutheran School in 1958 when it moved into the Centro. With the day school and late afternoon and evening classes, Winkler noted that the mission was getting "every nickel's worth of service" from the new building. At one time, more than 1000 people passed through the building each day.

St. Paul's Lutheran School settled into its new classrooms, with an enrollment of over 100 students. Harold Schmidt, Hong Kong Mission director of education after 1960, supervised Headmaster Timothy Lee, a board of managers, and the teaching staff of one man and five women.

Work with the Deaf

In 1962, two experienced teachers for the deaf, Mr. Peter Ip and a woman expert in sign language, began a program for the hearing impaired. Two years later, Synod called Rev. Bill Reinking to Hong Kong, as consultant for work with the deaf. Although he focused on programs in Hong Kong, he also became aware of the under-served deaf population of Macau. Louis Jasper, a St. Louis seminarian with a master's degree in deaf education, was called by the LCMS in 1967 to teach the hearing-impaired (see chapter 12). In Hong Kong, lessons were taught five evenings per week for about 60 students. Jasper's work in Hong Kong provided a model for a Macau school for the deaf.

As the mid-60s were unsettled times of riot and protest, Rev. Jasper initially spent little time in Macau. In 1968, he began making more regular crossings to help Mr. Ip's evening school for the deaf, and to lead mid-week evening worship services for about 40 deaf people. After five years of progress, Jasper arranged to mainstream all deaf students into the regular classes in St. Paul's Primary School in 1973. Miss Grace Lam Kin U provided tutoring and resources for deaf students. The number of adults and students diminished over the next five years while Dr. Jasper was on an educational leave to earn his doctorate in special education.

Classes began for mentally challenged students in October 1978, but closed after one term. Teaching staff had found it difficult to manage the combined deaf and mentally handicapped students. Titus Lee Fu Sheng determined to sell the *Centro Culture Luterano* in 1978, with an apparent goal of re-financing the Macau mission. Not long after the sale to commercial interests, Rev. Lee departed the territory, replaced briefly by Rev. Timothy Lee. Dr. Jasper and Rev. Lo Fuk Ki from Mongkok Lutheran School for the Deaf commuted by ferry to conduct mid-week worship services.

Revitalized Enterprise

Working together for several years, Missionary Eugene Seltz, Roy Karner, and the LCMS attempted clarification of *Centro Cultural Luterano's* legal ownership with the Macau government. The *Luterano* building was demolished, replaced by the 30-story Bank of China building. Later the LCMS was able to reclaim about $1.3 million from the sale, part of which became seed money for other LCMS and LCHKS projects, including the Martha Boss Lutheran Social Service Building in Hong Kong. The Macau mission has been cooperatively overseen by the LCMS and the LCHKS since 1976.

St. Paul congregation, numbering about 400 members, purchased ground floor wor-

 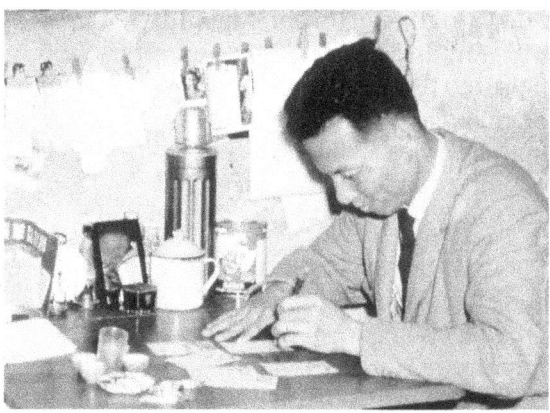

Handicraft production was an economic activity which refugee and displaced people could assemble or make to supplement some incomes from egg production and marketing.

Macau was under the supervision of Roy Karner for many years, but no missionary was resident in Macau until 1988.

ship space in the Edilficio Fei Chui Un, a commercial building. The deaf school was re-named St. Paul's Lutheran School for the Deaf and housed in the cockloft and part of the ground floor. Concurrently, the Roman Catholic Church had also initiated a ministry among the deaf of Macau. With the strong traditional influence of local Catholicism and help from the Social Welfare Department, the Catholics provided audiological services, vocational training, recreation, religious instruction, and worship services. Many deaf adults were drawn to these programs.

When the Macau government assumed control of all primary schools in 1979, the Hong Kong Synod decided to cease operating St. Paul's primary school, in favor of a school for the deaf, serving 27 children in three classes. The congregation declined under a string of short-term pastors. Mr. Lo Fuk Ki, religion teacher at the Mongkok Lutheran School for the Deaf, was recruited part time in 1984 to lead St. Paul's worship services. When the deaf school stopped charging tuition, it qualified for a financial subsidy and additional rent-free space from the Department of Education, and used classrooms in a new Macanese elementary school, the nearby Escola Barbosa.

In 1986 Patrick Hu, once a social work organizer from the Taiwan mission, accepted a position at the school. Along with his wife, Edna, he focused on social work, special education, and administration of the school until his retirement at age 70 in 1988. Mr. Hu held degrees in social work and had founded the Lutheran Service Center in Taipei with the China Evangelical Lutheran Church (CELC) in 1965.

Concordia School for Special Education

Local Chinese pastors maintained work at St. Paul's Church and school. The same pastor would also serve at St. Peter's and its preaching station for the elderly on Taipa Island. Continuity and energy were drained by the controversies and divisions within the Hong Kong mission in the mid-1970s. That power struggle, reflecting the distress within the LCMS at home and abroad, impeded progress in Macau. Yet, Charles Fox arrived in the mid-1980s, assigned as the first evangelistic missionary to Macau. His work with Pastor Lik Sang Yeung explored new potentials related to Macau's 1999 "changeover."

Pastor Yeung of St. Paul's, and the LCHKS decided in 1988 to open a for-profit kindergarten in the space formerly used by St. Paul's Lutheran School for the Deaf. At this point, Dr. Jasper and American businessman Fred Voightman formed and registered the Concordia Welfare and Education Society of Macau (CWESM), creating a local legal entity that could sponsor a school. CWESM also purchased an apartment to be available to Dr. Jasper and overseas volunteers. St. Paul's deaf school was closed, and students were then enrolled in the newly created Concordia School for Special Education (CSSE). The change in organization also anticipated work with Macau's new governance as a Special Administrative Region after the 1999 return to the People's Republic of China.

CSSE obtained a 5,000-foot open space on the ground floor of Edificio Jade Garden, a new high-rise housing block near the border gate. The school administration was responsible for finishing and furnishing classrooms, but the government provided a rent-free space, a subsidy to cover most of the school's operating costs, and a free hot lunch program. Additional space was used in the nearby Mayfair Garden building. CSSE was the first such government-subsidized school for the handicapped. Ms. Feng Xu Tong, trained as a teacher of the deaf in the U.S., brought new ideas and abundant energy to the staff in the mid-1990s.

The school continued operation with about 40 students, occasionally receiving donations from Church of All Nations and from Hong Kong International School. Secondary classes were added to the CSSE academic program beginning in 1989. Private tutoring

Chapter 15 — Macau - Not the Least of These

Friendship evangelism, and English instruction are offered at the Concordia English Center. The 6th floor facility is also the meeting place of a congregation.

for mainstreamed students in other schools was added. A number of deaf children living across the China border also enrolled. Some stayed with relatives in Macau, and returned to Guandong for weekends. The school recognized the need to build strong relationships with students and family, despite the challenges of emigration policies and other government changes. Advanced training for Christian educators in nearby Hong Kong was not possible due to that government's immigration restrictions. Professor Hank Rowold from Concordia Seminary in Kowloon conducted regular training classes when he visited Macau.

A 1991 mission strategy statement re-focused a vision for Macau. Activity at St. Paul's had languished at the Jade Garden building. The storefront premises continued to house a kindergarten for about 70 students, which financed the congregation. The St. Peter's facility near the Protestant cemetery was inconveniently located in a small and unattractive space, with access up a dingy stairway. Several rapid changes in Macau government had also meant new governorship and educational support.

Plans were made to start sign language classes for community members and parents of deaf students, in cooperation with the Rotary Club of Macau. Evening adult education of the handicapped was proposed. A study hall for children and adolescents of the community was to supplement the often-inadequate spaces available for study in crowded homes. CWESM and LCMS' joint focus on mission outreach and church planting would require dedicated staffing. Uncertainties preceeding of the much-anticipated 1999 changeover were interpreted as opportunities for the proclamation of the gospel, locally and abroad.

Concordia English Center - Friendship Evangelism

Several Las Vegas-based entrepreneurs and longtime Macau casino owner Stanley Ho re-vitalized once-somnolent Macau into Asia's gambling mecca following the 1999 changeover. A world-class airport, more bridges between islands, and new breakwaters appeared. Elegant hotel-casinos were built on reclaimed land between Taipa and Coloane Islands. So many workers for the 26 new casinos were required that the territory's workforce was not large enough. In the Chinese tradition of sojourners who send their earnings to their mainland families, hundreds of young people flooded into Macau as permitted contract-workers. Other migrants from neighboring Guandong Province had been working in Macau for many years at garment factories, hotels, and telecommunication companies.

Anticipating a new outreach, Anastasia Wilch arrived in 1996, along with Rev. Michael and Irene Paul, for the purpose of using ESL classes as a means of outreach and church-planting. During their year of intense Cantonese language training and relationship building, they worshipped at St. Paul's where LCHKS pastor Yeung led services in Cantonese. Aided by Tom Dunseth, they established the Concordia English Center in the Hac Sa neighborhood. Free English Bible classes, Mandarin Bible studies and worship were offered. Through these activities, soon there were five baptisms. One of those was Diana Lei, also a graduate of CSSE, who took deaconess training at Concordia, Fort Wayne and returned to serve her internship in Macau.

The CEC relocated in 1999 to a commercial building on Rua de Pequim so that it could be registered, becoming part of the International Lutheran Society of Macau (ILSM). With a consistent supply of one-year volunteer teachers, expansion of evening and part-time English education became possible. Many hundreds of contract workers have passed through the CEC. Learning and practicing English conversation with native English speakers remains highly desirable.

Opportunities for Christian staff to testify

Chapter 15 — Macau - Not the Least of These

Macau volunteer teachers   2005-2012

Long Term

2005
   Mary Elizabeth Eddy
2006
   Anna Horkey
   John Shmalcs
2007
   Carol Beske
   Doris Bowerman
   Lloyd Bowerman
   Family Latimer
   Anna Moore
   David Pfeifer
   Bryn Weicenbach
   Kali Williams
2008
   Mary Elizabeth Eddy
   Janet Foytek
   Jessica Luebbe
   Michael Ulrich
2009
   Cecilia Anita
      Dell'Immagine
   Elaine Mills
2010
   Serena Mae Derricks
2011
   Alissa Ann Asmus
   Allen Carl Piepenbrink
   Shirley Ann Piepenbrink
   Cecilia Anita
      Dell'Immagine
   Serena Mae Derricks

Short Term

2007
   Brian Bielfelt
2008
   Ron Bostick
   Jessica Flakne
   Janet Foytek
   Karen Friedrich
   Jane Moody
   Delwin Mahn
2009
   Carsten Bjornstad
   Laura Davis
   Donna Meyer
   Aida Popp
   Milton Popp
   David Risner
  Summer camp:
   Jennifer Hartsough
   Marjeen Pahl
   Gail Peck
   David Zimmerman
   Gloria Zimmerman
2010
   Christin Pfeffer
   James Rush
   Steven Wolf
2011
   Ryan Lee Napier
   Milton Norman Popp
   Aida Louise Popp
   Edward Earl Brandt
   Eileen Kay Brandt
2012
   Allan Carl Harlos
   Robert Edmund
   Karl Oettel
   Chuck Edelen

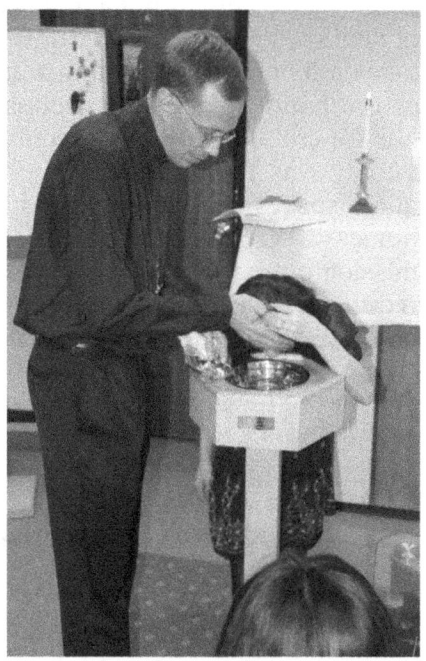

through friendship have introduced countless sojourners to the gospel. Witness happens one-to-one, as it has since the day of Phillip's discussion with the Ethiopian eunuch recorded in Acts 8. The Apostle Paul's first-century epistles provide the template for individual witness, conversion, and Christian living.

Friendship fills loneliness, and the Good News fills the void from a Communist/atheist environment. A variety of special activities include seasonal Christmas and Easter dramas put on by the students. Occasional evangelistic events are held with help from LCHKS teams directed by long-term HK-based Deaconess Carol Halter. Many seekers return week after week for both English and Christian instruction.

It is through personal relationships that evangelism opportunities present themselves. Trust is built over time; age is respected; loyalty is a commitment. Trained Chinese pastors, vicars and evangelists can capitalize on their valued longevity. Upon return to their homeland, CEC members have shared their faith with family and friends. In Chinese culture, the beliefs and enthusiasm of a fellow countryman is far more credible than that of a foreigner. Continued growth in faith and participation in sound Christian fellowship sustains and nurtures any fledgling Christian. More than 20 new believers were baptized within five years. Many new believers choose to receive training as leaders at the CEC.

Overseas Staffing

Rev. Tom Dunseth was called in 1994 to be the first Lutheran missionary pastor assigned to Macau. Dr. Jasper had advocated for a full time LCMS presence as work at the School for the Deaf and at Concordia English Center prospered. Among his outreach activities, Dunseth became a CSSE Board of Control member, learned Chinese sign language, and shaped a strong school with a more direct link to the LCMS.

Training and in-service programs for local educators of the deaf became feasible with the opening of Macau University. Hearing specialist Dr. Herman Holste spent more than a year conducting hearing tests. Barbara Holste taught many classes and deaf volunteer Jennifer Knaack worked with the youth. Dr. Jasper's worked part-time (four days a week in Macau and three with MLSD) until his departure to New Jersey in 1996. At that time, Jasper asked Dunseth to "look after" the Christian program at CSSE. Dunseth left in 2000, but continues to return for three one-month visits annually. Sponsored by the LCMS Michigan District and the Mill Neck Organization of New York, he manages the school and conducts worship services for the deaf whenever possible.

After the 1999 changeover, the Macau Education and Youth Affairs Bureau granted the school a new and more spacious facility in 2000, on the podium level of Edificio Zhu Kuan, a high-rise residential building near the jetfoil terminal. More children are served, including mentally-challenged students who are not deaf. Enrollment by 2010 exceeded a hundred students.

Volunteer programs

From the late 1990s, LCMS World Missions began revising the traditional "missionary model," encouraging the participation of the laity to serve in overseas settings. These GEO (Globally Engaged in Outreach) volunteers are placed in overseas situations with opportunities to share the gospel and witness their faith. They teach English, provide expertise for service projects, and support mission-related programs with knowledge and professionalism. Fewer career missionaries are thus needed to team with the short- and long-term volunteers to teach English and Bible studies, develop personal contacts and establish relationships. Career missionaries, long term volunteers, and GEO workers are responsible for their own support, usually fundraising when they are on "home service,"

Air travel was available briefly in the late 1930s between Hong Kong and Macau, via "Clipper" airships capable of amphibious landing. The service ended with the advent of World War II, and air service to Macau was not reinstated until after it became an SAR in 1999.

Lying amongst the islands of the western Pearl estuary, transportation and livlihood on the water give a timelessness and tranquility to a the Mediterranean climate and setting.

and with sponsorship from groups and congregations. Funds are channeled through the LCMS, which provides many support services.

The first GEO short-term Macau volunteer arrived in 1998. Within the year, long-term volunteers began developing programs of English instruction and Bible classes. Self-financed volunteers now form the backbone of the CEC center. Over 100 volunteers have served in Macau, typically recent college graduates (under age 25) and retirees (over age 60). GEO volunteers also serve in 23 other mission fields of the LCMS. Macau has utilized the largest number of volunteers, requiring several volunteers each year.

From Taiwan, experienced LCMS pastor Michael Wu relocated to Macau in 2003, as part of a partnership with the China Evangelical Lutheran Church (CELC). He had spent several years as chaplain and evangelist at Taiwan's Concordia Middle School and English Outreach Center (see Chapter 18). Wu spearheaded the worshipping congregation meeting at the CEC. Fledgling connections have grown into the training of evangelists and deacons, church leaders, and teachers in Macau and abroad.

While the original goal of the Macau LCMS mission team was local church planting, the center became a successful adult education language institution under the consecutive leadership of Tom Dunseth, Anastasia Wilch, Michael Paul, Sharon Owens, Matt Myers, and Vicar Daniel Ho. Christian witness to inquirers of the "one thing needful" is being carried into diverse areas of southern China by returning sojourners from the Macau SAR. The consequent sharing of the good news by Chinese speakers to family and friends in their home country holds great promise for the promulgation of the gospel over a wide geography.

From its historic six square miles comes a contemporary potential Christian revitalization of one-quarter of the world's population. Macau promises to be a mustard seed! The Word has power.

Significant Sources:

Coates, Austin	*A Macau Narrative*
Low, Harriett	*Lights and Shadows of a Macao Life*
Polland, Madeleine	*Mission to Cathay*
Porter, Jonathan	*Macau – The Imaginary City*
Thomas, T.	*Macau, A Glimpse of Glory*
Wong Shiu Kwan	*Macao Architecture*

Interviews with Tom Dunseth, Carl Hanson, Louis Jasper, Roy Karner, Kim and Matt Myers, and Michael Paul.

Chapter 16   Planting the Seed in Taiwan

Arrived

1951	Gruen	Olive	
1952	Suelflow	Roy	& Wanda
1953	Willenius	John	& Tellervo
	Schalow	Frederick	& Sarah
1955	Bringewatt	Ralph	& Martha
	Worthington	Van	& Alice
	Trinklein	Michael	& Janice
	Gremmels	Del	& Lela
1956	Riedel	Erhardt	
1957	Haffner	Victor	& Adeline
	Walter	Norman	& Donna
1959	Dingler	William	& Evelyn

Departed

1955	Schalow	Frederick	& Sarah
1956	Willenius	John	& Tellervo
1958	Worthington	Van	& Alice
	Gremmels	Del	& Lela
1960	Suelflow	Roy	& Wanda

So it is not the will of the Father who is in heaven that one of these little ones should perish... For where two or three are gathered in my name, there am I among them."

Matthew 18:14, 20

Chapter 16

Planting the Seed in Taiwan – The Missionary Stage

The LCMS China ministry has a longer continuous history on Taiwan than its first 39 years on the mainland. The sub-tropical island—80 miles wide, 250 miles north-to-south, and shaped like an elm leaf—straddles the Tropic of Cancer off China's southeast coast. Although there were fewer threats of major external warfare and devastation, the Missouri Synod and the China Evangelical Lutheran Church (CELC) struggled with its own internal challenges and skirmishes in its mission journey.

Three distinct phases mark LCMS history on the island of Formosa since Nationalist Chinese refugees first arrived in the late 1940s. During the initial decade, foundations were laid for a new church body, built mostly by first generation believers led by missionaries from the former LCMS China mission.

By 1962, the Taiwan church entered a second stage, one of shared responsibility, incorporating a new and younger second generation of missionaries and a youthful national church, described in chapter 17. By that time, two generations of Taiwan seminary students had graduated from Concordia Theological Seminary, mid-island at Chai Yi, and had assumed pastoral leadership of the church. Seeing itself as the successor of the Missouri Synod church on the mainland, the China Evangelical Lutheran Church (CELC) retained that name from the Fu Yin Dao Lo Deh Wei. Even as the Taiwan church was separating from the LCMS, the two bodies established their most successful project—Concordia Middle School at the city of Chai Yi.

The third phase, beginning about 1983 and detailed in chapter 18, is marked by the departure of all but two of the second-era missionaries. New missionaries arrived but a gradual reduction in ranks of long-term missionaries shrank LCMS forces mostly to the use of many shorter-term volunteers. The original group of pastors and evangelists had mostly passed away or retired. Times of intense and divisive struggle over financial and property resources lay ahead. As of this writing, a smaller sobered but hopeful church has begun to consolidate on Taiwan, led by a new corps of next-generation pastors.

Taiwan History

The *Ilha Formosa* (Isle of Beauty) impressed Portuguese sailors on the South China Sea as they first passed by lovely Taiwan five centuries ago, and what was initially a

Taiwan - LCMS Locations and the CELC

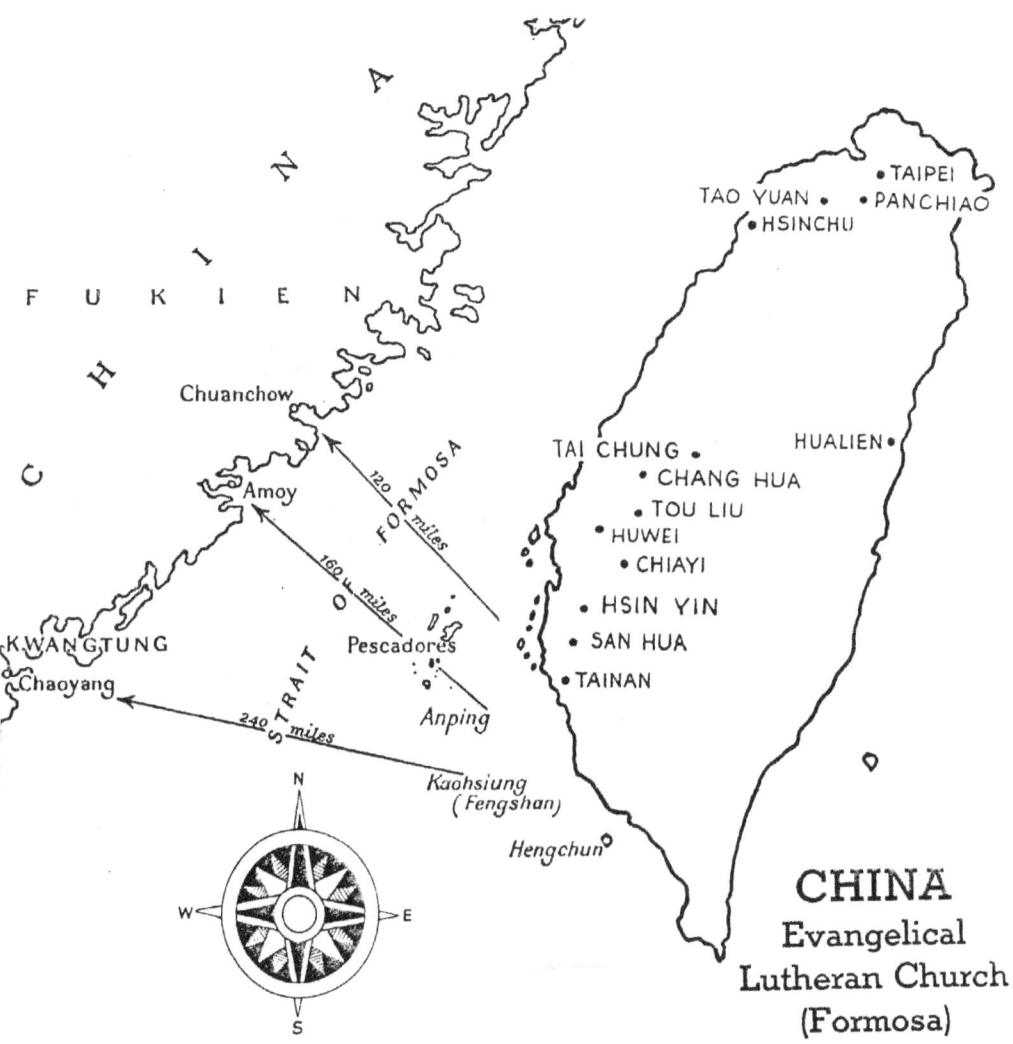

Refugees fleeing the Communist victory in China migrated to Formosa, a large island off the coast of Fukien [Fujian] Province, beginning in 1948. The island had been occupied by Japan from 1895 until the end of World war II in 1945. Cultural influences also include at least nine aboriginal groups. Quemoy Island, two miles offshore near the bay of Amoy, was also claimed by the Taiwan government (Republic of China) and highly contested in the 1950s. LCMS missionaries launched weather balloons carrying Bible tracts from that island. (see chapter 17)

mere description became the name by which western nations knew the island. Taiwan was also simply a description (Terraced Bay), but because it was a Chinese name, that's how the world refers to it today.

Early Portuguese traders and sailors didn't settle much in Taiwan, nor did the Chinese empire pay much attention to the island. Located 135 miles offshore, Taiwan was inhabited largely by immigrants from the southern portion of nearby Fukien [Fujian] Province, and what became known as the Taiwanese language (Hokkien) developed from that same part of China.

Also inhabiting Taiwan were several aboriginal tribes, more closely related culturally to maritime peoples of the south Pacific than to ethnic Han Chinese. Some were legendary headhunters. Just as formidable were the coastal pirates who marauded the surrounding seas, disturbing both local and trans-Pacific trade.

It wasn't until the seventeenth century that Taiwan took on western visibility, when the island was settled by three groups of outsiders: Spanish from the Philippines, Dutch from Indonesia, and remnants of the toppled Ming dynasty seeking refuge after 1644. Even with that occupation, Taiwan remained on the fringe, neglected in the Chinese world until it was granted status as a province of China in 1885.

The island had been part of the Japanese Empire since the Japanese defeat of China in 1895. Japan used Formosa and its people to further the empire by exploiting agricultural and mineral resources. The Taiwanese population was treated as a subclass. All education and communication were in the Japanese language, and a strong Japanese cultural element became part of Taiwanese life. While the native Taiwanese were relieved to be returned after WW II to the self-rule of the Chinese homeland in 1945, their joy was short-lived.

Taiwan comes into the scope of LCMS history shortly after the Nationalist government of China, led by Generalissimo Chiang Kai-shek, was driven out of the mainland by "red" Communist forces in the late 1940s, taking refuge on Taiwan (not unlike the Ming dynasty exodus of the 1640s). With the 1949 Nationalist Chinese troops of occupation (referred to as "mainlanders") came a wariness of the loyalties of the indigenous Taiwanese. The Nationalist migration quickly added two million homeless people, with backgrounds in education, the military, commerce, and religion (including Christian leaders and missionaries), to Taiwan's mostly rural population. Some early, bloody clashes, and a forceful suppression of Taiwanese people by the Nationalist (KMT) military, led to simmering tensions in the decades following.

Few resources go to waste in the Lord's kingdom, including missionaries driven out of China. The earliest worker to recognize both the need and the opportunity to follow the mass movement of mainland people to Taiwan was Olive Gruen, stranded in the U.S. on furlough as masses were fleeing the mainland. She had been the first female China missionary of the LCMS, with a lengthy ministry from 1921 to 1949 in three of the mainland stations. Her indomitable spirit showed as she worked in schools, clinics, and orphanages, mustering courage and tenacity in 1943 to join Gertrude Simon leading a 14-day evacuation of 20 young orphans ahead of advancing Japanese troops. Details of the wintertime 200-mile trek from Enshih to Wanhsien, is told in chapter 8. Gruen had even served a year-long teaching stint in India during World War II.

LCMS Contacts in Taiwan

Having heard reports from Taiwan via the Hong Kong mission concerning refugee Chinese Lutherans from Rennie's Mill, Gruen requested the LCMS Board for Foreign Missions (BFM) to send her as its first missionary to Taiwan. Hong Kong Missionary Herb

Chapter 16 — Planting the Seed in Taiwan

Long-time China missionary Olive Gruen (shown with an orphan group in Shinan, Hupeh) came to Taiwan in 1951 to find and organize Lutheran refugees who had resettled there from Hong Kong. Herb Hinz visited occasionally from Hong Kong, and the mission was formally established in 1952 with the arrival of Roy Suelflow. Soon a campus was under construction at Chaiyi. Olive retired at age 77 in 1960 after 40 years in the China field.

Hinz had twice visited about ten graduates of Concordia Bible School who immigrated to Taiwan. He and the three other Hong Kong missionaries knew of two pockets of mainland refugees, near Taipei and Chai Yi, numbering about fifty in total.

When Miss Gruen arrived in the summer of 1951, she knew no one in Taiwan and had no support system, but at age 68 this woman would not be denied. She found lodging in Taipei at the Friends of China Club, and immediately began teaching English classes, as Lorraine Behling had done in Hong Kong. At Taiwan University, she would make contact with educated society and recruit young Chinese into her English Bible classes. She befriended refugees who had once been respected middle class government, military, and business people.

As Olive gathered and mentored transplanted nationalists, worship was held in open air spaces. A small bamboo chapel was built on land provided by a Chinese family and with $468 from women's groups in America. It was dedicated in Chai Yi within two months of her arrival there. She also opened preaching stations in Taipei 150 miles north of Chai Yi. About 250 attendees signed a petition to the LCMS in 1952 that requested an ordained pastor to shepherd the small flocks.

In response, the BFM called Roy Suelflow, then in Japan, to pull the Taiwan mission effort together. Although his time on the mainland had been cut short when the Communist Party took power in 1949, he had served three years in Japan With his Mandarin language background, Suelflow's call was not only to minister to the fledgling flocks gathered in Taiwan but also to develop a seminary there to train local pastors.

The seminary students were primarily refugees who had fled the civil war via Hong Kong, without an established church to draw upon. At the Nationalist refugee camp there in Rennie's Mill, the men had come to faith, studying at Gertrude Simon's Concordia Bible Institute. After receiving long-awaited visas, most transferred to Taiwan, where they received further training, initially in Suelflow's living room. That influx of students quickly expanded the ability of the mission to reach out to Lutheran Chinese in several cities on Taiwan. Congregations were begun in Taipei, Banchiao, Huwei and Chai Yi. By the time Suelflow left on his furlough in 1953, not only had he begun the seminary, and overseen mission stations in half a dozen places, but he had also established broadcasts of *The Lutheran Hour* in Taiwan.

While Suelflow was on furlough, the mission added four new workers. John Wilenius and Frederick Schalow had previously been stationed in post-war China. Two Chinese evangelists joined the missionaries. Shen Yu Ch'ing agreed to work with the LCMS. An un-ordained Hankow seminary graduate, Tai Kuang Ming from Kweifu, was located and recruited, which then allowed for resident teams at Taipei and at Chia Yi.

Schalow, assisted by Mr. Tai, relocated the Lutheran Hour work and the seminary to Chia Yi. Though Suelflow had planned to relocate the seminary to the educational center of Taichung, land was purchased on a hill in Chia Yi for construction of a standard seminary campus. Seminary students helped with Lutheran Hour correspondence work. Eleven men graduated from the seminary in June 1954.

The next two years saw the missionary staff expand with the return of Suelflow and the addition in 1954 of Rev. Ralph Bringewatt, yet another former China missionary (1946-1949) called from Japan. He spoke both Mandarin and Japanese, which was understood by people on Taiwan because of the earlier Japanese occupation. Bringewatt was also assigned to further develop the Lutheran Hour and Bible Correspondence School ministries.

Chapter 16 Planting the Seed in Taiwan

Olive Gruen's work came to focus on nursery and child-care projects, in Taipei and other locations where refugees had settled. Work with pre-school children was more successful than opening parochial schools on Taiwan.

In 1955, Michael Trinklein and Delbert Gremmels were the first missionaries to come directly to Taiwan without service experience in China. Evangelist Tai would work with Gremmels and Lutheran Hour - Bringing Christ to the Nations. Van Worthington joined as the first non-ordained staff, filling the much-needed role of business manager. Ministry continued to expand, including evangelistic outreach with kindergartens, Lutheran Hour programs and church planting by seminary students and missionaries. However, the issues of Chinese governance of the growing local church and of cooperative efforts with other Christian and Lutheran missions were so divisive by 1956 that missionaries Schalow and Wilenius resigned, as did Evangelist Tai, who then came to the U.S.

In 1956, Dr. Herman Koppelmann, BFM executive secretary, visited Taiwan to help ease tensions and work through plans for continued outreach. The arrival of three new missionaries helped give renewed impetus. Two of these missionaries had been part of the former China mission. Dr. Erhardt Riedel, the first man to join with Edward Arndt in 1915, left his grown family in California, and would serve 15 more years in Taiwan. Rev. Victor Hafner, with two years experience in China and six years in the Philippines, was called from that mission field to operate the growing seminary. Rev. Norman Walter, with no previous Mandarin-speaking experience, was assigned to study the Taiwanese language in order to begin outreach to the majority population in Taiwan.

Language Soup - Culture, Politics, and Communications

Although all Chinese languages share the same ideographic written script, spoken regional languages and dialects numbers over 300. They differ by sounds, tones, expressions, and grammar. Given the same written characters (a Scripture reading, for instance), Chinese people from different language areas reading those characters together aloud would sound as though they're speaking in tongues. They would not be able to understand each other unless they communicated with written characters. Mandarin, developed from the regional language (*putonghua*) of the capital Peking [Beijing], is the national language throughout China, including Taiwan, and thus the norm for national communication in education, law, and mass media. Anyone with a basic elementary education functions in Mandarin.

Various regions cling to their local languages as a matter of identity and heritage. The major regional language on Taiwan comes from the Amoy region of Fukien, the Chinese province closest to Taiwan. Part of the tension between occupying mainlander and resident Taiwanese has been the Nationalist government's insistence that Mandarin is the proper and sole language. Taiwanese is forbidden in schools and public assemblies. Taiwanese people resented the minority government removing the legitimacy of the mother tongue of its local majority population. A smaller sector speaks Hakka, a totally different minority language, generally dismissed by both larger groups.

Linguistic and political tension did not adversely affect the early mission work of the LCMS because seven of the first ten LCMS missionaries came from the mainland already speaking Mandarin, even if heavily accented with Yangtze region dialects. They further worked with refugees with whom they felt not just sympathy but the shared experience of being expelled from home and a desire to return. The assignment of missionary Walter to study Taiwanese in order to reach the Taiwanese population was a well-intended but blundered entry which haunted the mission for several decades.

Starting Lutheran Hour Operations

Lutheran Hour radio ministry had been established in China in 1936, although the disruptions of war interrupted regular radio

Chapter 16 — Planting the Seed in Taiwan

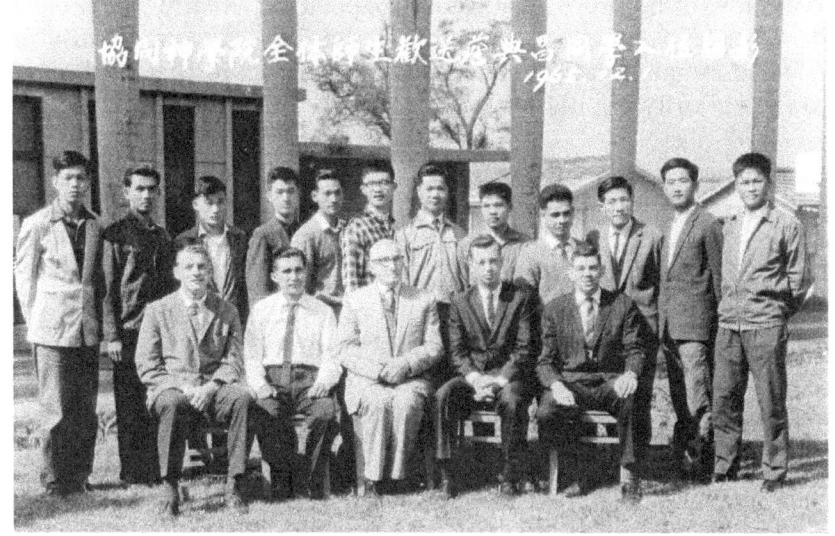

At the palm-lined seminary in Chaiyi, several missionary families lived in community, including the Michael Trinkleins, China veteran Erhardt Riedel, and the Bringewatt family. Son Ronald is shown on the motorcycle. Son Richard shown at his confirmation (far right), went on to become an LCMS pastor in Nebraska.

transmission. Suelflow had arranged for Lutheran Hour broadcasts in Taiwan, although the content in early years was basically English sermons produced in the States. Under Gremmels' directorship, the transition to local programming began. The next two directors were Taiwanese-speaking missionaries Norman Walter and William Dingler. Their Chinese language teacher, Mr. Henry Go H. J. Wu, would later become the only local director.

Essential to the Lutheran Hour plan was the Correspondence Bible Study course. Seminarians helped with the correspondence, but Bringewatt soon realized that neither the American content nor format was well-suited to Taiwan. While all seminary students went out on vicarage, Bringewatt spent seven months re-working the curriculum. Sermons were generated locally, written by Evangelist Tai until he left the island in 1960. A listing of Lutheran Hour correspondence students at Gemmel's time numbered 35,468.

A close bond of mutual respect and common purpose developed between the American and Chinese leaders. New mission stations were opened at Hsinchu, Hsinyang, Hualian, Tainan, Nantou, Taichung, Changhwa and Toului. Two additional chapels were opened in Chai Yi. Between 1951 and 1959, twelve churches were founded in Taiwan and there were 1221 communicant members in the CELC. Devotional and worship materials were prepared and published, as was the correspondence course. The seminary program was refined and in the second class, five men were preparing to graduate in 1964, by which time CELC membership had increased to 1906 communicants.

Gremmels and Worthington left Taiwan after their initial five-year term. Walter became business manager as well as Lutheran Hour director and supervisor of several mission stations, at the expense, however, of developing the Taiwanese ministry. In 1959, Dingler had been called as the second Taiwanese-speaking missionary, but was busy simply assuming Walter's roles when he left for a position in Hong Kong, within four years.

With all the starts and stops the church was continuing to grow and mature. Not only were mission stations planted which became congregations, but a variety of special ministries were operative (Lutheran Hour, Bible Correspondence School, literature production, the bi-weekly Truth magazine for members, and ministry to the deaf).

For unrelated reasons, three of the remaining missionaries left the field in 1961 (Hafner, Trinklein and Walter). Dr. Riedel also left for a year-long furlough. This meant the loss of almost the entire first generation of ministry and experience. Bill Dingler remained until 1963, which left only Bringewatt and Riedel (after his return from furlough) to provide continuity into the next era.

One final point of transition toward the next era lies in the matter of governance of the newly planted church. In the early days when churches were just being planted and when the local ministry had not yet been formed, planning and decision-making lay largely in the hands of the missionaries of the Missionary Conference. As the number of missionaries began to decrease, as local churches became more established, and as Chinese colleagues grew more experienced in ministry, the matter of local governance surfaced. By 1954, steps to involve laymen in church decision-making jelled into a 'Delegate Conference," but the concept was premature and dissolved by 1958.

More time and education would be needed to bring the newly converted Chinese into the organizational matrix of the established church. Missionary Vic Hafner observed that:

There is a possibility that our whole mode of operation is too institutionalized, that we cannot think of the kingdom of God except in terms of congregations with church buildings and schools. If we are willing to abandon the "fine display" of statistics, the tangibility of buildings

Chapter 16　　　　　　　　　　　　　　　　　Planting the Seed in Taiwan

Lutheran Hour Locations and the Mountains of Taiwan

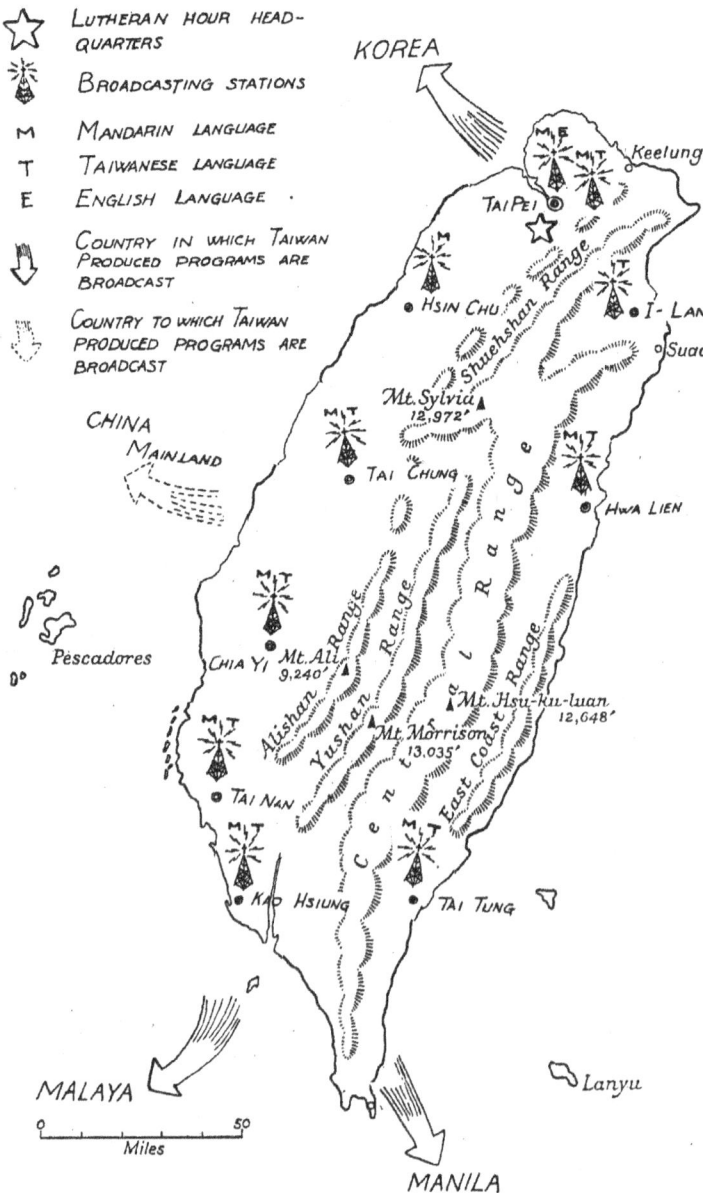

Localized broadcasting with ten towers enabled full coverage of Taiwan and also directed radio programs toward Korea, China, Malaysia, and the Philippines.

and organizations, and simply teach and preach in homes, parks, and on the street, then we do not need a building financal plan at all.

Hafner's vision was relegated into the same abyss with the suggestions of former missionaries Meyer, Voss, Martens, and so many others. It was not yet time for a different paradigm.

In 1960, movement toward a Joint Pastors' Conference (JPC) emerged, still advisory and clergy-centered, but nonetheless contributory toward planning and making decisions. This JPC would be preliminary toward the full establishment of a national church.

It became reality in the next era.

Lutheran Hour messages and drama presentations were aired in Cantonese, Mandarin, and Hakka languages.

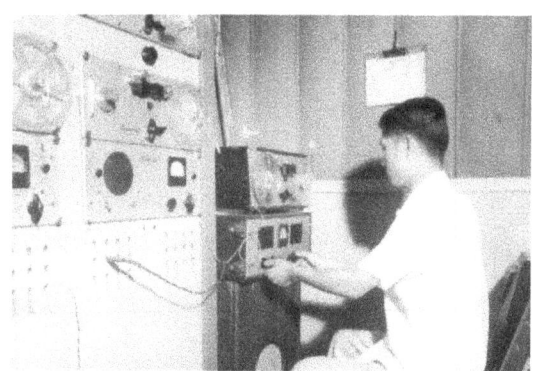

Significant sources

Albrecht, Ardon,	*The CELC in Perspective, 1965*
Gemmels & Walter,	*Christianity vs. Paganism, 1958*
Goddard, W.G.,	*Formosa: A Study in Chinese History*
Persbacher, Gerald,	*The Best is Yet to Come*
Rowold, Henry	*Notes on the China Evangelical Lutheran Church, 2013*

Interviews with Ardon Albrecht, Ed Bertram, Bill Dingler, and Hank Rowold

Chapter 17 — Progress and Transition – 1962-1983

Arrived

Year	Surname	First	Spouse
1961	Halamka	Ronald	& Claire
	Sprier	John	& Mary
	Bertram	Edward	& Marilyn
1962	Albrecht	Ardon	& Edith
1963	Zimmer	Robert	& Shirley
	Henningfield	Richard	& Delsena
1964	Frederick	Donald	
	Meyer	Arno	& Nina
1965	Goldhammer	Maurice	& Susan
	Hu	Patrick	& Edna
	Rowold	Henry	& Phyllis
1966	Winter	Clifford	& Lois
1967	Golnick	Merle	& Dorothy
1972	Kebschull	Lowell	& Elizabeth

Departed

Year	Surname	First	Spouse
1961	Trinklein	Michael	& Janice
	Haffner	Victor	& Adeline
	Walter	Norman	& Donna
1966	Sprier	John	& Mary
1967	Frederick	Donald	
1971	Albrecht	Ardon	& Edith
	Goldhammer	Maurice	& Susan
1972	Halamka	Ronald	& Claire
	Zimmer	Robert	& Shirley
1973	Bertram	Edward	& Marilyn
	Zimmer	Robert	& Shirley
	Henningfield	Richard	& Delsena
	Meyer	Arno	& Nina
	Hu	Patrick	& Edna

Lowland areas of western Taiwan were subject to nearly annual flooding, isolating villages and destroying property.

Train up a child in the way he should go; even when he is old he will not depart from it.
Proverbs 22:6 (ESV)

Chapter 17

Progress and Transition – 1962-1983

The first decade of LCMS activity in Taiwan was an era formative in establishing the fundamentals of mission ministry, including evangelism, church planting, *Lutheran Hour* programming, literature production, acquisition of properties, and human care ministries. Recruitment and training of over 20 potential clergy pointed toward a self-perpetuating and vibrant church, aimed toward local governance. The unplanned departure of six of the eight earliest missionaries, most with roots and experience in mainland China, left a significant void, moreso since trust in Chinese culture is based on long-term relationships. Only two of the early missionaries, Ralph Bringewatt and aging Erhardt Riedel, would serve terms longer than ten years with the CELC. An adjustment to new relationships with a second generation of missionaries signaled a revised and transitional era from 1962 to about 1983.

Within the first five years of this second phase, twelve new missionaries arrived in Taiwan. Virtually all the new pastoral missionaries were recent graduates from LCMS seminaries, eager to accept and begin their first call. In comparison, three teachers, the new business manager, and social worker were already well established in their careers. While the influx of youth allowed for new energy and new creativity, this called for an adjustment from the Chinese leadership since, by tradition, age was always more respected than youth, regardless of education.

Almost all of the Taiwan clergy had come to faith as adults and as refugees. This certainly gave them clarity of faith, a commitment to ministry, and an empathy with fellow refugees to whom they were reaching out. At the same time, it created a sort of generational mismatch with the new cadre of missionaries, who understandably did not have the first-hand refugee experience.

Chinese culture calls for students to respect teachers and for younger to respect older. In the first era, the missionaries were generally older and certainly more experienced in ministry than the national clergy. By 1962, the Chinese clergy were older than the foreign missionaries, and understood their own Chinese culture better. Those young missionaries had been raised in the heritage of North American congregational life and pastoral service, an unfamiliar model to the Chinese. Like all newly arrived expats, the Americans were also on a steep cultural and linguistic learning track.

Chapter 17   Progress and Transition – 1962-1983

Alan and Jeanine Meyer, affiliated with Concordia Middle School, experimented with a ministry of witness in the 1970s to churches and schools utilizing puppets acting out Christian drama situations. The innovative format successfully incorporated Alan's scripts with local Taiwanese theatric traditions.

The two major centers of Lutheran work on Taiwan were in the Taipei region, and at Chia Yi down is-land. Congregations were established, served by graduates of Concordia Seminary at Chia Yi. Visitors came from various Lutheran auxiliary organizations to encourage missionaries and new converts, and to implement non-traditional eduction projects. Due to government policies, Taiwan churches were unable to establish the tradition of parochial primary schools as had been done in china and in Hong Kong. Lack of schools impeded congregational growth and propagation.

Among the new arrivals were Ronald Halamka, John Spreier and Edward Bertram, all assigned to work in the Mandarin language. Halamka assumed presidency of Concordia Seminary. On faculty with Bertram and Rev. Donald Frederick, Halamka led three groups of pastors through to graduation and certification for ministry, five in the second class in 1964, two in the third in class in 1967, and two evangelists who graduated in 1969. Twenty pastors and evangelists were placed, mostly back into the congregations they had helped to form when seminarians. The work and growth begun in the first era had apparently come to fruition.

Taiwanese Language Ministry

Among the seminary graduates were two local Taiwanese men who pastored congregations in their native language. With strong encouragement from St. Louis to reach out to more of the majority population group on the island, the Missionary Conference drafted a "Taiwanese Evangelism Thrust." As a result, six of the next nine missionaries were called specifically to study the Taiwanese language and to work among the indigenous Taiwanese. Those newly-minted overseas seminarians included Ardon Albrecht, Donald Frederick, Arno Meyer, Maurice Goldhammer, Henry Rowold, and Clifford Winter.

A two-year Taiwanese evangelist training class was begun, which graduated seven evangelists. The burst of commitment to things Taiwanese in the mid-1960s was met with political alarm by many of the pastors with mainland roots. Accordingly, many of the Taiwanese evangelists were assigned to Mandarin-speaking congregations, resulting in a diluted Taiwanese outreach. Missionaries assigned to work in the Taiwanese language experienced cultural and administrative roadblocks which were not satisfactorily resolved at the time, and would eventually become an underlying and divisive struggle.

While several Taiwanese congregations were planted, not all of the "Thrust" goals were met. As decades and the passions have passed, the distinguishing lines are no longer so baldly drawn, the groups intermix (and intermarry), and the Taiwanese language is used much more freely. Mandarin is still the language of education, so that even CELC congregations of largely Taiwanese numbers worship in Mandarin. Among other Protestant churches, the Taiwan Presbyterian Church is an exception to this trend, which continues to see language as a matter of identity and cultural survival.

As second generation missionary ranks were filling out, the movement toward nationalization also accelerated. The Joint Pastors Conference (JPC) served its purpose for a transitional period as the local church sought a new status. After conversation and negotiation among church leaders and between the JPC and BWM, a protocol was forged and signed. In 1967, the China Evangelical Lutheran Church (CELC) was thus formed, and both the JPC and the Taiwan Missionary Conference were disbanded. One colleague referred to this as the biological miracle of a daughter church becoming a sister church. The preferred term is partner church.

The first chairman of the new partner church was the long-term first era missionary Rev. Ralph Bringewatt. The relationship of the CELC and LCMS represented a fulfillment, although provisional, of wishes and dreams from the earlier era for a successful new church body. Bringewatt provided institutional memory, good transition between the eras, firm pastoral leadership, and wise precedent for the fledgling CELC. Subsequent chairmen have all been pastors of CELC congregations

Changes at the Seminary

With three classes of theologically educated men graduated, CELC pastors all had calls to congregations and the congregations all had pastors. The impetus to continue to train younger pastors for new fields waned.

Chapter 17　　　　　　　　　　　　　　Progress and Transition – 1962-1983

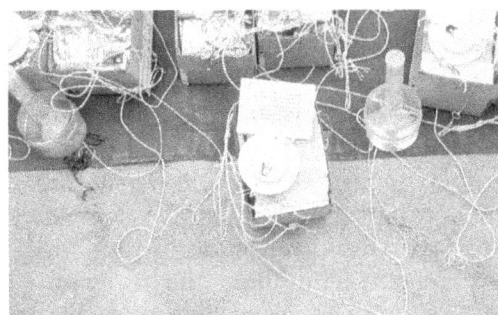

Lutheran Hour mail from China brought requests for Bibles to replace those burned by Red Guard forces of the Cultural Revolution. In response, missionary Ardon Albrecht, business manager Richard Henningfield, and Henry Go Wu raised funds through special broadcasts soliciting the support of donors across Taiwan. On March 22, 1967, 10,000 copies of the Book of John were flown in a Taiwan government airplane to Quemoy, an island within sight of the Mainland. There, bundles of the specially printed booklets (with a cover letter from president Chiang Kai-shek) were attached to helium weather balloons, launched, and wind-borne deep over Fukien province.

This seems short-sighted. During this lull, efforts were made to unite CELC's Concordia Seminary at Chai Yi with the Taiwan Lutheran Church (TLC) in forming a Federated Lutheran Seminary (FLS). This seemed possible as Lutherans worldwide were enjoying a decade of harmonious relations, in the Lutheran World Federation and LCUSA (Lutheran Council of the USA).

There were a small number of young Chinese men who felt called to the ministry, and plans for church expansion presumed a continuing supply of pastors. The possibility of any joint work with the LCMS seminary in Hong Kong was precluded by logistic and immigration considerations. However, without a full faculty or a full complement of students, FLS could only send its students to another seminary that would have some FLS faculty on staff to teach courses in Lutheran distinctives. Without full support, FLS disbanded and its director Halamka returned to the States in 1972.

Only Rowold remained to coordinate a seminary-level program. Disbanding the FLS meant that even fewer resources were available for the CELC to operate its own seminary program. An abbreviated FLS pattern continued for the remaining years of this era, so that a few new students were trained, the 1969 class of two Taiwanese evangelists were upgraded as pastors, and extension classes were conducted in other Taiwan cities. Rowold explored rekindling the vision of a cooperative Lutheran theological education program, which would bring together the six Lutheran churches and mission agencies on Taiwan. Possibilities included using either the campus of the Lutheran Bible School at Hsin Chu or the Concordia Seminary campus near Chia Yi. The timing was both too late and too early (see chapter 18).

Lutheran Hour Expansion

As noted in the last chapter, *Lutheran Hour* radio had been an integral part of the LCMS mission in Taiwan since the early 1950s, first arranged by Roy Suelflow. Although in early years the directors were missionaries, they were blessed with a creative and energetic assistant, Henry Go H. J. Wu. Early programming had generally re-broadcast sermons from Lutheran Hour speakers in the United States. Understanding local interest levels, Henry Go developed musical programming with brief devotional spots in the Mandarin, Taiwanese and Hakka languages.

Missionary Ardon Albrecht compiled a major publication explaining local Chinese religions and gods in the context of Christianity. Albrecht produced Cantonese devotions, sending those tapes to former China and Hong Kong missionary Wilbert Holt for re-broadcast in San Francisco. (Ironically, Cantonese programs are now produced at the Church of the Holy Spirit in San Francisco for re-broadcast in Asia.)

In the 1960s, programs also presented the Christian message in locally-produced theatrical episodes, similar to the ancient Chinese tradition of temple drama. That regional touch, generated by Henry Go, was affirmed when he was appointed director in 1971, a position he held until his death in 1997. Go also developed a very popular cassette ministry. Taped programs included evening devotions, scripture readings, prayers, and worship services with sermon helps and pre-recorded music, for use both as a model for church leaders and for people unable to attend public worship.

Among other creative Lutheran Hour activities was a campaign to airlift Bibles to the mainland. Using surplus weather balloons, this was an innovative plan borne of desperation to supply Christian material to the mainland.

Another mass media ministry was a television program, shared jointly with the Taiwan Lutheran Church (TLC). *Sunday Theater* was a prime-time drama that brought the message of the gospel to bear on issues of the day. A decade earlier, LCMS television had produced several seasons of an acclaimed

Chapter 17　　　　　　　　　　　　　　　　Progress and Transition – 1962-1983

Lutheran Hour operations improved as the Far East Broadcasting Corporation expanded its facilities and services. Programming, once originated at the KFUO studios on the campus of Concordia Seminary in St. Louis was now exclusively the product of local Chinese scriptwriters, actors, speakers, and technicians.

family TV drama series entitled *This Is The Life*. After a few years, declining financial resources allowed television stations, always a bit nervous about giving high visibility to Christian programming, to discontinue the program.

Mr. Richard Henningfield arrived as the second business manager in 1963. He put the mission and church on a solid financial footing, and oversaw a legal corporation established for registration of church properties. By Taiwan law, churches could not own property, so it came about that titles to land and properties of the General Conference of the CELC were to be held by the Legal Corporation Board of Control (LCBOC). As partner church, the LCMS became the "donating body," of the real estate it had purchased, entrusting its stewardship to the Legal Corporation and its officers.

Strange things sometimes happen when people conduct business in self-promoting ways. A later generation of corporation officers, seeking creative ways to secure financing after the loss of LCMS subsidy, would become mired in questionable dealings resulting in the loss of many church properties, despite years of litigation (see chapter 18).

Concordia Middle School

Refugees in Taiwan came mostly without families, adult men fleeing their homeland for political or economic reasons. Even though most growth in Christian communities is through its youth, the Taiwan pioneers had not focused on schooling, possibly since few had children with them. Survival was hardscrabble, but upheaval presented the opportunity to learn of and accept Christ.

The Taiwan government provided basic compulsory education, with particular emphasis on grades five and six. The heritage of schooling under the previous Japanese occupation had been aimed at keeping the Chinese subservient. There was scant tradition of Christian schooling, and even that was primarily for missionary children.

Middle school education was free but not required. There were not yet enough government middle schools, and there were only a few Roman Catholic, Presbyterian or Episcopal schools. To be competitive for placement in any middle school, students usually paid for extra "cram" courses after regular school hours and on weekends. Even taking time for church Sunday school was ill-advised. But, within the Lutheran mission, factors were coming together at the opportune time.

An early resolution of the Missionary Conference in 1955 had recommended opening a Lutheran high school on Taiwan, probably in keeping with the 1950s trend in America for establishing community Lutheran secondary schools in major cities. The time was not right then, nor when Hafner made a similar proposal in 1960.

To honor the pioneer work in Taiwan by Olive Gruen, the LWML set aside $20,000 in 1961 for up to ten $2,000 loans to individual Taiwan congregations for the construction of kindergarten or nursery facilities. Just five congregations eventually availed themselves of the funds, which had been re-directed from an incomplete project in Brazil. Gruen had long been an advocate of early childhood education, but it was not part of the program in Taiwan. No serious attempt at a Christian day school has ever been made, since government schooling is provided, and religious curricula are severely challenged.

Part of the emphasis by the new missionaries in the early 1960s included "Project 21," social welfare programs. With the creation of a BFM secretary for East Asia came the personalized services of an active missionary, Paul Strege. In this role, Strege was able to travel from his base in Tokyo to advise developing LCMS missions in Taiwan, Hong Kong, Korea, New Guinea, Japan, and the Philippines. Investigation of an educational strategy in Taiwan was one result.

Chapter 17   Progress and Transition – 1962-1983

Top left photo - Dr. Osward Hoffman came to Taipei for the 25th anniversary celebration of Taiwan operations in 1977.

Concordia Middle school was suggested by Mel Kieschnick (shown at a planning dinner with Erhrdt Riedel), and opened by founders Robert and Shirley Zimmer in 1967. The expansive campus included student quarters, classrooms, chapel, and a massive gateway.

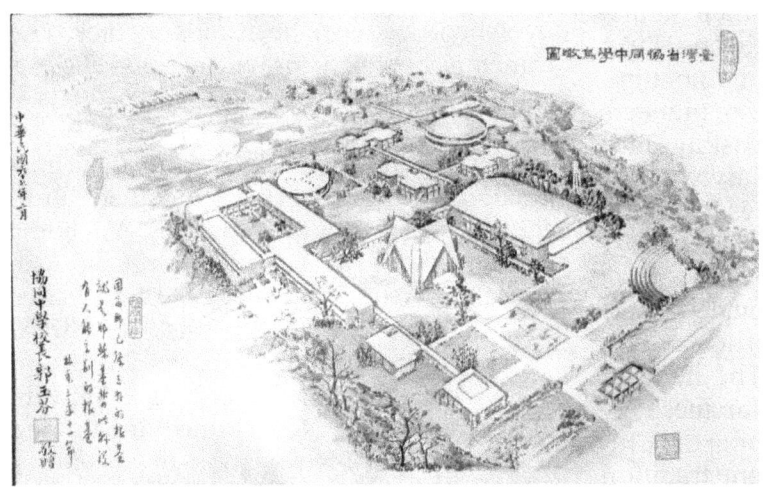

In January 1963, Mel Kieschnick, from the Hong Kong mission, was invited to spend three months accessing the educational potentials of the Taiwan mission. Kieschnick also had a background in volunteerism, having participated in Lutheran Volunteer School programs in his youth in America. At that time, the LCMS operated only four kindergartens. The Taiwan government was not supportive of religious schooling, and did not take a benevolent approach toward private schooling. From his survey, Kieschnick recommended that establishing a middle school (junior and senior high school) would be the most productive educational venture for the Lutherans in Taiwan. There were few quality schools at the secondary level, there was strong interest among local families for their children's higher education, and families were willing to pay sufficient tuition to make such schools self-sustaining.

Robert Zimmer, an experienced Lutheran teacher and principal from Maryland with a heart for civil rights, was called in 1963. After a year of language work, Zimmer surveyed all ten cities where there were CELC congregations. While each wanted a school in their neighborhood, all agreed that Chai Yi was the next best location choice.

With help from a consulting board, two major tasks were worked through. First was the identification of a 25-acre plot of dry sugar cane land about four miles north on the main road from Chia Yi at Min Hsiung. This meant sorting through a tangle of owners of several small fields, negotiating purchase prices, and drawing plans. Construction began in 1966. Architect Kuo Tien Lai designed the campus to be built in three phases. The building site was cleared and graded using loaned heavy equipment and volunteer operators from the nearby U.S. military base at Tainan. About $15,000 was saved through their labor.

The other major task was navigating governmental systems for permission and recognition of a private, church-run middle school; there were only a few such schools operating in Taiwan. Provincial Education Commissioner P'an Chien Ch'iu supported the proposals and applications of the CELC, glad for the promise of another quality middle school in his territory. Start-up costs—about $300,000—were approved and funded through the LCMS national Ebenezer thank offering of 1966. In 1967 Concordia Middle School (CMS) Phase One was finished, and classes began in September.

Concordia translates as "harmony" (*Hsieh Tong*)—a perfect and auspicious name for an institution bridging cultures. Implicit in plans from day one was a program of Christian exposure, without the structure of a curriculum. With no required religion classes, would all of the effort and expense yield a positive and appealing witness of the Christian beliefs of the administration and staff?

Unlike Hong Kong International School, coincidentally also opened in 1967, CMS was to be a local school, serving local students in the vernacular language with locally-hired national Christian teachers. The first years were difficult, as the school was a distance from the city and its reputation not yet well-established With intense work by gifted administrators and faculty, the school was slowly able to develop and demonstrate its mettle.

CMS evolved a uniquely successful English language program, developed with the guidance of experienced educator Merle Golnick. Called from Cleveland Lutheran High School in 1967, Golnick would dedicate 25 years to implementing creative English language instruction. On his first furlough, Merle did graduate work at the University of Hawaii in English as a Second Language. Using innovative techniques new to Chinese speakers, Golnick and his department were able to sidestep the normal pattern of rote memorization of vocabulary and grammar by developing conversational skills enabling lexicon and grammar to fit an everyday context. Key

Chapter 17   Progress and Transition – 1962-1983

VYM Volunteers 1978-2002

Year	#	First	Last
2002	75	Jason	Ball
2002	74	Andrew	Dinger
2002	73	Nate	Medlin
2002	72	Ben	Strohschein
2002	71	Robyn	(Gerber) Strohschein
2001	70	Nikki	Baldwin
2001	69	Sara	Hagemeyer
2001	68	Anne	Podoll
2001	67	Jessie	Vogel
2000	66	Laura	Loseke
2000	65	Krista	Noack
1999	64	Nicole	Dodd
1999	63	Jackie	Gronbach
1999	62	Rachel	(Schoenfuhs) Schmidt
1998	61	Jean	Beck
1998	60	Tonya	Eza
1998	59	Toby	Schmidt
1998	58	Krista	Wiesenauer
1997	57		
1997	56		
1997	55		
1997	54		
1997	53		
1996	52	Phil	Rigdon
1996	51	Steve	Wiesenauer
1995	50	Kim	Barnett
1995	49	Scott	Kroger
1995	48	Jenn	(Schutt) Castens
1995	47	Dan	Weiss
1994	46	Joel	Sievers
1994	45	Jeff	Snyder-Reinke
1994	44	Lena	(Yamasaki) Sievers
1993	43	Kurt	Buchholz
1993	42	Jenny	Buchholz
1993	41	Andrew	Fields
1993	40	Dan	Fingerlin
1993	39	Jeri	(Sibley) Pobanz
1992	38	Corey	Baden
1992	37	Ted	Groth
1992	36	Pat	(Stange) Hambaum
1992	35	Ann	(Wenger) Schmelge
1991	34		
1991	33	Scott	Perry
1991	32		
1990	31	Robin	(Dixon) Bomball
1990	30	Beth	Niermann
1990	16	Barb	Rebentisch (Hibbing)
1990	29	Kris	Rebentisch
1989	28	Andy	Safarik
1989	27	Johanna	Safarik
1988	26	Cindy	(Hass) Rasmussen
1988	25	Kip	Hoech
1988	24	Beth	(Schultz) Simmons
	23	Mark	Baumbach
	22	Kathy	Karlen
	21	Steve	Burke
	20	Carl	Hanson
	19		
	18		
	17	Denise	Buuck
	16	Barb	Hibbing
	15	Todd	Roeske
	14	Becky	Gimbel (Hsiao)
		Carol	Moser
	13	Mark	Busch
	12	Jennifer	(Hanson) O'Neal
	11	Mark	Wallace
	10	Luke	Armbruster
	9	Jeff	Bartells
	8	Betty	Meyers
	7	Shawn	Reynolds
	6	Deborah	Reedstrom
	5	John	Schirmer
	4	Ed	Strohschein
	3	Don	Bahr
	2	Fred	Lentz
	1	Rod	Ketcher

CMS volunteers and staff pose prior to taking home leave.

Students participated frequently in choral and drama presentations.

to success was quantity and quality conversation with native English speakers, a need filled by missionary wives and many shorter-term volunteer American teachers (see VYM below). The caliber and distinctiveness of this conversational approach soon gained island-wide and international recognition, bringing government officials, educators, and student teachers to observe it, to learn from it, and to adapt it.

The Christian character and context of the school remains a unique and dynamic feature of CMS, as of 2014. There has always been a LCMS missionary on staff, working with the religion department. One class period utilizes a weekly curriculum developed from Scripture - Old Testament in grade 8 and New Testament in grade 9. Supplemental regular chapel services, student service groups, Christian activities and celebrations—optional and outside classroom hours—are vital parts of student life. Many students enthusiastically participate in Bible class, choir, special camp sessions, and various organizations on campus. Trust and relationship evangelism mark the tenor of Christian living and working in community. A three-story gospel center was constructed on campus in 1991, funded by a $100,000 grant from the LWML. Groups from CMS have visited and worked regularly in recent years with mission outreach projects in Burma (Myanmar) among ethnic Chinese peoples there.

Zimmer returned to the States to work with Wheat Ridge Ministries in 1973. Lowell Kebschull succeeded him as CMS executive secretary, and worked closely with Principals Priscilla Kuo and Kenneth Chen. CMS experienced major growth in enrollment numbers and academic profile. Principals John Wan, Jeremy Lin, and Paul Yu have continued the strong Chinese Christian tradition of Christian leadership and high-quality education. From the earliest graduating year, CMS students have scored exceptionally high on national examinations, earning CMS an enviable reputation and a high profile among the best schools in Taiwan.

VYM - Volunteer Youth Ministry

Another energetic LCMS mission program has been the Volunteer Youth Ministry (VYM) program, conceived about the time the national Walther League met its decline. Begun in Japan as the Prince of Peace Corps (POPV) in the mid-1960s, VYM offered overseas mission experience to young Lutherans between college and career for periods up to two and a half years. The first half year was committed to language acquisition, after which the "VYMer" was assigned to a congregation or church agency assisting half-time in ministry, typically working with youth. The other half-time was for gainful employment, often teaching, with earnings given to the VYM program to support administrative and living expenses. The model is based in the tradition of the early Christian church community.

Success of the program in Japan led Cliff Winter, who also served as director of CELC youth work, to put together a similar program in Taiwan. The first VYMer, Rod Ketcher, arrived in 1978; within the next seven years, twenty VYMers served in Taiwan, at a variety of locations and churches, assisting Winter and the CELC youth department with youth camps, training sessions, and special events bringing young people together from congregations throughout Taiwan.

As many as five volunteers would arrive per year to assist with youth work at congregations in Chai Yi and the English language programs at CMS. These became essential in Golnick's English immersion program. Six strategies were developed to utilize student interests: clown/mime, art/crafts, puppetry, sports, English camps, and singing/music. Volunteers shared their faith by word and practice. Their mission statement reads:

..to assist the overall formal ministry of the China Evangelical Lutheran Church in Tai-

Chapter 17 Progress and Transition – 1962-1983

A highly innovative facility, sponsored by the Wheat Ridge Foundation, was opened and directed by Patrick Hu, a U.S.-trained social worker. The Lutheran Social Service Center in Taipei offered training and educational programs, interest groups, and services for families and youth for six years.

wan...by providing committed young, American, short-term workers...who will serve on both the congregational and church-wide levels....and who will earn the program's support through local employment.

Ken Boudreau was called in 1991 to continue administration of the program, which now lists nearly 200 former workers. Twenty alumni have gone on to further careers in the church, many in Asia. There have been at least ten VYM-sourced marriages. VYM transitioned into the GEO program in 2006 (see chapter 19).

Lutheran Social Service Center

Unique among the missionaries of this era is social worker Patrick P. C. Hu. His story of deliverance from dismal poverty in China to an American graduate degree in social work and to the Christian faith rates as epic. His understanding of American and Chinese ways, as well as his university training allowed him to begin ministry the minute he arrived in Taiwan. Hu had answered an advertisement in the Lutheran Witness for a social worker in Taiwan, and spent the summer of 1965 in St. Louis at mission school with newly-called missionaries Rowold, Winter, and Goldhammer.

Originally a component of Project 21, the Lutheran mission envisioned a social service center in Taipei as a joint effort with Wheat Ridge Foundation, Lutheran World Relief and the CELC. Missionary John Spreier was especially helpful in setting up the Lutheran Social Service Center (LSSC). Pat Hu recruited a staff of local social workers to provide services for the poor including vocational training, educational assistance, a safe place for students to study, tutorial help, marital and parental counseling, assistance in household management and basic hygiene, and referrals for medical needs. Social work students from National Taiwan Normal University, Provincial Chungshin University and the College of Chinese Culture were placed at LSSC for field work. Hu also taught at Tunghai University. The center worked with the Taipei orphanage run by Gladys Aylward, the former China Inland Mission pioneer well known for her anti-foot binding work depicted in the 1958 20th Century Fox movie *Inn of the Sixth Happiness*.

LSSC was an unqualified success. Local agencies referred their clients to LSSC for cooking and sewing classes, youth services, and orphan placement. There was joint work with other agencies for flood and typhoon relief projects. People were taught to help themselves. Local churches were encouraged to prepare for a time when funds from the LCMS would cease. One congregation, inspired by work in Hong Kong, developed the Lutheran Handicraft Center, making mostly Chinese dolls and selling them so as to become financially self-sufficient.

As had happened with Golnick at CMS, Hu's expertise quickly caught the attention of governmental and educational agencies as he provided internship training for social work students. In addition to his teaching, he served as consultant to the human care ministries of some congregations, particularly working with sight- or hearing-impaired people.

As seems true all too often, financial shortfalls led to the closing of the center in 1971 and to the eventual departure of Hu for America. He and his wife, Edna, served years later in Macau at St. Paul's School for the Deaf with Louis Jasper. Hu conducted various human care workshops in China in the late 80s and early 90s. As of this writing, he is 96, living in Colorado close to family, and proud of his black belt in karate.

Christian Salvation Service

Christian Salvation Service is a non-denominational entity which helps young unwed pregnant Chinese women with medical aid and emotional support. Taiwanese society places a harsh judgment on illegitimacy. Lillian Dickson, the Presbyterian founder of the Taiwan-based "Mustard Seed" ministry

Chapter 17　　　　　　　　　　　　　　Progress and Transition – 1962-1983

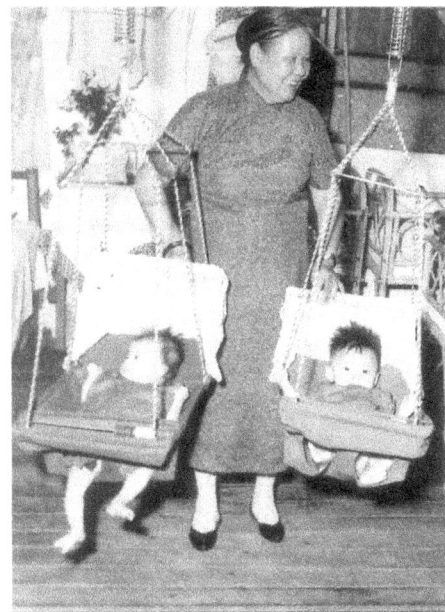

Kindergartens, nurseries, and activities at the Lutheran Social service Center all focused on training young people and exposing them to the care of Christian workers.

in 1952, died in 1983. Different branches of that human care ministry were entrusted to various Mustard Seed leaders. Among those branches was an infant/children-at-risk ministry, administered by LCMS member Paula Voigtmann. She revived the registered but inactive organization named Christian Salvation Service (CSS) as home for the Mustard Seed family program. In 1985, the LWML provided a $48,000 grant for a children's shelter, baby nurseries, and adoption placement services. Adoption fees and other reimbursements have since made the CSS operation self-supporting.

Together with Georgia Hsieh, a dynamic Chinese social worker, CSS was extended to include infants and young children at risk - many abandoned, born with deficiencies, or from families who could not afford to raise them. CSS facilitated a nursery, a short-term orphanage, adoption into Christian homes, active pro-life advocacy, and lab training for field workers and social work interns. Women & Teens' Program, Child Rescue Program, and Hospice Care Services have been developed by a staff of 20, both to provide assistance, but also to demonstrate the love of Christ to those who need a chance at a new life. The Mu En (Shepherd's Grace) Infant Care Facility has helped over 1000 prematurely born or special needs children.

CSS fills a social need with such competence that it has gained national prominence, and has received donations and funding from local sources in numbers virtually unprecedented in Taiwan. Though CSS is not institutionally part of either CELC or LCMS, its leadership and several board members and staff have come from both, and benefits all.

This second era, 1961-1985, was a time of significant growth: graduation of clergy and evangelists, formation of the China Evangelical Lutheran Church as partner to the LCMS in 1967, vision of cooperative Lutheran theological education, legal registration of CELC, outreach to Mandarin-speaking and Taiwanese-speaking populations, expansion of Lutheran Hour ministry, opening and growth of Concordia Middle School, operation of a human care center and Christian Salvation Service.

During this era, the first few Chinese pastors had passed away. Reminiscent of what happened at the end of the first period, by the end of the second era, several missionaries had departed Taiwan, with the exception of the Golnicks.

Painful issues, just beginning to surface, would prove very difficult in the third era. One was the growing expression of Taiwanese identity and the involvement of one pastor in a civil rights demonstration, which actually turned bloody when police came to disband the demonstration. Several ring leaders were identified and sought. A young Taiwanese CELC pastor provided safe haven for one of the fugitives, and was later arrested and sentenced to prison along with the fugitive. The CELC leadership defrocked him, which brought other tensions to the surface. Major turmoil followed, prompting the departure of one seminary student and the refusal of another to return to Taiwan from his graduate studies in the States. One missionary who expressed concern for the imprisoned Taiwanese pastor was dismissed.

Added to this atmosphere was the prospect of shrinking financial support from the LCMS, tempting some leaders in the CELC to begin reallocating resources already controlled by the CELC. As of the thirtieth anniversary of the CELC, 26 churches were rostered, with a total of 2,144 baptized or communicant members.

Chapter 17   Progress and Transition – 1962-1983

Students at Concordia Middle School submitted testimonies of their faith life and journey in 2012. They are presented on these pages, and on pages 202, 210, and 214

My personal story   *Christy*

God is good and we can experience love and grace from Him deeply. I started to know God when I studied at CMS and got baptized during that time while I was a grade two student in Senior High School. The reason I got baptized is very simple. I feel peace and fulfilled love from God that nothing can be replaced. In this few years, I learned that we just need to spend time with Him everyday and do our parts then God will help us the parts out of our abilities.

When I worked at VYM (Volunteer Youth Ministry: an organization in Taiwan to support missionaries coming from the United States.), we have FNBS (Friday Night Bible Study: missionaries lead Bible Study on Friday Night), it's good to see people coming to join with us singing songs, sharing Bible stories and chatting time. Originally, they come just for learning English, but frequently they start to learn God more and more and more people get baptized. To me, I love songs parts the most, so I start to pray and hope one day I can play piano while singing.

God is great, He answers my prayer, He gave me a classic piano teacher and I learned piano two years. At that time still can't play chords well. Now, VYM center is closed, but we still have FNBS at church, people still come and I can't believe that I already play piano at FNBS for about 2 years, God is amazing. it's hard for me to play songs just follow melodies, but every time when I play piano with the team at FNBS, there is always some creative notes coming out in my mind and works out well.

Philippians 4:19,"My God will meet all your needs according to His glorious riches in Christ Jesus."

Christian Personal Story   *Rita*

My mom is a Christian, and she took me to church since I was born. When I grow up, I learn about Jesus more and more, and I choose to believe in Him. So, I think my belief is not all because of my mom. My dad is not a Christian, sometimes he will argue with us about God is real or not. These years, we try very hard to talk to him about Jesus and we pray for him, so he began not to be that unbelief in Jesus.

Taiwan is a typical Buddhist society, many of my friends and families are Buddhist. It may be a challenge to being Christian in Taiwan. For an example, when my great-grandfather died, we needed to take incense sticks in the funeral, but that could be worshiping to another God, so my mom refused it (also refuse for me), I guess it would be little embarrassing. Sometimes, they would ask us why did we care so much about this or they would say this is not important at all. They just think we don't need to obey it.

I share my faith when I see someone need help, including both physical and mental trouble. I will pray for them, and tell them that they can also try to pray to God when they feel helpless. For an example, one of my friends got poor score on her monthly test, her parents are very strict, and she kept crying not wanting to go home. I told her to pray to God and we did it together, on the next day, she said she didn't get any blames from her parents!

Living with Jesus makes my life fill with more confidence and brightness, I think He can give me courage and strength to face some hardships. When I have quarrel with somebody, God help me to get through it. When I felt frustrated and wanted to cry in the midnight, He is the one who gives me comfort.

Christian Personal Story   *Grace*

> During winter vacation in 2000, my family found a small but beautiful church in Summertown, Oxford. The secretary of the church, Beryl, who became my Godmother in 2006, was very friendly to us when we first stepped into the Summertown United Reformed Church. Ever since then, we would always visit the church when we go to England (almost every year). This church is quite different from those in Taiwan. The Summertown URC has very peaceful lectures, while churches in Taiwan have emotional speeches. My family seldom goes to church now in Taiwan, because we are not used to them.
>
> At the time when I'm baptized, my religion was just something I liked. It was when I entered senior high school that my belief grew stronger. Both my teachers and my friends encouraged me to attend the gathering in the school chapel every Friday. They also introduced me to a small group formed by students to pray and sing. Praising Jesus in a song is one of my favorite things to do now. My friends and I in the small group would sing every Friday morning in the school chapel, and that is the time I've always anticipated. Thanks to the environment my school has provided me, I'm now really proud of my being a Christian!

Hupeh Province and Missouri on the same scale

Taiwan (Formosa) and Illinois on the same scale

Significant Sources:

Hu, Patrick	*Why Me, Lord*
Rowold, Henry	*Notes on the China Evangelical Lutheran Church, 2013*
Strege, Paul	*How Small is Small?*
Zimmer, Robert	*Dreams Come True*

Interviews with Richard Bringewatt, Maurice Goldhammer, Merle & Dorothy Golnick, Ron Halamka, Elizabeth Ketcher, Hank & Phylis Rowold, Cliff Winter, and Bob Zimmer

Chapter 18	Regrouping, Trauma, and Hope -1983-2012

Arrived

1983	Brandt	Robert	& Harriett
1986	Molitoris	Craig	& Joyce
	Ketcher	Rodney	& Elizabeth
	Found	Jim	& Sue
1988	Fox	Chip	& Hannah
1989	Peterson Merlin		
1993	Burke	Steve	& Ming Hwei
1994	Boudreau	Ken	& Janice
	Oschwald	Jeffrey	& Jill
1996	Tursic	Richard	& Kathy
1997	Buchholz	Kurt	& Jenny
	Hanson	Carl	& Chenhsi
	Oliver	Stephen	& Shu Hua
	Paul	Michael	& Irene
	Wasmunds	Matt	& DeeDee

Departed

Information unavailable

Summer camp was held at the Lutheran Social Service Center in Taipei where children learned responsibility, hygiene, and social skills in addition to playing games, studying, and worshipping.

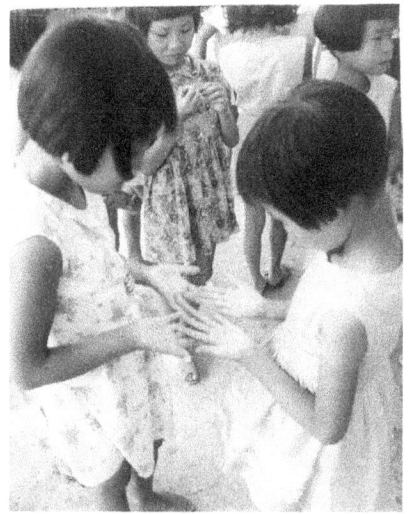

If you have faith like a grain of mustard seed, you will say to this mountain, Move from here to there, and it will move, and nothing will be impossible for you.

Matthew 17:20 (ESV)

Chapter 18

Regrouping, Trauma, and Hope - 1983-2013

Thirty years after the first Chinese Lutheran refugees arrived on Taiwan, an indigenous Lutheran church body (CELC) had been established as a partner church with the LCMS. As the third era of Lutheran activity began, twenty congregations were blessed with pastors and evangelists; a vigorous Lutheran Hour reached airwaves over far corners of the region; a nationally recognized middle school was flourishing at Chia Yi; social ministries were growing in various congregations; and there was renewed yearning for a theological education program.

In the mid-1980s, relocation or retirement of significant overseas and local staff would once again shift direction and focus of the CELC. Virtually all missionaries departed, and several Chinese pastors passed away within a short period. In seeking new opportunities and further transitions, tensions underlying the mission from earlier periods continued to fester, erupt, and divide. Inevitably, scars remained from the healing process, but new promising strengths have emerged as the CELC finds focus in local and overseas growth.

With healing comes health; with health comes vigor; with vigor comes action.

The CELC has been led by several leaders, designated as chairmen, not presidents:

Missionary Ralph Bringewatt
Rev. Winston Chu (WenSheng)
Rev. Richard Yi (RenYang)
Rev. Harold Ren (ZhiPing)
Rev. Andrew Miao (QiHwa)

New Staffing and Programs of the 1980s

The departure of all but two LCMS missionaries presented an opportunity for LCMS World Mission (formerly the BFM) and the CELC to reevaluate the role of "missionary" in the mission and ministry of the Taiwan church. As a result, World Mission during the third phase sent six new missionaries within five years, men very different from the foreign missionaries of earlier eras. Five of these men came with levels of previous church service experience. Three arrived with a head start in Mandarin language acquisition. None were called to work with Taiwanese language outreach.

Four of these mid-1980s workers were assigned specifically to church planting, separate from program work such as adminis-

CELC Churches as of 2008 - listed by founding dates

Year	Chinese	English Name	Status
1951	永生堂	Eternal Life, Taipei	80-100 members
"	和平堂	Peace, Banchiao	30-60 members
"	錫安堂	Zion, Huwei	closed & auctioned
"	施恩堂	Grace, Chiayi	less than 10
1952	真光堂	True Light, Taipei	less than 20
"	真理堂	Truth, Taipei	Legal lean against it
1954	救主堂	Saviour, Chiayi	less than 10
"	文山佈道所	Wen Shan PS, Zhonghe	closed 1990's
1955	生命堂	Life, Tainan	closed - un-sellable
1956	新生堂	New Life, Hsinchu	to be auctioned
"	救恩堂	Salvation, Chiayi	30-40 members
"	恩典堂	Grace, Hsineng	closed & auctioned
1957	聖保羅堂	Saint Paul, Hualian	maybe 20 members?
1958	頌恩堂	Glory Grace, Tainan	60-80 members
1959	迦南堂	Cannan, Tapei	lean/less than 10
1960	聖三一堂	Holy Trinity, Nantou	20-40 members
"	嘉興佈道所	Chia Hsing PS, Chiayi	less than 20
1961	台中佈道所	Tai Chung PS, Taichung	less than 10
"	甘露堂	Heavenly Dew, Zhanghwa	closed & auctioned
"	靈恩堂	Spiritual Grace, Toului	20-30 members
1963	仁愛堂	Mercy, Tauyuan	tenuous
1964	榮恩堂	Glorious Grace, Shenzaopu	20 members
1965	新莊佈道所	Hsin Chuang PS, Hsinchuang	less than 10
1969	鴻恩堂	Abundant Grace, Shilin	less than 10
1976	松山佈道所	Sung Shan PS, Sungshan	less than 10
1978	高雄區佈道所	Kaoshiung Area PS, Kaoshiung	closed 1980's
1983	安中佈道所	An Chung PS, Tainan	30-40 members
1985	信愛堂	Faith Love Church, Taichung	closed 1991
1988	大福教會	Da Fu Church, Kaoshiung	closed 1996
1989	信望愛	Faith, Hope, Love, Tainan	20 members
1989	天牧堂	Heavenly Shepherd, Taipei	closed 1998
1998	崇恩教會	Chong En Church, Taichung	No longer meets

tration, the Lutheran Hour or theological education. Robert Brandt was called out of a very successful U.S. parish ministry. Rodney Ketcher, Charles (Chip) Fox, and Craig Molitoris were recent graduates of the St. Louis Seminary, each with a year or more experience in the China region.

This "New Work," as it was called, was the first joint ministry effort between the CELC and LCMS in the wake of internal turmoil in the CELC, including dismissal of one missionary. As part of the effort to restructure future cooperative ministry, a "protocol document" was developed to define the nature, relationship and finances of mutual work.

Brandt, Molitoris, Ketcher, and Fox, were all called to a new paradigm of church planting. Each was paired with a younger CELC pastor as a church planting team, joined in some cases with a VYM volunteer. The teams would work in a specific geographic area to witness, convert, and facilitate a worship group. Ketcher, who had served as the first Taiwan VYMer, returned after seminary graduation to establish and serve with CELC Pastor Wu Ming Hui at Da Fu Church in Kaoshung.

It was hoped that the new approach might circumvent some of the other relational problems within the congregations. While creative beginnings were made, the pairings and personalities were not always harmonious. The task of planting a church is rarely easy or smooth, moreso when foreign cultures and personalities are involved or a timeline imposed. By the early 1990s, both missionaries and local pastors were reassigned to other congregational settings.

Concordia Middle School and the VYM

LCMS World Mission brought over additional educational missionaries to assist in the ministry of CMS, Jim Found in 1986, followed by Kurt Buchholz in 1997.

In addition to honing its academic programs, the scope of activities within the school's religion department has diversified into three branches: ministry to students, ministry to teachers, and ministry to community. Building on earlier practices, student ministry has involved evangelistic witness with school-wide celebrations at Christmas and Easter. Special activities reinforce understanding of the Christian message of salvation. Second and third year junior high students are invited to join small "Growth Groups" providing fellowship, follow-up, and formation in the faith. Discipleship training is available in the Stewards' Club, a Christian club for senior high students, and also in small leadership training groups. A series of drama, literature, leadership, and special interest winter camps are held annually, often assisted by returning alumni leaders.

A ministry of Christian witness to the non-Christian teaching and support staff is a unique opportunity for Christian faculty and students. It is an adult ministry of in-house witness through daily relationships. Campus Christians offer prayer, visitation, and Bible study with weekly devotions and prayer meetings. The annual all-school faculty retreat is also a special time for gathering to grow in fellowship and team-building.

The third element of CMS ministry brings focus to social services beyond the school walls, both local and overseas. On the island, the Mercy Club members volunteer at Chia Yi Christian Hospital. They team with classmates and teachers to share God's love with patients and families in need. Volunteers also serve at the Ro Ju School for the mentally challenged. Each spring, a team of graduating senior high students travels to help the Zo Zu mountain people in Cha Shan. This gospel team carries Christ's love to children in the isolated community.

Integral to the verve and life of CMS, and to the several extra-curricular opportunities, has been the presence and contribution of over 80 VYM volunteers from America since

Chapter 18 — Regrouping, Trauma, and Hope - 1983-2012

Roster of LCMS Pastors in Taiwan

A – Concordia Seminary, Chia Yi, First Class	
B – Concordia Seminary, Chia Yi, First Class (delayed, military duty)	
C – Concordia Seminary, Chia Yi, Second Class	
D – Special Evangelists	
E – Concordia Seminary, Chia Yi, Evangelist Class	
F – Concordia Seminary, Chia Yi, Evangelist Class (delayed)	
G – Joint Program with Tainan Theological Seminary	
H – Joint Program with Taiwan Theological Seminary	
I – Joint Program with China Evangelical Seminary	
J – Hsi Luo Seminary	
K – China Lutheran Seminary, Hsin Chu	
L – CELC House of Theological Studies	
M – LCMS Seminary Graduates	
N – Other	
♦ - Deceased	

	Name	Name Romanized/Pinyin
A1♦	張叔華	Chang Shu Hua/ Zhang Shuhua
A2	趙 健	Chao Chien/Zhao Jian
A3♦	朱文生	Chu Wen Sheng/Zhu Wensheng
A4♦	朱毓書	Chu Yü Shu/Zhu Yushu
A5♦	璩泰開	Ch'yu T'ai K'ai/ Qu Taikai
A6♦	徐 晏	Hsü Yan/Xu Yan
A7	任治平	Jen Chih P'ing/Ren Zhiping
A8♦	李壽林	Li Shao Lin/Li Shaolin
A9	魯振華	Lu Chen Hua/Lu Zhenhua
A10♦	劉心平	Lyou Hsin P'ing/ Liu Xinping
A11	梅篠峰	Mei Hsiao Feng/Mei Xiaofeng
A12	萬良心	Wan Liang Hsin/Wan Liangxin
A13	宜仁揚	Yi Jen Yang/Yi Renyang
B1♦	許竹軒	Hsü Chu Hsuan/Xu Zhuxuan
C1	向介明	Hsiang Chieh Ming/Xiang Jieming
C2	李約翰	Li Yue Han/Li Yuehan
C3♦	廖海全	Liao Hai Ch'uan/Liao Haiquan
C4♦	曹國強	Ts'ao Kuo Ch'iang/Cao Guoqiang
D1♦	許靖華	Hsü Ching Hua/Xu Jinghua
D2♦	馬寶箴	Ma Bao Chen/Ma Baozhen
E1	何人助	Ho Jen Chu/He Renzhu
E2	林朝宗	Lin Ch'ao Chung/Lin Chaozhong
E3	林阿連	Lin Ya Lien/Lin Yalian
E4	施正雄	Shih Cheng Hsiung/Shi Zhengxiong
E5	王茂雄	Wang Mao Hsiung/Wang Maoxiong
E6	宜信一	Yi Hsin Yi/Yi Xinyi
F1	蔡貽慕	Tsai Yi Mu/Cai Yimu
G1♦	李仲秋	Li Chong Ch'iu/Li Zhongqiu
G2	吳文	Wu Wen/Wu Wen
H2	莊光明	Chuang Kwang Ming/Zhuang Guangming
H1	萬德樹	Wan Teh Shu/Wan Deshu
I1	任仂德	Jen Le Teh/Ren Lede
I2	苗其華	Miao Ch'I Hwa/Miao Qihua
I3	萬德成	Wan Teh Ch'eng/Wan Decheng
J1	陳平安	Ch'en P'ing An/Chen Pingan
J2*	趙世輝	Chao Shih Hwei/Zhao Shihui
K1	鄭玉章	Cheng Yü Chang/Zheng Yuzhang
K2	璩亞稐	Ch'yu Ya Lun/Qu Yalun
K3	范紀明	Fan Chih Ming/Fan Jiming
K4	林中一	Lin Chong Yi/Lin Zhongyi
K5	劉坤昌	Liu Kun Ch'ang/Liu Kunqiang
K6	吳明輝	Wu Ming Hwei/Wu Minghui
K7*	宜約堂	Yi Yue T'ang/Yuetang
L1	朱運平	Chu Yun P'ing/Zhu Yunping
L2	蕭正賢	Hsiao Cheng Hsien/Xiao Zhengxian
M1	吳政勛	Wu Cheng Hsün/Wu Zhengxun
M2	吳山大	Wu Shan Ta/Wu Shanda
N1	劉	Liu Meng Wei

1978. Changes in restrictions for missionary visas as well as tensions within the CELC led to the need to find alternate access to visas for the volunteers. CMS stepped forward to apply for educational (rather than missionary) visas, and to provide housing and on-site funding. Renamed as Volunteer Missionary Service, the volunteer program became a part of CMS, and volunteers no longer serve and live in local congregations. In conjunction with World Mission restructuring, VYM changed its name once more—now GEO (Globally Engaged in Outreach)—and changed its operation to a more flexible but still clearly focused ministry.

The volunteer ministry has enlisted the energy and commitment of well over 200 volunteers. Missionary Clifford Winter was the founder of the program, but subsequent leaders have all been selected from volunteers themselves: Becky (Gimbel) Shaw, Jennifer (Hanson) O'Neal, Krista (Noack) Alexander, Ken Boudreau, and Matt Wasmund. Some twenty have entered the pastoral, educational, or deaconess ministries, and another ten have married into those ministries. Others have taken leadership in congregations back home. Still others have returned to overseas service in a variety of places, including Taiwan and China. In other words, aside from the energy and creativity that the volunteers brought to the CELC and to CMS, volunteer programs have focused the dedication of gifted people for service to the Lord, the church, the Chinese, and the world community.

Concordia Middle School continues to be the flagship ministry of the CELC. Its excellence of education and its enviable record of graduates who have advanced their way through a national system of college entrance exams are its heritage. It has a full complement with students on a waiting list. In addition to the middle school curriculum, CMS has also opened Concordia English Language Academy and an English-intensive after-school program for kindergarten and primary school children.

CMS has been led by five principals in its forty years: Ch'eng Ch'ung Ch'uen, Hsu Chien Chang, John Wan, Jeremy Lin, and Paul Yu, each promoted from years of service within the CMS community. Each has been strongly committed to academic excellence and to Christian witness, and each continuing to live and work in community at CMS.

One singular innovation of this era is the outreach program, mentioned above, that CMS has developed with Chinese-speakers in the far north of Myanmar (Burma). Many of those Chinese-speakers are Miao or Hmong tribal peoples that spill over the border between Myanmar and China. Some are refugees fleeing the devastation of China's civil war (Communist vs. Nationalist) or the more recent Cultural Revolution in the People's Republic. CMS students and faculty have provided school furnishings and educational materials, as well as intensive training for Myanmar teachers and students alike, all the while sharing the Christian faith that takes them there.

Supported by a foundation named for CMS founder Robert Zimmer, Concordia has become both 1) an internationally-oriented school, not so much within Taiwan but in its outreach abroad, and 2) a missional school, both in its internal school life and in its mission outreach.

China Lutheran Seminary

Merlin Peterson, with a career in theological education, joined the LCMS in Taiwan in 1988. When CELC discontinued the earlier Federated Lutheran Seminary (FLS) model of theological education, it called Peterson to establish a "house of studies" model. The plan would gather students to a central location for scheduled intensive study periods, returning each to their home community with assignments and projects to be discussed on the next regular visit.

Concurrently, another vision of a cooperative Lutheran seminary was activated by

China Lutheran seminary in Hsin Chu brought together six smaller seminaries into the largest Chinese language Luther Studies program in the world. Staff and visiting professors from several countries enrich the program, now housed in a large campus and extensive library, dedicated in 2008.

Former LCMS seminarian Liu Teng-sheng, kneeling at right, a 1936 student at the original Concordia Seminary in Hankow, was still attending Taipei's Eternal Life church in in 2008.

the former bishop of the Taiwan Lutheran Church, the largest of many Lutheran bodies in Taiwan. Dr. Thomas Yu (and perhaps only he) had the stature, the commitment, and the diplomacy to bring together six Lutheran church bodies and mission agencies (two Norwegian, one Finnish, two American, and one international) to form China Lutheran Seminary (CLS), on the campus of the former Lutheran Bible School at Hsin Chu. Dr. Waldemar Degner, in his retirement as professor at Concordia Theological Seminary, Fort Wayne, joined the ministry at CLS and helped to expand its Bachelor of Theology program. Though the beginnings were tenuous, with minimal financial resources, few students, limited faculty, and aging buildings, the strong commitment of all parties has led to a first-rate seminary. With new facilities completed in 2008, a young and gifted faculty, and the finest theological library facility in Taiwan, (including the collections of the "house of studies" and FLS), it also houses the only Mandarin-language graduate program in Luther studies.

This seminary formed at a critical time for the CELC; virtually all of the CELC's first generation of pastors and evangelists have passed away. As part of its contribution to this ministry, LCMS WM has sent Professors Jeffrey Oschwald (1994-2002), Michael Paul (2002-2003), and Stephen Oliver (2001-current), to serve as faculty, plus occasional part-time faculty - Carl Hanson; Bruce Hartung; Hank Rowold; and guest lectures in the Luther's Studies program, including Robert Kolb and Charles Arand.

Church Planting

The *New Work* congregational experiment, discontinued in the early 1990s, was replaced by a plan focused on Taiwan's emerging urbanism. With martial law ended in 1986, there was a subsequent allowance of former mainlanders to return to their homelands. Opportunity for businesses to operate abroad, and in the PRC, built momentum for Taiwan to become an international economic hub. Taiwan became one of the five so-called "Asian Tigers," with a growing middle class, increasingly sophisticated technological and electronic industry, and a growing economy. Gone is the refugee generation. Most young and professional families preferred to live in gated high rise apartment dwellings in new housing estates within trendy metropolitan areas.

Nurturing the hope of planting churches through Bible study and small groups, a new TEAM ministry attempted to form worshiping communities in several newly-developed urban areas. Living in the same building complexes, the missionaries could take advantage of common or community space for large activities, and members' apartments for Bible study and relational evangelism.

Steve Burke arrived in 1993, having been a VYM'er from 1986-88. Richard Tursic was a recent seminary graduate who had years of English teaching and business management experience in China. Carl Hanson brought five years of VYM experience (1986-91). Internal and external pressures left the team with only two years to accomplish its task of planting a self-sustaining church. Even though they were able to expand to three locations and began joint worship services as large as any of the CELC congregations, the missionaries were eventually reassigned: Tursic to Yunnan, China, in 1999, and Hanson to CMS at Chia Yi, in 2001. Burke repatriated in 2004 as part of a World Mission 25% reduction of its expatriate force. The new believers joined existing CELC or other Lutheran congregations, but the idea of planting a new church in Taiwan externally had run its course. These three were the last LCMS missionaries to be called to Taiwan for church planting.

Lutheran Hour Ministries

For the Lutheran Hour, this new era was a particularly exciting one, because not only was its ministry growing in Taiwan, but Chi-

Chapter 18　　　　　　　　　　　　　　Regrouping, Trauma, and Hope -1983-2012

Mr. Liu Teng-sheng, once a student in the LCMS seminary in China, is pictured with Rev Carl Hanson, in 2008. Mr. Liu was a member of Eternal Light congregation in Taipei

Sewing and other programs in domestic science were among the courses offered at the Lutheran Social Services Center. Training enabled women to gain employment.

180

na was beginning to re-open. Together with an assistant, Rev. Stephen Xu, Director Henry Wu visited China several times to explore possibilities both for ministry inside China and also for setting up operations inside China, the dream of earlier generations of missionaries. For a variety of reasons, one of which was avoiding political complications, the International Lutheran Hour decided to separate ministry in China from the Taiwan Lutheran Hour, and appointed Go's assistant, Xu, to assume leadership in China.

Growing opportunities and interest in China together with declining financial resources led eventually to reduction of funding of the Taiwan Lutheran Hour. It struggled on for a brief time, but simply could not sustain a ministry that relies on sophisticated and expensive technology as well as costly air time. Programs came to a complete halt when Henry Go died suddenly in 1997. The International Lutheran Hour sought to maintain at least a presence in Taiwan by cooperating with *Lutheran Voice*, a radio ministry operated by the Taiwan Lutheran Church, but eventually discontinued all ministry in Taiwan.

Sorting out the Details

As mentioned in chapter 17, the most contentious issue of the current Taiwan era is that of land and property. In hindsight, the CELC committed an ill-advised decision early in this period. The constitution of the CELC stipulated that its General Conference (GC) is the final authority over all matters in the church, and the Executive Committee is such when the GC is not in session. This includes authority over the Legal Corporation Board of Control (LCBOC) as well as the CMS Board of Control, and election of members to both Boards. By contrast, the government in Taiwan recognizes only the LCBOC as a legal entity because it is the registered body, and holds title to land and properties of the General Conference.

At a moment of confusion, distraction, and lack of definition, the resolution passed at a General Conference meeting which surrendered to the LCBOC the right to elect its own members. In other words, the LCBOC became an independent, self-appointing board with full legal rights and with deeds to land and properties. Though there are laws protecting and limiting non-profit organizations, the LCBOC pursued avenues to raze CELC buildings in order to enter into joint venture building projects without the knowledge or approval of the wider church or the donating body (LCMS). Monies were raised without accounts kept or reports given. When challenged, the LCBOC sought to assert itself as the CELC, with power to disburse monies, to ordain pastors, to open or close congregations, and to refuse to issue visas.

Eventually, a long, tortuous legal battle was engaged in by the leadership of the CELC, with support and involvement also by the LCMS, designated as "donor" of the contested properties. Final court judgment affirmed the position of the CELC and LCMS World Mission, and several of the LCBOC members were convicted of fraud. In the end, a number of church properties were lost over debts arising from illegal building contracts. A few legal cases are still pending in 2014. This has resulted in the loss not just of property but of congregations, pastors, members, confidence, energy, momentum, and reputation.

What was once a church body of nearly 3000 members, numbers between five- and six-hundred at the time of this writing. Stark as this is, clarity of legal issues has finally been granted, which in turn makes possible trustworthy management of current resources. This allows the CELC, much sobered, bruised, and diminished, to focus again on the mission and ministry of the gospel in Taiwan.

Unmentioned to this point is the evolving political relationship between Taiwan and the People's Republic of China. Beginning about 1986, when former mainlanders who fled to Taiwan were allowed to return to their

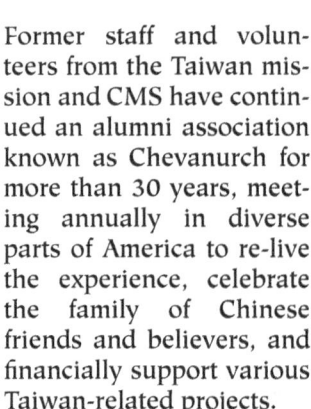

Former staff and volunteers from the Taiwan mission and CMS have continued an alumni association known as Chevanurch for more than 30 years, meeting annually in diverse parts of America to re-live the experience, celebrate the family of Chinese friends and believers, and financially support various Taiwan-related projects.

home provinces, a new dawn of relationship has emerged. Joint business ventures have multiplied. Travel from Taiwan has become commonplace, and direct flights between Taiwan and China are scheduled. Delegations, tour groups, and individuals have bridged divisions on every level. LCMS and CELC connections now exist with Christians in the mainland. Through networks, respectful contacts, and family links once impossible for westerners to understand, the Chinese Christian world is connected and alive. Actually, it thrives.

Not all of the story of the CELC is positive, nor are all of the issues settled. The loss of the Taiwan Lutheran Hour ministry is unfortunate, as well as the loss of the Social Service Center in Taipei and of the church planting experiments. More tragic is the loss of congregations and their ministries.

On the other hand, some ministries have borne enormous fruit for the ministry of the gospel. From the loss of Concordia Seminary in Taiwan and the inability of the Federated Lutheran Seminary to sustain itself came the formation of China Lutheran Seminary, with a growing Chinese faculty, state-of-the-art facilities, an extensive offsite lay training program, its residential program, and the only Chinese-language graduate program in Luther studies worldwide. Concordia Middle School, from its modest beginnings, has been blessed with leaders of vision and competence, and has become both one of the finest middle schools in Taiwan and a clearly Christian school with both internal and external mission commitment. Christian Salvation Service provides care for some of the most vulnerable of all human beings, infants at risk, and serves as advocate for the sanctity of life in Taiwan.

These details may form the hiatus of the story for now, but not the end of the Lord's continuing outreach for his children. The church is standing at a point of a new, challenging, but hopefully less-contested future. Perhaps a future writer of CELC history will select precisely this point as the beginning of a fourth and much more productive era, when legal issues are solved, Mandarin-Taiwanese problems have subsided, and the next generation of well-trained clergy are in place.

Of course, every time and every place, every era and every situation will have its challenges. One observation, however, both a comfort and an encouragement, is that the Lord is not without resources, even when the church is tired, or distracted, or feeling betrayed or bereft of material or human resources. The Lord's resources are much more powerful, and since they are the Lord's, they do not stop when human resources give out. Those resources shared richly and undeservedly, are the Spirit, the gospel, word and sacraments, and the fellowship of the Lord's faithful.

Thus, the work in Taiwan started, thus it progressed, thus it overcame, thus it survived, and thus it continues.

To God be the glory!

Significant sources:

Interviews with Edward Bertram, Ted Englebrecht, Carl Hanson, John Mehl, Stephen Oliver, Michael Paul, and Hank Rowld

Chapter 19 — Looking Back - Looking Forward

Arrived

1981	Halter	Carol
1983	Rimbach	Jim
1984	Rowold	Hank & Phyllis
1991	Molitoris	Craig & Joyce
	Birner	Dave & Lois
1997	Rimbach	Jim
1998	Rittmann	David & Doris
	Weber	Michael & Louise
	Krenzke	Tim & Betty
	Luedtke	Todd
1999	Strohschein	Ed & Shauna
2002	Schmidt,	Al & Sandi CISS
2004	Scheiwe	Joel & Iantha
2005	Hanson,	Carl & Chenhsi
2006	Mehl	John & Susan
2007	Lange	Josh
	Kerschen	Jim & Joani
2010	Wiesenauer	Stephen & Krista
	Cagnin	Michelle
	Kincaid	Megan
2011	Winkelman	Steve
2012	Brockberg	Kevin & Susan

Departed
Information unavailable

The skyline of modern Shanghai could never have been visualized by missionary Elmer Zimmermann when he prepared his inforative booklet about the mainland Mission in the late 1930s

Give generously, for your gift will return later. If you wait for perfect conditions, you will never get anything done! Keep on sowing your seed, for you never know which will grow, perhaps it all will.

Ecclesiastes 11:1, 4, 6 (New Living Bible)

Chapter 19

Looking Back - Looking Forward

The Christian enterprise is dynamic: unscripted, blessed, consistent, hopeful.... add your favorite adjective here

Situations on the Chinese mainland, in the Special Administrative Regions (SAR), across the Straits, and throughout the greater diaspora of the Overseas (nanyang) Chinese, have diversified and grown exponentially since the late 1970s. Opportunities and innovations proliferate in the evolving modernization of East Asia. Over the course of the last 40 years, the enthusiasm has become two-sided.

Historic attempts to harmonize, coordinate or complement the one-sided western desire to bridge gaps with China have been legion. Marco Polo, Matteo Ricci, Robert Morrison, Karl Guetzlaff and Edward Arndt each felt that "now is the time." Abraham Lincoln's visionary Secretary of State William Seward predicted that the two great civilizations were destined to meet on the coasts and islands of the Pacific Ocean. The American Minister to Peking in 1913, Paul S. Reinsch wrote "all previous interactions with China were but the slightest of frontier skirmishes in the drama of China's rise from seclusion."

Perhaps the best way to conclude Lutherans on the Yangtze is to celebrate that there is no epilogue, but that under the richest blessings of Almighty God, the Lutheran Christian enterprise continues:

Go therefore and make disciples of all nations baptizing them in the name of the Father and of the Son and of the Holy Spirit, teaching them to observe all that I have commanded you. And behold, I am with you always, until the end of the age.

Matthew 28:19-20

Religion in China after the 1949 Revolution

Bleak, dismal, and frustrating seemed the prospects for Christianity in Communist China when Elmer and Frieda Thode were finally allowed to leave in May 1952. Based on a report as he saw the China mission in 1950, the Lutheran Witness declared as "dire" the Chinese government declarations of policy regarding the existence of religions. Freedom to practice any religion was theoretically guaranteed by the PRC (People's Republic of China) constitution, yet restricted by the 1952 policies of the Communist regime.

Chapter 19 — Looking Back - Looking Forward

Li Yen San, who worked with the Mainland mission in the 1940's, left his family in China to attend a year of classes at Concordia seminary in St Louis with the intention of serving as translator and evangelist. He was a good friend with the Ziegler family (pictured with Everett and Howard). Because of his earlier connections with the nationalist government, he was reportedly killed in the early 1950s.

Major Lutheran Women's Missionary League grants in the China Field

Date	Program
7/15/10	Church Led Community Health Education Program (China)
7/15/07	Prevention Education in Xi'an Elementary Schools - China
7/15/05	Healthcare Worker Training in China for Management of Children with Cerebral Palsy (China)
7/15/02	Village Doctor Training and Community Sanitation Project in China (China)
7/1/00	Physical Rehabilitation Training Course in Qingdao, China (China)
1/15/00	Community Center of Shanghai (China)
5/1/99	Physical Rehabilitation Training Course in Guanganmeng, Inner Mongolia (Mongolia, China)
5/1/98	Physical Rehabilitation Training Course in Kunming, China (China)
5/1/97	Bracing Training Course at Second People's Hospital, Qingdao China (China)
3/15/95	CHINA REHABILITATION PROJECT 1995-1997 (China)
9/15/93	REHABILITATION TRAINING SEMINARS (China)
12/11/89	Young Teen Rehabilitation Program (China)
11/10/83	Social Service Project (China)
1/1/68	Lutheran Education Conference - Hong Kong (China)

Most of the displaced missionaries felt that events in China were simply just another interruption of the work, similar to that in 1926 or 1937, and that return to evangelistic activity in China was a matter of time once the two-party struggle would blow over. Several were becoming first-time parents, became immersed in their new Japan, Philippine, or Taiwan mission fields, and only after a few years came to the full conclusion that the LCMS endeavor in China was terminated

As the government of China sought to modernize and develop a socialist country, several five-year programs were implemented, each with a patriotic title and its own thematic focus on changing individual and national behaviors. Most plans resulted in social upheaval and traumatic geographic changes for millions of people in every walk of life, and especially former peasants—farmers or indentured agricultural families. Intellectuals, artists, and "capitalist roaders" (those who accepted western ways) were equally subject to "re-education." In theory, all citizens were to experience a rise from poverty to a higher quality in living conditions and social status. Large posters proclaimed the merits of the people's revolution. In practice, party members maintained a privelage status, and some of the "people" were more equal than others. Everyone wore blue jackets, some of cotton, some of silk. Millions were relocated and re-educated. Uncounted millions starved.

Nationwide programs were designed and implemented in attempts to modernize China, socialize the population, and eventually raise the People's Republic to a level of international status under Mao Zedong. Planners wanted to adapt the highly centralized and heavy-industrial Stalinist model to post-revolution China. Several long-range plans were implemented, with questionable results:

1952 - 1957 - The First Five-year Plan
1956 - 1957 - One Hundred Flowers Blooming Everywhere
1958 - 1961 - The Great Leap Forward (and the Great Hunger)
1958 - 1962 - The Second Five Year Plan
1966 - 1976 - The (Great Proletariat) Cultural Revolution

As concerned faith and spirituality, five religions were recognized and overseen by the Religious Affairs Bureau - Buddhism, Taoism, Islam, Roman Catholicism, and Protestantism. Each could exist under some form of "three-self" structure, the concept originally promoted by early mission leaders, and endorsed in a slightly different context by Sun Yat Sen. Each recognized religion was to be self-propagating (no proselytization outside the group), self-financing (no external sources of income or support), and self-governing (no control, influence, or management from outside the country).

Li Yen-san, a promising committed Lutheran from Hupeh, enrolled for a year at the St. Louis seminary. He had worked with the mission in the early 1940s, especially with Paul Martens in Enshih. After the Japanese war, he traveled to America for further education, financed both by Chiang Kai-shek personally and by the mission. His role was to include literature work and teaching, and he was also to be the first business manager for the mission. Mr. Li returned to his homeland in 1948, sailing with new missionaries Richard and Lois Meyer, nurses Heidi Muelller and Norma Lenschow, and teacher Lorraine Behling for active service to the church. News reached the LCMS in 1950 that because of prior connections with Americans and the disgraced Nationalists, he was killed shortly after arrival. Many hopes for advancing a Chinese church were dashed by his death.

Any chance of LCMS support - manpower, financial, or philosophic - was eliminated. News articles and reports of 1953 noted that many Christians, unable to escape persecution because of their links with westerners, were imprisoned in the People's Republic (PRC). Some of these believers were martyred. The number of congregations was reduced from about 20,000 to less than 100.

Chapter 19   Looking Back - Looking Forward

Two student groups from Hong Kong International School were among the earliest to enter China in 1979 and 1980. They experienced a China in transition, dynamic and enthusiastic to be entering the community of nations.

Leading the student groups was HKIS art teacher Dave Kohl (holding camera).

Organized religion was overseen by the Three-Self Patriotic Movement (TSPM). Re-introduced in 1951 by a Chinese Christian, the TSPM became official government practice in 1954. The TSPM would eliminate foreign influences and insure that religions were unflinchingly loyal to the PRC. Concerned primarily about any "disharmonious" thinking, the government could effectively examine and control organized religious activity. Government interest in Christianity was not doctrinal.

Although the other four recognized religions (Daoism, Buddhism, Islam, and Catholic Christian) operate with a form of "three-self" policy, only the Protestant Christians include the "Three Self" term in their official name.

Occasional mention of isolated Christian activity filtered across the Hong Kong border, including news of the death of Li Yen-san about 1950. Select foreign "guests" were shown limited and officially approved aspects of Communist society; with its militarism, and communal lifestyle for both agricultural and industrial workers. Certain communes were selected as model brigades for the country to emulate successful models of excellence were publicized - "In agriculture, learn from Dazhai (a model commune).". Individual folk and military heroes became the focus of popular socialist songs, stories, and posters. Heroic comrades, like peasant-soldier Lei Feng, were honored in art and literature.

In the 1960s, several LCMS missionaries in Hong Kong became aware of conditions across the border from their amahs (domestic servants) returning from holiday visits to Guangdong province. These women would load up with food, consumer goods, and electronics to take as gifts for annual Lunar New Year visits. They often returned with great sadness and a reluctance to share any information about their family, communities, or general living conditions. Related exodus movements in 1952, 1957, 1962, and 1966 have been previously mentioned in the Hong Kong chapters.

During the Cultural Revolution of 1966-1976, any expression of religious activity (Christian and non-Christian alike) in China was effectively banned; even that of the TSPM, which was also shuttered. Implemented by Red Guard youth with a goal of eliminating historic and foreign influences, most religious buildings of all faiths, even historic cultural Chinese relics, were damaged or destroyed. As a result, Christians met in secret for fear of persecution – an underground church.

Surprising developments of the 1970s

Kinks in the Bamboo Curtain were few until the efforts of U.S. statesman Henry Kissinger and PRC Premier Zhou Enlai brought about the 1971 breakthrough of "Ping Pong Diplomacy." Soon thereafter came the historic visit of U.S. President Richard Nixon in 1972, and the loan of pandas to select American zoos. The deaths of Zhou Enlai and Mao Zedong in 1976 portended changes in Communist Party policies regarding international contact. While Canadians had been able to visit the mainland for many years on cultural exchanges, only in 1979 were average U.S. citizens officially allowed to visit the country, and to tour select communal factories, farms, and historic landmarks. The itineraries were determined and limited by the government's China Travel Service (CTS).

The first recorded Missouri Synod visitors to the new China were three staff from Hong Kong International School, two in 1969 (Les Zimmermann and Edith Burvett) and this author in 1977, during the chairmanship of Hua Kuofeng. They observed little visible evidence from the Christian era, reduced to a few former church buildings converted into factories or shops, and those that were spotted had no known LCMS links. A tradition of week-long tourist visits to China by students from HKIS began in 1979, as part of

Chapter 19 — Looking Back - Looking Forward

Statement of Faith - Three Self Patriotic Movement adopted January 2008

The Chinese Church takes the contents of the entire Bible, the Apostles' Creed and the Nicene Creed as the foundation of our faith, the main points of which are as follows:

Ours is a **Triune God**, everlasting and eternal.

God is Spirit. God is loving, just, holy, and trustworthy. God is almighty **Father**, the Lord who creates and sustains the cosmos and all that is in it, who keeps and cares for the whole world.

Jesus Christ is the only **Son** of God, born of the Holy Spirit, the Word made flesh, wholly God and wholly human. He came into the world to save humankind, to witness to God the Father, to preach the gospel; he was crucified, died, and was buried. He rose again and ascended into heaven. He will come again to judge the world.

The **Holy Spirit** is the Comforter, who enables people to know their sinfulness and to repent, who bestows wisdom and ability and every grace, leading us to know God and to enter into the truth, enabling people to live holy lives, and to give beautiful witness to Christ.

The **church** is the body of Christ and Christ is its Head. The church is apostolic, one, holy, and catholic. The visible church is called by God to be a fellowship of those who believe in Jesus Christ. It was established by the apostles as Jesus instructed them. The mission of the church is to preach the gospel, to administer the Sacraments, to teach and nurture believers, to do good works, and to bear witness to the Lord. The church is both universal and particular. The Chinese Church must build itself up in love and be one in Christ.

The **Bible** has been revealed by God and written down by human beings through the inspiration of the Holy Spirit. The Bible is the highest authority in matters of faith and the standard of life for believers. Through the leading of the Holy Spirit, people in different times have gained new light in the Bible. The Bible should be interpreted in accordance with the principle of rightly explaining the word of truth. It should not be interpreted arbitrarily or out of context.

Human beings are made in the image of God, but cannot become gods. God has given humanity dominion over all God's creation. Because of sin, human beings have diminished God's glory, yet through faith and the grace of Jesus Christ, human beings are redeemed and saved, and are granted resurrection and everlasting life.

Christ will come again. According to the teachings of the Bible, no one knows the day of his coming, and any method to determine when Christ will come again violates the teachings of the Bible.

A Christian's faith and works are one. Christians must live out Christ in the world, glorifying God and benefiting people.

the school's interim program. "Tourist money," spendable only in Friendship Stores, was the sole currency available to foreigners.

Chairman Deng Xiaoping assumed party leadership in 1978, two years after the deaths of Premier Zhou and Chairman Mao. In a deviation from 30-year policies and practices, smatterings of free enterprise were gradually permitted. The commune system began a decline at both factory and farm. Individuals were permitted to earn their own *renminbi* (national currency). Fearfully at first, religious Chinese began to surface after years of secretive activity. Their existence had been unknown to the west, and their numbers apparently surprised many officials. A glimmer of hope for contact with mainland Christians excited watchers in Hong Kong and in America.

Under Deng's reforms and "normalization," numerous Chinese citizens began redirecting their search for spirituality, stability, and fulfillment. Individuals could cautiously question religious practices previously reinforced by ritual, worship of the Emperor, or adulation of Communist leaders. In many rural areas where there had been no historic missionary activity, active and enthusiastic "underground" Christians became visible. Clusters of urban "inquirers" quietly started meetings in homes. Rare copies of the New Testament or of Gospel portions, some hand-copied, were treasured. Denominational linkage with foreign churches was still impossible. Christians identified themselves as *Jidutu*. Unregistered Christians held steadfast in the political turmoil, even promoting revivals after 1978. In some cases, these house churches grew in number and confidence to request recognition as independent churches, a status rarely permitted by the RAB or TSPM.

To counter the growing trend of unregistered meetings, in 1979 the government officially restored the TSPM thirteen years after its disappearance. The China Christian Council (CCC) formed in 1980. Together, the two entities are known as the *lianghui* (two organizations) which form the structure of the registered Protestant church. The CCC serves an ecclesiastical role, focusing on the internal management and affairs of the church. The TSPM role is to liaison with the government, through appointed local provincial representatives of the Religious Affairs Bureau (RAB).

Deng's solution in 1984 to China's eventual re-unification of Hong Kong (1997) and Macau (1999) was the principle of "one country- two systems." Extrapolating any solution that "saves face" for all parties gave hope to creative thinking by Christian leaders. One significant development was the payment by the Hong Kong government for the LCMS mission facilities at Rennie's Mill. After the handover, the government proposed operating a new school in that area (now known as Tui Keng Leng). The government would provide the land and building for a school and the Hong Kong Synod would provide the furnishings and teachers. The offer gave a signal that the authorities would not separate schools from their supporting churches. This unexpected request from the SAR authorities to a religious organization such as the LCHKS portended a continuing harmonious arrangement with the department of education.

Christian evangelism has always been based on individual witness and testimony, and so it remains in post-Mao China. The approach is "relational ministry," personally building trust and understanding through connecting with people in different contexts. These programs promoted by the LCMS of caring for others, education and helping to build up local people to meet their own needs are identical to the historic evangelism themes from Scripture.

Man's plans are not God's plans

An electrifying letter dated September 24, 1980 reached former China missionary Eugene Seltz, living in Minnesota. LCMS Chi-

Chapter 19 Looking Back - Looking Forward

Mr. Zhong was baptized by LCMS missionary Wilbert Werling following the Han River floods of 1935. Rev Luther Li, serving in Chongqing since 1946, with visiting LCMS pastor Bill Harmon; another veteran pastor was found in Qingdao in 1995.

In Three-Self Patriotic Movement churches across the border, congregations of non-denominational Protestant Christians have been able to worship openly in sanctuaries old and new. Churches pictured are at ShenZhen, Zhongshan, Shasi, and Makou.

nese pastor Tai Kuang-ming (a 1937 graduate from the Hankow Seminary) had just returned from his first visit to China in 30 years. He reported visits with remnant LCMS Christians in Fengjie, Wanhsien, and Hankow. Reverend Tai was the second son of the tenacious teacher Tai Chin-tang in Kweifu [Fengjie]. Tai Ch'iu-tao, his older brother, had remained pastor in Kweifu during the Japanese occupation of the 1930s and endured persecution during the more recent Cultural Revolution. Kweifu, the station not served by a full time LCMS missionary since 1927, had been harboring an active Christian community faithfully surviving oppression and militarism.

In Wanxian, where he was vicar in the late 1930s, the younger Tai learned that his seminary classmate Chang Tung-chin was still pastor. Chang had endured "re-education" during the Cultural Revolution, pushing handcarts. His resilience in the face of persecution is a strong witness to the power of God in one person's life.

Pastor Tai was also able to report meeting with several high-ranking officials, professors, and grass-roots Christians. Through conversation and observation, he found that the way of life in China was changing incrementally. Temples and churches were being reopened. Politics, education, the economy, and religion were more openly discussed. He surmised that freedom of religion could be eventually restored.

An alignment of forces was stabilizing that would enable LCMS involvement in the reviving Chinese Church. Communist party leader Deng Xiaoping was setting a different paradigm, replacing Marxist dogma with new economic liberalization; arranging an orderly government of technocrats with fixed terms of office; and modifying revolutionary foreign policy in favor of tacit cooperation with trade partners including the U.S. The PRC was admitted into the United Nations and recognized as the governing expression of China.

A delegation of 13 synodical leaders was invited to visit China in 1985. Included were LCHKS President Titus Lee Wa-tao, LCMS President Ralph Bohlmann, as well as Dr. Louis Nau and Dr. Ed Westcott from the Board for Mission Services, Mr. Robert Zimmer, president of the Wheatridge Foundation (and founding Headmaster of CMS), Professor Cliff and Bette Horn from Concordia College in Portland, and Dr. Henry Rowold, former Taiwan missionary. President Bohlmann spoke to 150 faculty and students at the Nanjing Union Theological Seminary. In return, the U.S. delegates also heard personal testimonies from Christians who had endured under the Cultural Revolution.

During those eleven days, sessions with RAB officials and church leaders explored possibilities for sharing Jesus Christ in the People's Republic of China. While direct financial aid or the placement of missionaries was not appropriate, programs were explored to include the provision of theological library materials, seminary faculty exchanges, and educational assistance.

Within a year, Rowold, a Mandarin speaker, spent another two weeks in China investigating the situation of the churches in WuXi, Nanjing, Wuhan, and beyond. In Wanxian, where the LCMS once had congregations and schools, he made contact with Rev. Li Muqun, a 1941 Hankow Seminary graduate. Rev Li was still serving a very large congregation. Worship services of nearly a thousand Christians took place in a church designed to seat 400. The link through Pastor Li back to the China mission prior to Japanese occupation was inspirational. Li lived to see construction of a new prominently located sanctuary in 2002.

On succeeding visits in the late 1990s, Rowold visited several former mission locations. Contact was re-established with three men who had served the China mission as pastors or evangelists, and widows of two others:

Chapter 19 Looking Back - Looking Forward

Three-self congregations in Yichang, Chongqing, Shasi, and Wanxian trace their roots partially to LCMS missions in those cities.

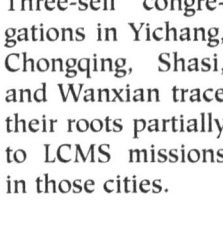

Churches pictured are Wanxian, Chongqing and Makou.

Wuhan - Rev. Wei Xiangbo John Wei; Concordia Seminary
Wanxian - Rev. Zhang Dongjin (Chang Tung chin)
Chongqing - Rev. Li Muqun; Savior church
Shashi - Wang Mei Yu, widow of Rev. Liu Lan'gen;
Fengjie - Tai Ch'iu-tao, son of teacher Tai

Rowold found that these leaders had remained faithful, serving believers since 1949. This visit, after 50 years of isolation, energized the long-term survivors and their believing families and friends. At Yichang, near the Three Gorges Dam project, he also found Luther School, Grace Church, St. Paul Church, and St James. Church from the days of missionary Thode.

Relationships also developed with several of the seminaries of the registered church. LCMS seminary professors Jim Rimbach and Henry Rowold had opportunities to serve as guest lecturers at three of these. Other LCMS educators have taught on staff at other universities in southern China. Several descendants of LCMS missionaries have visited and taught in Engish language programs in diverse parts of China.

During the ensuing 20 years, Rowold returned many times as a guest professor at seminaries, networking with Chinese Christians and pastoral candidates. He founded the LCMS China Ministry Center in Hong Kong, which in turn was developed and extended by Rev. Craig Molitoris.

Other connections with mainland Christians by LCMS people in the 1990s were individual and episodic. Several adults, children born during the China mission era, were able to visit their birthplaces if the tourist itinerary included Wuhan or Yichang, gateway to the Three-Gorges Hydro-electric Dam Project. The Concordia Seminary compound in Hankow still stands, presently housing the Wuhan City *Yu T'sai* ("to foster talent") Kindergarten for over 800 students. Visited by this author in 2013, the seven-acre compound was immune from the effects of the Cultural Revolution. Its pedimented-classroom building and the five sturdy brick faculty residences are now surrounded by high-rise residential constructions. The location, once swampland, is near the heart of modern Hankow [Hankou].

Siblings of the Klein, Riedel, and Ziegler families rediscovered childhood friends and former neighbors during visits. In 2005, the Zimmermann children reunited with John Pan, age 95, who was their father's first baptismal candidate in 1929. At Shashi, Mr. Pan, together with Evangelist Wang Meiyu, had faithfully kept together the band of Lutheran Christians from Zimmermann's two congregations. In 2007, this author was introduced to Mr. Liu Tien-shang, a 1936 student at the Hankou Concordia Seminary, whose later years were spent at Eternal Life Lutheran Church in Taipei, Taiwan. In an all-too-familiar scenario, Liu had fled China, expecting his fiancée to soon follow. She never reached Taiwan.

An almost imperceptible but growing spiritual exodus from government orthodoxy followed the democracy movement and activities of 1989. In a post-denominational age, there are no longer Lutheran, Baptist, or Methodist distinctions. Christianity has ceased being perceived as a foreigner's religion. Jesus Christ and the Christian church are now led by local Christians.

In 2010 it was estimated that 20 - 30% of Christians on the mainland associated with the registered church and about 70-80% functioned within home churches. An average of estimates suggest there were about 80 million adherents in these unregistered churches, not including "underground" churches.

Leaders of the LCMS in Hong Kong and the Lutheran Church Hong Kong Synod quietly sought for many years any possible

Chapter 19　　　　　　　　　　　　　　　　　　　　Looking Back - Looking Forward

Henry Go Wu was an essential link in work with Amity Foundation, printers of Bibles in Nanjing.

"Good News from Jesus" booklets were written originally by former HK missionary Len Galster, and have now been translated into 24 Asian languages, with over 100,000 distributed. They are available electronically from a website;

www.jesusevangilism.com

contact across the border which might offer promise of witness, service, or reconnection. Verification of the home church phenomenon encouraged Lutherans in America and Hong Kong to seek individual opportunities to re-connect and support the emerging Christian communities in the PRC.

Cooperative programs with the PRC State Administration for Religious Affairs and the registered church are based on a delicate and mutually respectful relationship. LCMS representatives in Hong Kong and St. Louis have continued exploring avenues of mutual cooperation. Concordia Unversities in Portland and Irvine continue to seek working relationships in education, service, business, and the arts.

The Chinese government is proud of its ascent among world nations. No longer consigned to third-world status, China is in a position to advocate its own best interests. As such, China joined the World Trade Organization in 2000. Altering the communal model, diversification and modernizing of manufacturing, and open exchanges of business leaders and students have meant rapid progress in all sectors, even if not evenly spread through all provinces and minority areas. China has assumed equality of status in the international community.

Literature

In traditional Chinese society the written page has always been esteemed. Opportunities for Christians to read Scripture for oneself are prized, and if an individual owns a Bible, it is usually carried to worship and heavy with marginal notes. During the Communist era, Bibles or Bible portions were carried across borders and entry points, casually and openly in small numbers, but surreptitiously in larger numbers. In the 1950s, Bible portions and tracts were even attached to weather balloons, airlifted over Fujian province from Taiwan. (See chapter 17)

Among several worldwide enterprises to generate Christian literature for the Chinese, is a Minnesota-based group founded by former Lutheran missionaries. These volunteers and old "China hands" have worked to produce and distribute a Chinese version of the Bethel Bible Series and other Christian materials. Former missionaries of the LCMS and other Synods have initiated many personal exchange and education programs on both sides of the Pacific.

Former LCMS Hong Kong missionary Len Galster composed a 40-page booklet, arranging Bible verses into a chronological explanation of God's plan for salvation through Jesus. Financing the project has been very grass roots, with donations from individuals and groups. The most recent translation of this booklet–in simplified Chinese characters - was translated with the help of the LCHKS and financed primarily by one congregation, Living Savior, in Tualatin, Oregon.

Translations of major Lutheran writings into Chinese have been produced by China Lutheran Seminary in Taiwan, the LCHKS' Literature Department, and Concordia Seminary in St Louis in connection with Lutheran Hour Ministries. These include contemporary translations of the Lutheran Confessions and several volumes of Luther's Works.

Lutheran Hour Ministries

With increased opportunities for witness in the mainland, Lutheran Hour Ministries explores, develops, and supports several enterprises. The constitution of the PRC has made it possible for congregations to legally proclaim the gospel, worship formally, train church workers, and produce and distribute Christian materials within the churches. Two specific needs being met through LHM work are the supply of reliable print and electronic resources as well as the training of lay evangelists.

Chapter 19 Looking Back - Looking Forward

Deaconess Carol Halter and Martha Boss

Hong Kong Lutheran Social Service

Nursery Division
  Community Centre Division,

Martha Boss Lutheran Day Nursery	Homantin, Kl...
Heng Fa Chuen Lutheran Day Nursery	Chai Wan, H.K.
Chan En Mei Lutheran Day Nursery	Cheung Chau, H.K
Lui Kwan Pok Lutheran Day Nursery	Cheung Chau, H.K.
Lei Tung Lutheran Day Nursery	Apleichau, H.K.
Leung King Lutheran Day Nursery	Tuen Mun, N.T.
King Lam Lutheran Day Nursery	Tseung Kwan O, N.T.
Cheung Ching Lutheran Day Nursery	Tsing Yi, N.T.
Maritime Square Lutheran Day Nursery	Tsing Yi, NT.
Fu Tai Lutheran Day Nursery	Tuen Mun, NT.
Sun Chui Lutheran Children Centre	Shatin, N.T.
Lutheran Family Life Education Unit	Shatin, N.T.
Lutheran Parents Hotline	Tsuen Wan, N.T
Touch The Bug Hotline	Tsuen Wan, N.T

Foster Care Service Division

Lutheran Foster Care Unit	Homantin, Kln.

Elderly Centre Division

Cheer Lutheran Centre	Sheung Shui, N.T.
Evergreen Lutheran Centre	Kwun Tong, Kln.
Sunshine Lutheran Centre	Tai Po, N.T.
Rainbow Lutheran Centre	Sai Kung, N.T.

School Social Work Division Counseling Service Centre

School Social Work Division & Elderly Centre Division
  Children and Family Service Division,
  Integrated Children & Youth Service Centre Division,
  Community Development Division
    Jockey Club Wah Ming Lutheran Integrated Service Centre
    Jockey Club Fu Shin Lutheran Integrated Service Centre
    Jockey Club Yung Shing Lutheran Integrated Service Centre
    Jockey Club Riviera Gardens Lutheran Integrated Service Centre

Lutheran School Social Work Unit	Homantin, Kln.
	ShamShuiPo, Kln.

Martha Boss Lutheran Community Centre	Homantin, Kln.

  Group & Community Work Unit
  Integrated Employment Assistance and School Based Service

Shek Wu Lutheran Community Development Project	Fanling, N.T.
Shek Kip Mei Lutheran Centre for the Blind	ShekKipMei Kln.
Cheung Ching Lutheran Centre for the Disabled	Tsing Yi, N.T.
Martha Boss Lutheran Day Activity Centre	Homantin, Kln.
Lei Tung Lutheran Day Activity Centre	Apleichau, H.K.
Lei Tung Lutheran Hostel	Apleichau, H.K.
Lung On Lutheran Day Activity Centre	Wong Tai Sin Kln
Homantin Lutheran Hostel	Homantin, Kln.
Homantin Lutheran Yung Lok Centre	Homantin, Kln.
Lutheran Supported Employment & Training Scheme	Tsing Yi, N.T.
On Lutheran Centre for the Elderly	Tuen Mun, N.T.
Sun Chui Lutheran Centre for the Elderly	Shatin, N.T.
Peninsula Lions Club Jubilee Lutheran Centre for Elderly	Homantin, Kln.
Ma Tau Wai Lutheran Centre for the Elderly	Ma Tau Wa, Kln.
Sai Cho Wan Lutheran Centre for the Elderly	Kwun Tong, Kln.
Harmony Garden Lutheran Centre for the Elderly	Chai Wan, H.K.
Rhythm Garden Lutheran Centre for the Elderly	Choi Hung, Kln.
Martha Boss Lutheran Day Care Centre for the Elderly	Homantin, Kln.
Mrs Leung Kwai Yee Lutheran Home for the Elderly	Tsing Yi, N.T.
Fung Tak Lutheran Home for the Elderly	Diamond Hill Kln.
Mr & Mrs Lawrence Wong Lutheran Home for Elderly	Chai Wan, H.K.
Mr & Mrs Lawrence Wong 2nd Lutheran Home for Elderly	Tseung Kwan O
Jockey Club Lutheran Home for the Elderly	Homantin, Kln.
Mr & Mrs Lawrence Wong Lutheran Rehabilitation Centre	Homantin, Kln.
Martha Boss Day Care Centre & Elderly Home Division	Homantin, Kln.
Lutheran Educational Complex	Tsuen Wan, N.T
Lutheran Family Counselling Centre	Tsuen Wan, N.T

Nearly 1.5 million audio cassettes and compact discs have been produced and distributed. Recordings include Christian sermons, a teaching series based on the Apostles Creed, the Psalms and selected Bible stories, Christian hymns, and other Christian instrumental and choral music. Funding has provided for tape players for rural congregations.

LHM cooperates in the support of Amity Foundation, a faith-initiated entity based in Nanjing, which prints Bibles and other Christian materials. It is one of the first non-governmental organizations in China, begun when an association of international Christian organizations formed Amity Printing Press in the 1980s. Dr. Oswald Hoffman, long-time speaker of *The Lutheran Hour*, participated in its establishment, especially as chair of United Bible Societies. With the approval of the RAB, Amity has published some 70 million Bibles in simplified characters. Editions include the Chinese Union Version of 1919, the most common version used by the Protestant church, and the Pastoral Bible used by Catholic churches. A million Bibles now come off the press monthly, distributed through a network of officially registered churches. Amity also supports programs for social and medical work, disaster relief, education and environmental protection. In addition to work with the Amity Foundation, LHM has also supported the Aiji Press, a supplemental printing operation of the Christian church in the Shanghai region.

In cooperation with Yilin Press, a secular mainland publishing company, LHM and the China Christian Council have published books in simplified Mandarin since 1993. One major tome is the Book of Concord, based on the translation by pioneer LCMS missionary Erhardt Riedel in 1971. Other books include *The Theology of Martin Luther* by Paul Althaus, *Here I Stand* by Roland Bainton, and *The Two Natures in Christ* by Martin Chemnitz.

Besides involvement with publications and media, LHM also offers training workshops that provide instruction for lay volunteers wanting to share and proclaim the good news. MP3 players augment "Equipping the Saints" (ETS) workshops, in which the laity are trained to share the gospel on a grassroots level. Benefiting from the ETS program, one congregation in Hebei Province celebrated the baptism of 261 new believers at one single event in 2012.

Human Care and Welfare ministries

With a goal of improving the lives of impoverished rural communities in Asia through education and service, a number of Non-Governmental Organizations (NGOs) have been founded by a number of Christian organizations including Lutherans. Partnering with local communities and governments, these NGOs help to identify the sources of poverty that can be addressed by volunteers. The types of projects in the region include programs in English language and infrastructural improvements such as clean water systems and hygiene projects.

Many of these organizations send volunteers for week-long projects in several urban and rural settings. Long- and short-term overseas volunteers and secondary students are sent as work parties across the region. Working with the people they are serving, volunteers improve the lives of those living in poverty through training and education. They help people discover ways to help themselves. In the process, they also witness to their Christian commitment. Relationships build trust and trust enables credibility.

MOST (Mission Opportunities Short Term) is yet another U.S.-based group which sends service teams worldwide. Teams of volunteers focus on medical needs with health clinics, sight testing and glasses-fitting within impoverished communities.

Chapter 19 — Looking Back - Looking Forward

Artwork done to publicize LCMS mission endeavors in Asia appeared in the 1960s.

In the next 30 years, various programs emerged whereby self-financed non-professionals, young or older, could volunteer to teach English. ELIC (English Language Institute for China) has coordinated over 1000 volunteers in 25 years. Young LCMS volunteers also came to SW China in 2012 to work with health and sanitation projects.

Interdisciplinary thinking

Several concepts practiced in contemporary business with China may be useful as the church looks to its future enterprise.

- Invite Chinese leaders to visit workers and leaders in America;
- Promote growth in relationships - personal, professional, and philosophic;
- Provide materials for positive media coverage;
- Utilize existing links with individuals working abroad, written or electronic;
- Seek situations to interface with individuals with similar interests;
- Explore mass communication technologies, social media, web sites, etc.;
- Facilitate student and professional exchanges at institutional levels;
- Exhibit mutual respect; learn more about national and local cultures;
- Welcome and enable settlement and adjustment of newly arrived workers;
- Model good citizenship, community care, harmony with authority, etc.

Scholars and China-watchers have proclaimed that the 2000s may be the "Chinese Century," as the PRC continues its unprecedented modernization and growing political and financial importance in the world community. Religious, educational, and service groups around the world seek avenues for interaction with the Chinese people at home and abroad.

Many have identified a major need for English-speaking educators in PRC high schools and universities. Several co-operative U.S.-based non-profit organizations are involved in helping people to connect with this work. English Language in China (ELIC) volunteers finance their own travel expenses to China, and teach spoken American English for terms from two weeks to two years.

Institutional Programs

Beginning in 2005, the LCMS restructured how it supports and sends people into all overseas mission service. Career missionaries are identified as Network-Supported Missionaries (NSM). This means that their financial support from the Synod is provided 100% through designated gifts for each individual missionary. In addition to the NSM program, short-term "Globally Engaged in Outreach" or GEO missionaries are sent to the field for as much as two years of service. These individuals are not salaried, and like the NSMs are responsible for raising their own support, which may be composed of donations from congregations, auxiliaries, family, and private sources.

Mission Central is the enterprise begun by one LCMS layman in Iowa. Gary Thies established a residential retreat center for missionaries and mission support, using his house, barn, and other buildings, near Mapleton. The center is a conference and planning center where missionaries on furlough network with each other, coordinate with LCMS officials to evaluate and plan programs, and worship with up to 300 people at statewide mission events there. Mission Central is the largest mission-supporting agency working with the LCMS to support missionaries in the field. Tens of thousands of visitors from hundreds of congregations have utilized the facility since 2003, and hundreds of mission workers have benefited from financial and spiritual support.

In Taiwan:
Contemporary LCMS presence.

Concordia Middle School

From its founding in 1847, the LCMS has placed great importance on education, student and adult, biblical and secular. So it is that in Taiwan, the most successful on-going outreach of partner China Evangelical Lutheran Church (CELC) is Concordia Middle School (CMS), mid-island at Chai Yi. The English programs begun in 1967 by Merle

Chapter 19 — Looking Back - Looking Forward

In Chia Yi, Concordia Middle School has attained high academic recognition while carrying on optional religion programs. In Taipei, Eternal Life congregation is on the street level of a residential building.

Personal Christian Story — *Justin*

I was born and raised in the United States as a child. I met and received the Lord at a very young age. Since I grew up in a Christian family, I tended to take Christianity for granted. Going to church and reading the Bible became typical chores. It wasn't until I came back to Taiwan did I truly experience God's love and grace!

It was very different for me when I first arrived. I had become the minority. I could no longer expect everybody to know the story of Christmas or understand why I wasn't available on Sunday mornings. Most people had their faith in idols and ancestors. To them, the Lord was insignificant, just another god to worship, if at all. With most people worshipping idols for protection and their ancestors as a sign of filial piety, it was an arduous task to get the more traditional people to even think about Christianity.

My father comes from a very large and traditional family of Hokkien people. Annually, the entire family of over two hundred people would get together at my great-great-grandfather's (who had many children) tomb to offer incense and practice ancestor worshipping. The first time I witnessed such an event, I was stunned. Even though I didn't know the names of more than half of the people present, I was amazed by the fact that distant relatives from all over the country would get together to pay respects to one person. In truth, I felt very awkward just standing around while hundreds of other people were bowing and kneeling before a portrait and tomb of my great-great-grandfather. Thankfully, my father quietly led me in prayer, praying both for our family and our faith in the Lord.

One of the greatest challenges of being a Christian in Taiwan is getting through the traditional beliefs. Having people renounce worshipping ancestors is difficult mainly because the motive is out of respect and protection. With so many temptations and opposing forces in Taiwan, it is extremely important for Taiwanese Christians to have good fellowship and unity.

Despite all of the challenges and difficulties Christians have to face in Taiwan, I have thoroughly enjoyed all the growth and lessons God has blessed me with. After all, God's will will never lead you to a place where his grace cannot keep you!

Golnick have flourished, and the school, partially residential, enrolls over 2000 students. CMS students use a standard Chinese curriculum, taught in Chinese, with an additional emphasis on high quality, trustworthiness, and focus on morality. About 30% of the faculty is Christian, and 15% of the students identify as believers. The school is among the most respected schools on the island.

Mandatory religion classes at CMS are not allowed by the Republic of China (ROC) government, but the school does have an active worship program and voluntary study programs that supplement the normal curriculum. After-school programs supplement English language instruction with a Christian curriculum. Bible study is a popular extra-curricular choice, utilizing short-term American LCMS teaching volunteers. Youth groups also meet regularly at a Chia Yi congregation.

Mission trips during winter and summer breaks have taken CMS students to northeast Myanmar (Burma) as part of the school's international outreach. In the late 1990s, teachers from CMS made a connection with Shin Bang (Hope) Middle School (HMS) at Lashu, where Mandarin is the local language. Curriculum links in mathematics and the teaching of English and Chinese have resulted. Originally, the CMS groups walked in from the Thai border, but now enter from Yangon (Rangoon). At nearby Holy Light School (HLS), a former Baptist school, CMS faculty has conducted workshops in Bible study, evangelism, and drug rehabilitation. The Taiwan students go to build relationships and have collected funds to support science and library improvements.

Exploratory excursions have also taken CMS people into Vietnam, where the LCMS has opened Concordia International School at Hanoi. In coordination with Concordia International School, Shanghai, CMS has also begun similar exchanges in some mainland provinces.

Christian Salvation Service

Providing a home and/or medical assistance to abandoned babies, Christian Salvation Service continues to serve women and children in need. Originating in Taiwan, the multi-focus human care agency has also reached into the PRC to provide supplementary educational resources for children in remote villages. Other infant-related issues came to be part of the ministry—right to life, home development, education, advocacy, employment, and adoption.

This loving and holistic human care ministry of CSS has gained recognition from social, educational, and governmental bodies in Taiwan, and receives unprecedented local support, financial and otherwise.

In Macau:
Contemporary LCMS activity

Concordia English Center

Concordia English Center in Macau provides English Bible study, English, Chinese, and deaf worship opportunities, and a venue for personal witness. In cooperation between the LCMS and LCHKS, programs have developed and operate with the essential help of overseas volunteers involving actual on-site teaching. An on-going flow of short-term volunteers enables a variety of services and personal contacts.

English language instruction attracts many Chinese workers who aspire to higher-paying jobs. With growing emphasis on careers in the business and international world, Chinese benefit from many levels of English instruction. In the earliest courses, the focus is on interaction and language help for people at a very basic level. The second tier of language education involves more English skills and fostering relationships with potential local community leaders.

Chapter 19 — Looking Back - Looking Forward

In the Hong Kong region, Buena Vista Concordia International School serves local and expat primary and middle school students, stressing instruction in English. Hong Kong International School operates four divisions, elementary schools in Repulse Bay and secondary levels at Tai Tam.

Elementary students and teacher Karin Marken were among the founding student body at Concordia International School Hanoi in 2012.

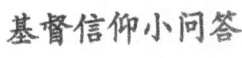

The LCHKS has fostered these two approaches at the Concordia English Center in Macau since 1988. Many young workers, enlightened by the gospel, have returned to homes and villages in the Pearl River Delta. (See chapter 15.)

In Hong Kong:
Contemporary LCMS Partnership

Lutheran Church Hong Kong Synod-maintained most of the original mission education and service programs continue to serve local children. Lutheran schools founded in the 1950s survived in cooperation with benevolent government social agencies and generous funding. Those in Macau fell on hard times and languished for a number of years until the recent developments recorded in chapter 15. Forty-one locations operated by the LCHKS within the Hong Kong Special Administrative Region (SAR) educate 20,000 pre-school, kindergarten, and primary students. Original storefront rentals have been replaced with large efficient multi-storied buildings, which also house the supporting churches. Individual congregations help improve the education and well-being of pre-school and lower primary children with after school programs, Vacation Bible School, summer camps, and other outreach activities.

LCHKS continues its highly visible network of schools, centers, clinics, clubs, and seminary programs. In cooperation with Lutheran Theological Seminary, visiting professors teach courses on both sides of the SAR border. Communication and exchange with several seminaries in China is supported by the LCMS.

Hong Kong Lutheran Social Services continues as a major force for welfare and social services, and their many divisions described in chapter 13 continue as a witness in the Hong Kong community.

In International Schools:
Hong Kong, China, and Viet Nam:

Hong Kong International School (HKIS) Repulse Bay and Tai Tam

Described in chapter 14, HKIS was initially envisioned for 600 students in one seven-story building. Its Christian philosophic base is evident in curriculum, administration, outreach and service programs and in personal care for students. It is now comprised of four divisions with 2700 students, pre-school to grade 12, located on two campuses, on the south side of Hong Kong Island. Representing over 30 countries, all instruction is in English with an American curriculum. Heavily staffed by LCMS-trained teachers during its first 20 years, faculty now hails from many different backgrounds and countries.

Concordia International School Hong Kong

Overseas Chinese professionals returning to the Hong Kong area after living or working abroad often desire that their children continue in the educational systems of the west. To meet this growing need for Chinese-language international schools, the LCHKS added Concordia International School of Hong Kong to its ministry. Located at the Synod headquarters building, adjacent to Concordia Middle School, instruction is in Chinese and English. Any local or international student may apply.

Buena Vista Concordia International School (BCIS) Shenzhen, SEZ

In addition to Concordia international school and some 40 other local schools, in 2011 the Lutheran Church Hong Kong Synod partnered with several educational experts in

Chapter 19 — Looking Back - Looking Forward

**Concordia International School Shanghai
Founding LCMS Staff, 1998**

Alan & Sandy Schmidt
Mike & Louise Weber
Pat & Sue Frerking
Anna Hu
Timothy & Betty Krenzke
Todd & Jan Luedtke
Vicci & Steve Henderson
Bill & Betty Morse

LCMS Staff since 1998

Don & Phyllis Bahr
David & Christine Bickel
David & Evelyn Chaveriat
Lucas & Michelle Gerlach
Carey & Jamie (Engerer) Halula
Matt & Jodee (Filmer) Johnson
Joel & Jane Klammer
Jim & Joanie Koerschen
Kay Lindsay
David Lyon
Gregg & Melanie Pinick
David & Doris Rittmann
Terry Umphenour
Gretchen Wiesner
Joel & Trixy (Hesskamp) Zielke

Since 1998, Concordia International School in Shanghai has continued the traditions of HKIS, with several founding staff members transferring from the Hong Kong School. An emphasis on the fine arts is a hallmark of the school, serving the expat community.

Traditional Dragon dances were performed in front of Concordia, Hanoi, in 2012. Ground was broken for a new self-contained campus in 2014.

China to open Buena Vista Concordia International School, (BCIS) in a large urban development across the border in the Special Economic Zone (SEZ) of Shenzhen. BCIS has an enrollment policy open to local Chinese and international students. BCIS portends a new phase of Lutheran educational ministry in the region, because with such a school available to their children, China nationals living abroad know that their children will continue to receive international-quality education when they relocate in the SEZ.

The head of school through 2014 was Dr. Kevin Brockberg, an educator with 30 years of teaching and administration experience, six as a staff member at HKIS. Sixty students enrolled for the opening year in grades K-8. Another grade will be added each year until a full K-12 student population is served.

Concordia International School Shanghai (CISS)

In 1998, the first Lutheran International school to open in China was made possible by HKIS' reputation as an outstanding school - Concordia International School Shanghai (CISS). Groundwork began in the late 1980s, with the concerted work of LCMS leaders in St. Louis and Hong Kong, and the international business community in Shanghai. Founding headmaster Allan Schmidt directed a core of several LCMS educators. A number of HKIS faculty transferred to initiate the academic program of CISS with Dr. Schmidt, including the elementary administrator for a number of years, Mrs. Louise Weber.

Schmidt was followed by David Rittmann, former HKIS headmaster, who set a tone of academic quality, an emphasis on the fine arts, and encouragement to reach beyond the school walls in community involvement and service projects. Rittmann was followed by Dr. James Kerschen and currently by Gregg Pinick. In the developing Jinqiao residential area of Pudong, the school has expanded into a spacious four-building complex for 1200 students. Like HKIS, CISS is a community ministry and witness among students holding passports from over 30 countries.

CISS and HKIS are operationally self-supporting from tuition resources. Each has benefited and contributed to the LCMS system in curriculum and program, and provides a new awareness of expatriate mission possibilities to the constituency of the Missouri Synod. Probably the most exemplary schools connected with the LCMS, they are recognized as among the finest of international schools anywhere.

Concordia International School Hanoi, Vietnam

Success in Hong Kong and Shanghai inspired LCMS visionaries to explore possibilities of establishing another such school in Hanoi, Vietnam. Close cooperation between the LCMS, Vietnamese and international business interests, and Hanoi's government led to opening a school serving about 50 elementary students in September 2011. The efforts of LCMS missionary Ted Engelbrecht and Asia Lutheran Educators Association Director Allen Schmidt have been instrumental in the rise of this school from its inception.

In its second school year, CISH had an enrollment of 44 boys and 52 girls from 18 countries. The school currently serves only expatriate students. Founding head of school, Steve Winkelman leads an international faculty with the motto "Building Our Community." It is the first such school in the country.

Congregational Involvement

Bringing these 19 chapters into perspective, its time to cite British missionary Andrew Murray, writing about the "key to the missionary problem" in 1901. His thoughts may well have influenced Edward Arndt. Still valid in 2013, Murray's observations identified three areas where the Christians should focus their efforts.

1. "Pastors in the pulpit" need to be energizers of their people;

Chapter 19 Looking Back - Looking Forward

Congregations serving large Chinese populations are spread across America. Several churches are clustered in the San Francisco and Los Angeles regions. In New York City, True Light continues a community outreach ministries in english and Chinese, where the family of first Chinese pastor, Paul Chang, continue their involvement.

Members of CLiMB(Chinese Lutherans in Missionbuilding met in May, 2014 in Vancouver BC to strategize effective church planting and to share in their ministry to 36 Chinese congregations in the LCMS in North America.

2. Top quality inspirational, scholarly and focused literature must be continually produced, competitive with the finest contemporary secular equivalents;

3. Committed involvement of the *people in the pew* to spread the good news at home and abroad, in public and in private, to family and neighbors is essential

Chinese-American congregations

True Light, New York City – The pioneer LCMS Chinese congregation in America – was begun in 1936 by Ms. Mary Banta, a former missionary to Liberia serving the Chinese department at the city's Methodist Church of All Nations. Forced to retire by age, she learned about the LCMS through *Lutheran Hour* messages of Walter A. Maier. She started an independent group of Chinese worshippers, worked with LCMS district president A. W. Meyer and Pastor Louis T. Bucheimer, was confirmed in 1935, and served the people of Chinatown and True Light Chinese Church until her death in 1971.

The majority of members over the last 60 years have been Cantonese immigrants, many with roots in Hong Kong, including their first Chinese pastor, Paul Chang.

Since 1980 newly arriving Mandarin-speakers and other international citizens participate in worship, educational, and social programs. Faithful service by Evangelist Mrs. Wonner Yee, Secretary Carol Wong and countless other believers has provided energy and humble leadership. Six pastors have been Chinese-speakers. Four were not. Congregational activities have included a Walther League group, a caring network, Chinese and English choirs, gospel fellowship, leadership training, family prayer gatherings, retreats, and the constant of all LCMS churches - Sunday coffee hour!

True Light is a beacon in Chinatown. Outreach activities have included immigration services, Boy and Girl Scouts, Chinese school, elderly support, and many sports programs in its fourth-floor gymnasium. The church is located within a mile of "Ground Zero," and the September 11, 2001 destruction of the nearby World Trade Center towers brought many challenges. While no members lost their life that day, health concerns and neighborhood disarray left their mark. Street traffic patterns were changed, most parking places eliminated, and shifting demographics have relocated much Financial District activity. The area now supports diverse residential usage. Many Chinese neighbors have moved into other Asian population centers in the area. Many non-Chinese now live in high-rise buildings near True Light. The congregation's outreach encompasses a broad cross-section of citizens. To reflect the shift, the congregation is now named "True Light Lutheran Church." Current pastor Chu Leong-wa is the son of 1954 graduate Hon Chung Chu from Gertrude Simon's original Concordia Bible Institute at Rennie's Mill.

Lutheran Church of the Holy Spirit, San Francisco not only serves its own Cantonese and Mandarin language parish, but works with the community in outreach to youth. Furloughed China missionary Herb Hinz was to begin work in San Francisco in 1950, but when he was called to help the Hong Kong missionaries, the project floundered. Not until Wilbert Holt left the Hong Kong mission for health reasons in 1963 did energetic work begin in the Bay area. Mrs. Amy Mui, parish worker and evangelist, has been on the church staff since its early days and has generated Lutheran Hour programs in Cantonese that are sent to Southeast Asia for local broadcast.

Chinese Lutherans in Mission-Building is a council of thirty-six LCMS congregations currently serving Chinese believers, in Cantonese or Mandarin language, bilingual ministries, or by their location in or near densely populated Asian neighborhoods across America.

Looking Back - Looking Forward

My Personal Story — Roy

I was born in a family of traditional religion, and my grandmother considers a temple in our neighborhood as her second home. On the contrary, my parents' thoughts about religion are absolutely different from my grandmother because they are atheists. My parents have been sharing liberal upbringing of me, so I have been exposed to a variety of things, including something related to gospel. Also, they always support me no matter what decision I make.

When it was time for me to be a seventh grader, my parents sent me to Concordia Middle School due to the famous English teaching and the excellent scores which students in Concordia got on every entrance exam of university. As I was in tenth grade, I taught my class to get the first prize in the carol competition, so my Chinese teacher invited me to join the worship band. At that time, I didn't know anything about worship anymore, but I finally said yes because I loved singing very much. After the first practice of the band, my teacher told me that I should attend the Bible study regularly to build relationship with God since I needed firm belief in Jesus Christ. I only knew a little bit about Christianity on account of the Bible class that we had every week, so I just couldn't entirely understand what my teacher said, but I tried to think why I needed God through the lyrics of some carols. Finally, I started to pray by myself and was determined to give my life to Jesus Christ.

In my summer vacation to senior two, I went to Myanmar to do missionary work and teach disadvantaged students. The experience made me know that I must cherish what I owned because they are all God's arrangements. In my second year in high school, I attended a Christian training course. In those five days, I gave my heavy burdens to God, asking him to heal the wound in my heart. With the help of the Christian training course, I believed in Holy Spirit's leading. I asked him to exercise control in my studying career and help me live on God's will.

After I believed in God, my life changed greatly. I was optimistic toward my life because I expected for every step Jesus lead me to walk, even when I was in dejection. I knew God would like to complete His plan for me through sufferings.

Volunteers from Fort Collins, Colorado, prepare to board a flight to serve for a month in Hong Kong. Their congregation has supported projects with workers and funding because of longtime links with individual missionaries in south China.

Loosely unified in purpose as Chinese Lutherans in Mission-Building (CLiMB), pastors and representatives of these congregations meet annually to explore and strengthen their ministry to an ethnic minority, and to become more recognized as a positive force in the church. Many of these pastors and leaders have come from Hong Kong or Taiwan already ordained; others have been educated at the seminaries in the U.S. Utilizing their knowledge and understanding of things Chinese, a major focus is reaching peoples of their homelands, especially in the mainland and Southeast Asia.

While the two legendary congregations in New York and San Francisco have established an admirable template, many LCMS congregations serve Asian Lutherans.

Many other LCMS congregations in the U.S. hold Chinese services and have a Chinese community outreach. Nearly all Chinese in America are bilingual. Many don't require Chinese language worship, but they desire to celebrate their uniqueness and heritage.

Non-Chinese congregations
the bulk of LCMS churches

Several stateside LCMS congregations have been involved in financial, prayer, and material support of specific mission personnel, dating back to the earliest LCMS missionaries. Zschiegner, Theiss, Behling, Gruen were each supported by a congregation, district, or the Walther League and Lutheran Women's Missionary League (LWML). Today, a number of congregations share support of specific workers in the field. Workers usually visit and report to their benefactors when they are on "home service" or furlough bringing up-dates of their work to their constituency.

Specific mission projects are financed by individuals or congregations. In one example, over 40 students and adults from Beautiful Savior Lutheran Church of Omaha, spent three summer weeks in 2011 leading VBS programs at six primary schools of the LCHKS. They reached over 500 kindergarten and primary-aged students in the Kowloon vicinity. Redemer Lutheran Church in fort Collins, Colorado has sent teams for several years to volunteer in China. The Northwest District of the LCMS supports a specific Asian-Pacific Rim program.

Expatriate congregation –
Church of All Nations (CAN)

In Hong Kong, Church of All Nations in Repulse Bay has endeavored to be a "sending congregation." The congregation composed primarily of expatriates holds a unique position as a springboard for witness in Hong Kong and throughout Asia. Many congregants hold business, educational, and consular positions requiring regular international travel, especially into China and throughout Southeast Asia. Concepts, materials and inspiration they receive on Sunday are taken with them to airports, boardrooms, and markets worldwide.

In addition to incorporating Chinese and other Asian customs with LCMS leadership, the congregation has developed several community service and outreach ministries. Several CAN members in the 1980s became aware of the unique needs of the Filipino community in Hong Kong. Thousands of women work in Hong Kong to earn money for their families in the Philippines. On Sunday, after morning chores, they are off-duty for the remainder of the day, and gather with friends and fellow sojourners. They have few places to socialize other than parks, arcades, and other covered spaces. Women separated from their families, speak and laugh with others in the same situation, share food, and discuss common problems.

A CAN committee generated the Filipino Prayer Share and Care group (FPSC) which recently celebrated 25 years of ministry. In brief, the FPSC offers a safe place for its

Church of All Nations is a congregation within the Northwest District of the LCMS. Pastors have included Len Galster, Karl Boehmke, Paul Tuchardt, Hank Rowold, Bruce Betker, Hu Temme, Dale Koehneke, and Joel Scheiwe. Overseas "alumni" of CAN gather whenever two or three are gathered together, usually over dim sum or a Chinese new year feast.

members to gather and rest on their one day off. The women gather for worship with other CAN members at Repulse Bay, share lunch, and have Bible study, singing and prayer. The group also typically organizes a retreat at Chinese New Year. The FPSC women also participate as members of the CAN community with service in altar care, ushering, reading lessons, singing as a choir on occasion, serving on boards and attending congregational retreats. Other activities have included craftwork, informative lectures, beach barbecues, outings aboard Chinese junks, hikes, and service projects in the Hong Kong community.

A project for many years has been the purchase of Christmas gifts for distribution to residents at the Home of Loving Faithfulness, a residence for the severely intellectually and physically disabled. The FPSC usually travel to the home to sing carols and distribute the gifts.

There is a constant flow of new participants and a rotation of women returning to their families in the Philippines. The faces change, but the fellowship remains a very important highlight in the lives of these women. . Long-term CAN coordinators have included Teri Betker, Donna Oetting, Asha Satharaj, and Mary Ewing.

CAN works with local LCHKS schools and churches by supporting English conversation programs. Volunteers from CAN visit Concordia Lutheran School North Point weekly for English conversation activities. This involves working with small groups of students to improve their English language understanding and confidence with conversation.

CAN youth and adults tutor English conversations at Concordia English Center, a ministry of the LCMS in Macau. English conversation events are a chance for CEC students to practice conversational English over a meal. Many workers in the hospitality industry or gambling centers take advantage of free language sessions that include optional Bible study. Fees are charged for more extensive English courses. The witness and service of short-and long-term American volunteers provide opportunities to share the "one thing needful."

Street Sleepers are Hong Kong's homeless or low income dwellers. A significant contingent of CAN members provides support to LCMS Deaconess Carol Halter, who monitors a ministry of mercy to these individuals. Since the mid-1990s volunteers hold an annual Street Sleeper Christmas party at Concordia Middle School in Kowloon. The effort includes preparing & serving refreshments and treats, organizing donated second-hand clothes for distribution, and performing as a choir to sing Christmas carols. Volunteer Chinese language speakers from New Life Mission Station, Abundant Life Lutheran Church, and several other churches join to share the gospel with the "sleepers." Work with individual street dwellers continues throughout the year.

CAN utilizes its overseas connections to participate in ongoing overseas service activities, including providing scholarships to Guangdong Province girls who might otherwise not be able to attend secondary school. Donors also provide support to the Concordia Children's Service orphanage in Manila, Philippines. Members from CAN have traveled for service trips supporting welfare and educational in China and Vietnam.

Prayer... Witness... Commitment... Innovation... Teamwork

The Christian church is the world's largest fraternity, the universal body of Christ.

Avenues of contact and service with Chinese peoples in America and Asia are constantly being sought and discovered. On-going innovations in electronic media promise wider availability and distribution of the good news, the "happy sound," as non-Chinese and Chinese Christians seek to share the love of Christ.

Chapter 19 — Looking Back - Looking Forward

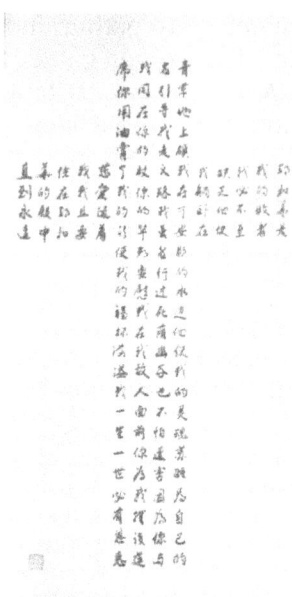

Being a Christian in Taiwan-   *Amy*

My father and my mother are both Christian, so we won't get angry with each other when I tell them that I want to go to church to do something. Unlike my parents, they have been having a big quarrel with their parents, my grandparents are afraid of that when they die, no one can worship them.

" You should realize that to worship us after I die is an very important thing, if no one burned the money for us after we died, then we won't have any money in the other world, we will starve and be very unhappy! Be a good kid!" my grandparents told my dad.

"But…but…father, can you just please let us choose our own believe?" My dad begged. The conversation and conflicts repeat again and again in our family. That is something happen often in Taiwan family.

Jesus is my life, He leads me through all the difficulties. Whenever I need Him, I just pray to Him, and He will answer. Sometimes He did not give you what you want to get but he said," You do not realize what I am doing, but later you will understand."

Last year, I have a chance to be one of the members of "red cross" in our school. However, the first day of the meeting was the day that I went to Korea with my church to learn how to tell strangers about God. Then, the leader said that I can not be the member of that group. I was very sad and felt confused that why God would let this thing happened. After a year, that is, this year, I got another great chance to go to Myanmar to worship God and teach some of Myanmar students. I suddenly found that if I am one of the members of "red cross" I may not have the chance to go to Myanmar because there are a very important activity held by them at that time.

Sometimes I felt that the life is filled with sadness and guiltiness, when I pray to the Lord, my heart will be joyful and full of energy again!

Jesus is the only God that can give you the true peace in your heart.
Jesus loves you.

With the centennial of the China enterprise of the Lutheran Church Missouri Synod in 2013, the church celebrates the bounty of activities and programs in place, projects in process, and ever-increasing possibilities for sharing the gospel of Jesus Christ with all people.

Sola Deo Gloria

Significant sources

Charbonnier, Jean-Pierra	*Christianity in china*
Lambert, Tony	*China's Christian Millions*
Langerwey, John	*China – A Religious State*
Leys, Simon	*Chinese Shadows*
Liao Yiwu	*God is Red*
Meyer, Richard	*Messiah in War and Peace, LW Dec 2000*
Smith, Carl	*Chinese Christians*
Yee, Edmond	*Abundant Harvest – Stories of Asian Lutherans*

Interviews with Kevin Brockberg, Adam Gawel,, Carol Halter Dennis & Donna Oetting, Ken Rohrs, and Joel & Iantha Scheiwe

Individual Index of mission personnel
Hong Kong -Taiwan -Macau

D = Deaconess
E = Educator
HK = Hong Kong
M = Macau
N = Nurse
R = Reverend
T = Taiwan

A
Albrecht, Ardon (R), 157-9

B
Beaver, Pierce, 65
Behling, Lorraine (Sonnenberg) (E), 0, 13-9,
    20, 25-7, 33, 47, 147, 187, 211
Berndt, Manfred (R), 60, 77
Bertram, Ed (R), 157
Beske, Carol, 124
Betker, Bruce (R), 104
Blau, Carrie, 124
Boehmke, Karl (R), 60. 104, 117
Boss, Martha (D), 0, 13-9, 49-51, 53, 71, 75, 279
Boudreau, Ken, 177
Brandt, Robert (R), 175
Brockberg, Dr Kevin (E), 207
Bringewatt, Ralph (R), 3, 147, 151, 155, 173
Buckholz (E), 175
Burke, Steve, 179
Buuck, Lorenz (R)

C
Chang, Paul (R), 9- 19, 25, 41, 105, 119, 129, 209
Chang, Silas (R), 17, 25, 131
Chen, Cromwell (R, 59)

Chen, Kenneth (T), 165
Ch'eng Ch'ung Ch'uen, 177
Chiang, David (R), 89
Chiang, Martin (R), 31, 37, 47, 53, 73
Chiu, Andrew (R), 17, 25, 65, 105, 129
Chiu, James, 124
Chow Sing, 53, 75
Christian, Robert (E), 60, 104, 115-8
    Arlene (E), 60, 75
Chu, James (E), 17, 47, 105
Chu, John (E), 17, 47, 105
Chu, Winston (R), 173
Coates, Thomas (R), 60

D
Deli'Immagine, Ceciia, 124
Dickhudt, Robert (E), 60, 69
Dingler, William (R), 60, 119, 151
Dull, Chuck (E), 104
Dunning, Kevin (E), 104
Dunseth, Tom (R), 124, 137-9
Duval, Liz, 115

E
Eddy, Mary Elizabeth, 124
Engelbrecht, Ted (E), 207

F
Feiss, Julie, 124
Fox, Charles (R), 124, 135, 175
Found, Jim (E), 175
Frederick, Don (R), 157

G

Galster, Leonard (R), 20, 59, 66, 77, 106-17,
 Ruth, 20, 77
Gihring, Ralph, 20, 53
Geissler, Herb (E), 87
Gimbel, Becky (Shaw), 177
Go, Henry H.J. Wu, 151, 159
Goldhammer, Maurice (R), 157
Golnick, Merle (E), 163, 203
Gremmels, Delbert (R), 149
Gruen, Olive (D), 27, 145, 211

H

Haffner, Vic (R), 3, 60, 113, 149, 151, 161
Halamka, Ron (R), 157
Halter, Carol (D), 104, 139
Hanson, Carl (R), 179
Hanson, Jennifer (O'Neal), 177
Hartung, Bruce, 179
Henningfield, Dick
Hinz, Herbert (R), 0, 19, 20, 27, 31, 41, 53,
 59, 129, 131, 147, 209
Ho, Daniel (R), 141
Ho, Paul (R), 131
Ho, Phillip Wan Chien (R), 25, 63, 69, 73, 77, 106
Holste, Herman, 124
Holt, Wilbert (R), , 3-19, 23, 39-41, 209
 Geri (N), 19, 39, 57, 73
Hoeltje, Wilbert (see Holt)
Horney, Anna 124
Hsu Chien Chang, 177
Hu, Patrick, 124, 135, 167
Hui Ming Kin (R), 71

I & J

Ip, Peter, 133

Jasper, Louis (R), 60, 71-3, 133, 167
Jiang, Martin (R), 37
Jen, Harold (R), 17

K

Kan, sunny, 124
Karner, Roy (R), 20, 53, 60, 75, 131, 134
 Betty, 20, 53, 60, 119
Kebschull, Lowell (E), 165
Kerschen, Dr James (E), 207
Ketcher, Rodney (R), 175
Kieschnick, Mel (E), 20, 47, 77, 10617, 163
 Jane, 20, 55
Koehneke, Dale (R), 104
Kuo, Priscilla (T), 165

L

Lai, Mark (R), 89
Lai Oi Man (E), 47
Lam KinU, Grace, 133
Lan, Timothy, 25
Latimer, 124
Law, Richard (R), 89
Lee, Daniel Wing Ching (R), 25, 31, 41, 105
Lee Kwan Rau (R)(HK), 37
Lee Ming, Benjamin, 75
Lee Fu Sheng, Titus (R), 131-3
Lee, Timothy (R), 133
Lee Wei Tao, Titus (R), 53, 69, 71, 193
Lenschow, Norma (N)
Lesemann, Bruce 124
Lik Sang Yeung (R), 135
Lin, Jeremy, 177
Lo Fuk Ki, (R), 133, 135
Luebbe, Jessica, 124
Luedtke, James (E), 60, 104

M

Mah, Isaac (E), 27, 41, 47, 105, 131
 Mrs. Isaac, 39
Mak, Luke (R), 89
Martens, Emily 124
Meyer, Arno (R), 157
Miao, Andrew (R), 173
Mills, Elaine, 124
Molitaris, Craig (R), 175, 195
Moore, Anna, 124
Mueller, Heidi (N)
Mueller, Reinhold (R)
Mueller, Richard (H), 104
Mui, Jason, 9
 Amy (D)
Myers, Matt & Kim, 124

N & O

Noack, Krista (Alexander), 177

Oliver, Stephen (R), 17
Oschwald, Jeffrey (R), 179
Owens, Sharon, 124, 141

P

Paul, Michael (R), 124, 137, 141, 179
Peterson, Merlin (R), 177
Pfeifer, David, 124
Pinick, Gregg, 207
Proft, Ruth (Dennehl) (N), 20, 27, 35, 53, 60, 65

R

Ranta, Hillard (R), 60
Reinking, William (R), 60, 69-71, 132-3
Ren, Harold (R), 25, 173
Richards, Bea (D), 75
Riedel, Erhardt (R), 149, 155, 199
Rittmann, David (E), 118-9, 207

Rohnke, Ruth, 124
Rohrbach, Roger (E),, 104 87
Rowold, Hank (R), 137, 157, 179, 193
Ruprecht, Bob (E), 116
Russell, Andy (E),104, 87

S

Schalow, Fred (R), 23, 27, 147
Scheiwe, Joel, 124
    Iantha, 124
Schmalcs, John, 124
Schmidt, Dr. Allan (E), 207
Schmidt, Harold (E), 20, 53, 67, 113, 133
Schmidt, Walt (E), 123
Schroeder, Mel, 116
Seltz, Eugene (R), 20, 53, 65, 112-3, 117, 133, 193
    Clara Rodenbeck (D), 20, 53, 73, 73
Shen Yu Ching, 147
Simon, Gertrude (D), 0, 3, 15-9, 25-7, 29, 37, 47, 55, 60, 75, 129, 145
Sprier, John (R), 157
Suelflow, Roy (R), 147

T

Tai Kuang Ming (R), 147
Temme, Hugh (R), 104
Thode, Elmer (R), 20, 35, 41, 55, 60, 185, 195
    Frieda (E), 20, 35, 41
Trinklein, Michael (R), 60, 149
Tuan, John, 73
Tuchardt, Paul (R), 104
Tursic, Richard, 179

U & V

Ulrich, Michael, 124

Von Behren, Werner (E), 1167
    Timothy Paul, 120-1

W

Walter, Norman (R), 149
Wan, John, 177
Wasmund, Matt, 177
Weber, Louise (Mrs)(E), 207
Wehrenberg, Bill (E) 104
Wei (Wen) John Yunnan (HK), 23, 131
Weleenbach, Bryn, 124
Westrick, Earl (E), 122
Wilch, Anastasia, 124, 137, 141
Wilenius, John (R), 147
Williams, Kali, 124
Winkelman, Steve (E), 207
Winkler, George (R, 20), 53, 55, 106, 133
    Florence (N), 20, 53, 55, 57, 69, 73
Winter, Cliff (R), 157
Witt, Sue (E), 115
Worthington, Van, 149
Wu, Michael (R), 141
Wu Ming Hui (R), 175

X

Xu, Stephen (R), 181

Y

Yeung Lik Sang (R), 135, 137
Yeung Yok Wah (E)
Yi, Richard (R), 173
Yip Miss Wai Ying, 69
Yu, Paul, 177
Yung, Allan (R) 95

Z

Ziegler, Albert (R), 3
Zimmer, Robert (E), 163, 177, 193
Zimmermann, Les (E), 116, 189

The Asian Lutheran Education Association held its bi-annual conference in Hong Kong in March, 2014. Representing over 150 Lutheran schools in South and East Asia were representatives from India, Australia, Thailand, Laos, Vietnam, Philippines, Taiwan, China, Macau, Hong Kong, Japan and Korea.

Index

D = Deaconess
E = Educator
HK = Hong Kong
M = Macau
N = Nurse
R = Reverend
T = Taiwan

A

AiJi Press, 199
Airports
    Chek Lap Kok
    Kai Tak, 9, 31, 43, 75-7
amah, 189
AmCham (American Chamber of Commerce), 111
American Women's Association (AWA), 39
AMITY, 199
ancestors, 13
Anglicans, 37
Anglo-Chinese, 23, 49, 87, 106
Arndt, Edward (R), 65, 149
Arrand, Charles, 179
Aylward, Gladys, 167

B

Bamboo curtain, 1, 67, 189
Banta, Mary (NYC), 41, 131, 209
baptism, 23
Baptist, 37, 195, 203
Bartling, Paul, 61
Basel Mission, 5, 9-11, 31, 35
BCC (British Crown Colony; HK before 1997), 1, 21
Behling, Robert, 13
Bertermann, Eugene (R), 27, 131

Betker, Teri (Mrs), 213
Bible Portions, 31
Bible Women, 39
blind, 39, 57
Board of Foreign Missions (BFM), 33, 55, 59, 145
Board of managers, 117
Bohlmann, Dr Ralph, 193
Bombay, 125
bombs, 79
Bowring, Sir John, 129
braille, 57, 73
Brazil, 161
Bringing Christ to the Nations, 131
Buchheimer, Louis (R), 41, 131, 209
Buddhism, 9, 25, 128, 189
Burma [Myanmar], 177, 203
Burtt, Mary, 73
Burvett, Edith (E), 189
business managers, 75, 149, 155, 161

C

Canton (see Guangzhou), 127
Cantonese 7, 35, 69, 159
CARE, 33
Caritas, 119
Castle Peak Hotel, 67
catechism, 17, 35
Catholic (Roman) Church, 37, 39, 63, 77, 119, 129, 161, 189, 199
Causeway Bay, 3
Central (Victoria), 3
Centro Culture Luterano, 133
Chai Yi (T), 145-7, 161-5, 173
Chan Cheng, Mrs, 117

Chang Tung-chin (R), 193, 195
chaplaincy, 39
Cheung Chau Island, 17
Chiang Kai-shek [Jiang Jieshi], 145, 187
China Christian Council (CCC), 191, 199
China Evangelical Lutheran Church (CELC), 157, 173-5, 203
China Lutheran Seminary (T), 177-9
chinatowns, 41, 209
Chinese Lutherans in Mission-Building CLiMB), 41, 211
"chinglish", 105
chinoiserie, 127
choral music, 37, 199
Christian Childrens Fund, 43
Christian Salvation Service (CSS)(T), 167, 183, 203
Chu Leong-wa (R), 209
Chung Hom Kok(HK), 114-5
Church of All Nations
    Hong Kong (CAN),119, 135, 211
    Jerusalem, 119
    New York City, 209
churchcraft, 15, 31
Clark, Maureen, 77
Clippers, 127
Coloane island CoTi), 126, 137
compradore, 7
Concordia Bible Institute/School (CBI) (HK), 25-7, 37, 55, 65, 105, 147, 209
Concordia College
    Fr. Wayne, 137, 179
    Portland, 193, 197
    River Forest, 105, 117
Concordia English Center (CEC) (Macau), 136, 203, 213
Concordia English Language Academy (T), 177
Concordia International School
    Buena Vista (BCIS) ShenZhen, 207
    Hanoi (CISH), 203, 207
    Hong Kong, 205
    Shanghai (CISS), 203, 207
Concordia Lutheran Middle School (HK), 47
Concordia Middle School (see Taiwan)
Concordia Publishing House (CPH, 15
Concordia School for Special Education (CSSE)(Macau), 135
Concordia University System (CUS), 197
Concordia Welfare and Education Society (CWESM) (Macau), 135
Conferences
    All Asia Missionary, 61
    Asian Pacific Regional___for the Deaf, 73
    Bandung, 87
    Ephphatha, 69
Confucian; confucius, 7, 128

congregations, LCMS
    US   Holy Cross (Deaf) - St. Louis, 69
           True Light - New York, 11, 41, 47, 119, 209
           Beautiful Savior - Omaha, 211
           Living Savior - Tualatin, OR, 197
           Holy Spirit - San Francisco, 9, 41, 159, 209
           Immanuel, Bridgeman, MI, 13
           Redemer, Ft. Collins, CO , 210
    Hong Kong (see LCMS Mission HK)
        Chatham Road, 94
        *Concordia (Yau Yatchuen), 55
        *Eternal Life (Shau Kee Wan)
        Grace (Sai Wan/Western Market), 31, 63, 131
        *Holy Cross (Tsuen Wan), 63
        *Holy Trinity (Kwun Tong), 59, 106
        *Nathan Road (Tsim Sha Tsui), 71, 77
        *Redemption (Lai Chi Kok), 63
        *Savior (Sham Shui Po), 17-9, 25, 27, 31, 47, 57, 63, 71, 73
        St. Johns (Rennie's Mill?), 25
        *St. Matthews (Hgau Tau Kok)
        *St. Phillips (Cha Kwo Ling), 47, 63
        *Sharon (Yau Ma Tei), 71
        *True Word - Chatham Road (Hung Hom), 69
        Zion (North Point), 63, 71
    Macau
        St. Paul's, 71, 131
        St. Peter's (Taipa), 130-1
    Taiwan
        Eternal Life, 174, 202
correspondence courses
    Bible Correspondence School (Taiwan), 147
    Lutheran Hour Correspondence Course, 151
consumption (see tuberculosis)
Cultural Revolution, 79, 125, 177, 189, 193, 195
Curtis, Darien, 71

D

Danker, William, 61, 65
Daoism, 9, 189
deaconess, 5, 37, 41
deaf, 69-73, 133-7
Degner, Dr Waldemar, 179
Delegate Conference (T), 151
Deng Xiaoping (Teng Shao-ping), 193
DePree, Gordon (R), 39
Der Lutheraner, 65
Dickenson, Lillian, 167

disturances, 53
Dominicans, 129
Dow Chemical Corporation, 115

E

early childhood education, 161
EbenezerThankoffering, 163
Education Department (HK), 43, 49, 111
English language (ESL), 163, 199
Enshih [Enshi], 145
Episcopal, 161
"Equipping the Saints", 199
evangelism, 31, 187
Ewing, Mary (Mrs), 213
ex-pats; expatriates, 67, 71, 155

F

"Faith Forward", 113
Far East Broadcasting, 156, 179-81
Fengjie (Kweifu), 193
Fenwick Pier, 39, 57, 67, 73
Feng Xu Tong, Ms, 135
Filipino Prayer Share andCare (FPSC), 213
filmstrips, 39
Finnish Lutherans, 179
fires, 25, 41
flannel board, 31
Fleet Club, 67
Franciscans, 129
friendship evangelism, 139

G

Gertrude Simon College (HK), 97
GEO (Globally Engaged in Outreach), 139, 177, 201
Glenn, John, 109
Great Hunger, 65, 131
Great Leap Forward, 65
Gregg,William, 111
Guangzhou (Kwangchow), 189
Guetzlaff, Karl, 185

H

Habel, Norman, 119
Hakka, 11, 105, 159
Handicrafts, 29
Handover; handback; return
Hankow [Hankou], 11, 27, 193, 195
Haven of Hope Sanitarium, 49-53
Heung Kong College (HK), 9, 15, 19
Hoffman, Dr. Oswald, 119, 199
Hooijberg, Trudy, 119
Holste, Dr Herman, 139
Home of Loving Faithfulness (HK), 213
Hong Kong International School (HKIS), 163, 205

Hong Kong Letter, 13, 29, 106
Hong Kong Lutheran Handicrafts Society, 75
Hong Kong Society for the Blind, 57, 73
Hong Kong Society for the Deaf, 71
Horn, Dr Clifford, 193
hospitals
    Kwang Hwa, 27
    Tung Hwa, 13, 27
house church, 195
Hsieh tong (harmony; concord), 163
Hua Kuofeng, 189
Hung, Prof C.S., 55, 109
hymns, hymnals, 35, 37, 39

I

India, 61
indignation, 79
inquirers, 191
International Lutheran Hour, 181
International Lutheran Society of macau (ILSM), 137
International Schools
    Buena Vista Concordia International School (HK), 207
    Concordia International School Shanghai, 207
    Concordia International School Hanoi, 41, 207
    Concordia International School Hong Kong, 205
    see Hong Kong International School, 163
Ip, Peter, 133
Islam, 189

J

Japan (see also LCMS Japan Mission), 145
Jehovah's Witnesses, 37
Jesuits, 128-9
Jesus Christ, 193, 195
Jidutu, 191
Jockey Club (HK), 198
Joint Pastors Conference (JPC) (T), 153, 157
Junk Bay (HK), 49

K

Kadoorie, 29
kindergarten, 161
King George V School (KG5), 111
Knaack, Jennifer, 139
Kolb, Dr Robert, 179
Koppelmann, Herman H (R), 33, 61-3, 109, 113, 149
Korea, 33, 35, 61
Kowloon Walled City, 21, 75-7
Kwun Tong (HK), 59, 63
Kuo Ming-tang (KMT)(GMD),13

Kuo Tien Lai AIA, 163
Kwan Yin, 127
Kwang Hwa Hospital (HK), 27
Kwangchow [see Guangzhou]
Kwangtung [Guandong], 189, 213

L

Lau, John, 9
Lee Ming, Benjamin, 75
Legal Corporation Board of Control (LCBOC)(T), 161, 181
Lei, Diana, 137
Lenschow, Norma (N), 187
Li (Zi), Nancy, 109, 119
Li Muqun (R), 193
Li Yen-san, 186-7
lianghui, 191
Liu Lang'gen (R), 195
Lo Wan Sing, 73
Liu Tien-shang, 195
LoWu (HK), 5, 65
Luther, Martin, 125, 179, 197
Lutheran Bible School (T), 159, 179
Lutheran Church - Hong Kong Synod (LCHKS), 191, 205
Lutheran Church Missouri Synod (LCMS)
LCMS Mission (HK) (see also Missionary Conference), 9, 29, 33
LCMS Mission (Japan), 27, 61
LCMS Mission (Taiwan), 27, 61
Lutheran Council of the USA (LCUSA), 159
Lutheran Deaf Evening School, 71
Lutheran Fellowship for the Blind, 73
Lutheran Handicraft Center (T), 167
Lutheran Handicrafts (HK), 29
Lutheran Hour, 27, 33, 63, 119, 183
Lutheran Hour Ministries, 179, 197
Lutheran Layman's League (LLL), 27
Lutheran Messenger, 73
Lutheran Missions Literature Society (LMLS), 39
Lutheran News, 91
Lutheran Salvation Service (T), 169
Lutheran School for the Deaf, 73
Lutheran School of Nursing, 35
Lutheran Service Center (LSSC) (T), 167, 183
Lutheran Voice, 181
Lutheran Volunteer School (LSV), 163
Lutheran Witness, 33, 106
Lutheran World Federation (LWF), 29, 33, 41, 159
Lutheran Womens Missionary League (LWML), 29, 41, 49, 75, 106, 165, 211
Lye Muen (HK), 25

M

Macau, 124-141
    Centro Cultural Luterano, 132-3
    Chapels, 131
    Concordia English Center, 136, 203
    Deaf work, 133
    History, 5, 21, 79, 125-129, 205
    Mission, 23, 53
    Sao Paulo Church, 124, 129
    Schools, 131-33
Mache, Joe, 109
    Dottie, 109
Mahlke, Bill, 121
Maier, Dr Walter A (R), 41)
mainland (see also PRC)
Majestic House (HK), 107
Malaya; Malaysia, 152
Man Kam To (HK), 5, 65
Mandarin, 75, 149, 173
Manila, 125, 152
Mao Tse-tung [Mao Zedong], 1, 187, 189
Martha Boss Lutheran Community Center (MBLCC), 133
Martens, Paul (R), 153, 187
Marty, Dr Martin, 121
Maryknoll, 33
May, Edward (R), 51
Methodist, 195, 209
Meyer, Herbert (R), 153
Meyer, Richard (R), 187
milk, 33, 77
Mill Neck Manor, 139
Mills, Verent (R), 43
Min Hsiung (T), 163
Ming Kei College, 71
Mission Central, 201
Missionary Conference
    Hong Kong, 29, 53, 77
    Taiwan, 151, 161
Missouri Evangelical Lutheran China Mission (MELCM)
Mongkok Lutheran School for the Deaf (MLSD), 71, 135
Monroe, Florence, 43
Moody Bible Institute, 31
Morrison, Dr Robert, 185
MOST (Mission Opportunities Short Term), 201
Mount Davis(HK), 13
Mueller, Heidi (N), 187
MuEn (Shepherd's Grace)(T), 169
Mui, Amy (Mrs), 41, 209
Munroe, Florence
Mustard Seed (T), 167

N

Nationalists, 13, 145
Nau, Dr Louis, 193

Naylor, Fr Harold, SJ, 121
Nelson, Daniel (R), 127
New Territories, 3
Nitz, Arthur, 61
Nixon, Pres Richard, 189
North Point (HK), 3, 53, 69, 79, 213
Northerners, 7
Norwegians, 179
NSM (Network Supported Ministry), 201

O

Oetting, Donna (Mrs), 213
opium, 77, 127
organists, 33, 37, 77
Oriental Mission Society, 43
Ott, Harold (R), 13
Ottley, Marge, 119
Outlying Islands, 3

P

pak pai, 115
P'an Chien Ch'iu (T), 163
Pan American airlines, 115
Pan, John, 195
paternalism, 61
Pearl River, 7, 125-6
Penang, 125
People's Republic of China (PRC), 23, 79, 125, 177, 183, 187-9
Philippines, 3, 149, 187, 211
pidgin, 9
Pok Fulam (HK, 13)
polio, 52
Portals of Prayer, 73
Portuguese, 125-9
Presbyterian, 157, 161
Preuss, Dr. Jack, 119
Project Concern (HK), 77
Project 21 (T), 161
provisional school, 114-5
putonghua, 149

R

Rae, John, 71
Red Guards, 79, 81, 189
Red Hill (HK), 117
"Red Tide", 21
Redifusion, 26, 131
refugees, 3-9, 21-5, 33, 161
Reinbrecht, Charles (R), 43
Religious Affairs Bureau (RAB), 187, 191
Rennie's Mill (HK), 13-5, 23-7, 29, 35, 51, 131, 145, 191
Republic of China (ROC) see Taiwan, 53
Repulse Bay, 79

Repulse Bay Hotel, 107
Repulse Bay Lutheran Church (see also CAN), 107
Resettlement Estates, 43-5
Ricci, Matteo, 129
Rhenish, 37, 43
"rice bowl", 29
Ricci, Matteo, 129, 185
rooftops, 43, 49, 65, 69, 73
Rotary Club, 137
Royal Mail, 75, 77

S

Sai Kung (HK), 25
SAR - (Hong Kong after 1997), 1
St. Peters Commercial School, 11
Saint Paul (airplane), 3
St. Paul's Lutheran School for the Deaf (Macau), 135
Satharaj, Asha (Mrs), 213
Schalk, Carl, 121
Schmidt, Otto H (R), 9, 27
schools, 37, 47
    Concordia (St. Pauls) Macau, 132
    Concordia (St John's) S, Rennie's Mill, 47
    Concordia Lutheran S, Kowloon, 47, 71, 106, 111
    Kwun Tong Lutheran S, 57, 69, 105, 111
Selle, Rev August, 17
Seminaries, 61
    Concordia Theological Seminary
        Hankow, 35, 193, 195
        Hong Kong, 57, 65
        St. Louis, 5, 105, 175, 187
        Springfield, 55, 59, 105, 107
        Taiwan, 157
        Federated Lutheran Seminary, 177, 183
        Lutheran Theological (Tao Fung shan), 35, 39
        Nanjing Union Theological, 193
Seventh-Day Adventists, 37
Sham Shui-po (HK), 5, 123
Shanghai, 11
Shek Kip Mei, 31, 35, 41, 53
ShenZhen(SEZ), 207
sign language, 137, 139
simplified characters, 197
Singapore, 125
Skau, Annie, 49-53
Social Welfare Department (HK)
social workers, 155
southerners, 7
special education, 135
Stanley (HK), 25
Star Ferry, 29, 75, 106
Star Ferry riots, 113-5
street sleepers, 213

Strege, Paul (R), 119, 161
student learning results (SLRs), 119
Sun Yat-sen, 187
sunday school, 33, 37, 79

T

Tai Hang Tung (HK), 43, 49
Tai Ch'iu-tao (R), 193, 195
Tai Kuang-ming (R), 193
tai-pan, 127
Tai Tam (HK), 11
Taipa island, 126, 130, 135
Taipei, 147
Taiwan, 143-83; 204
    see China Evangelical Lutheran Church
    General Conference, 181
    History, 27, 143
    Concordia Middle School, 161, 163, 175-7, 203
    Locations
        Banchiao, 147
        Chai Yi, 147
        Changhwa
        Hsinchu, 151
        Hsinyang, 151
        Hualien, 151
        Huwei, 147
        Kaoshung, Da Fu church 175
        Nantou, 151
        Taichung, 147
        Tainan, 151, 163
        Toului, 151
    Schools, 161
Taiwanese language, 149, 151, 157-9, 173
Taiwan Lutheran Church (TLC), 159, 181
Tang, Charles, 71
Tao Ho, AIA, 117
Taoism, 9, 128
Teen Times, 73
Term Controversy, 93
Thailand, 203
third-culture kids, 111
This Is The Life, 31
Theis, Gary, 201
Theiss, Henry O (R), 211
three-self, 11, 87, 189
Three Self Patriotic Movement (TSPM), 189, 191
Tiao Ching Ling Bible School (see CBI), 25
Timothy Paul Study Center (HK), 89
Tin Hau, 125
Tiu Keng Leng (HK) 13
Tokyo Lutheran Center, 27
Triads, 77
Treaty of Nanking, 127
Tropic Lisland Hotel (HK, 13)

Truth Magazine, 151
Tsin Sha Shui (TST), 106
tuberculosis, 17, 19, 49
Tui Keng Leng (HK), 191
Tung Hwa Hospital, 13

U

underground, 191, 197
United Bible Society, 199
United Nations, 33, 43, 193

V

Vatican II, 65
Vietnam, 39, 123, 203, 207
Voightman, Fred, 135
volunteers, 139, 199, 213
Volunteer Youth Ministry (VYM), 165
Voss, Kurt (R), 153

W

wai-tang preaching, 11
Walther League, 13, 19, 31, 51, 121, 211
Wanchai, 3, 65
Wang Mei Yu (Mrs), 195
Wanhsien [Wanxian], 11, 145, 193
water rationing, 23
Wei Xiangbo (John), 195
Welfare Handicrafts, 29, 75
Wescott, Dr Ed, 193
Wheat Ridge, 19, 51, 165
Wong Tai Sin (HK), 75
Wong, William, AIA, 111
Woo, John (HK) 53
worker-priest, 89
World Council of Churches, 33
World Mission (BFM), 173, 181
Wuhan, 195

Y

Yamashita, Carol, 119
Yee, Wonner (Mrs), 209
Yichang, 11, 195
Yilin Press, 199
Yip Wai Ying (Miss)
YWCA, 29
Yu, Dr. Thomas, 177

Z

Zenith Theater, 31, 53
Zhang Dongjin (R) 195
Zhou Enlai (Chou en-lai), 11, 189
Zschiegner, Max (R), 211

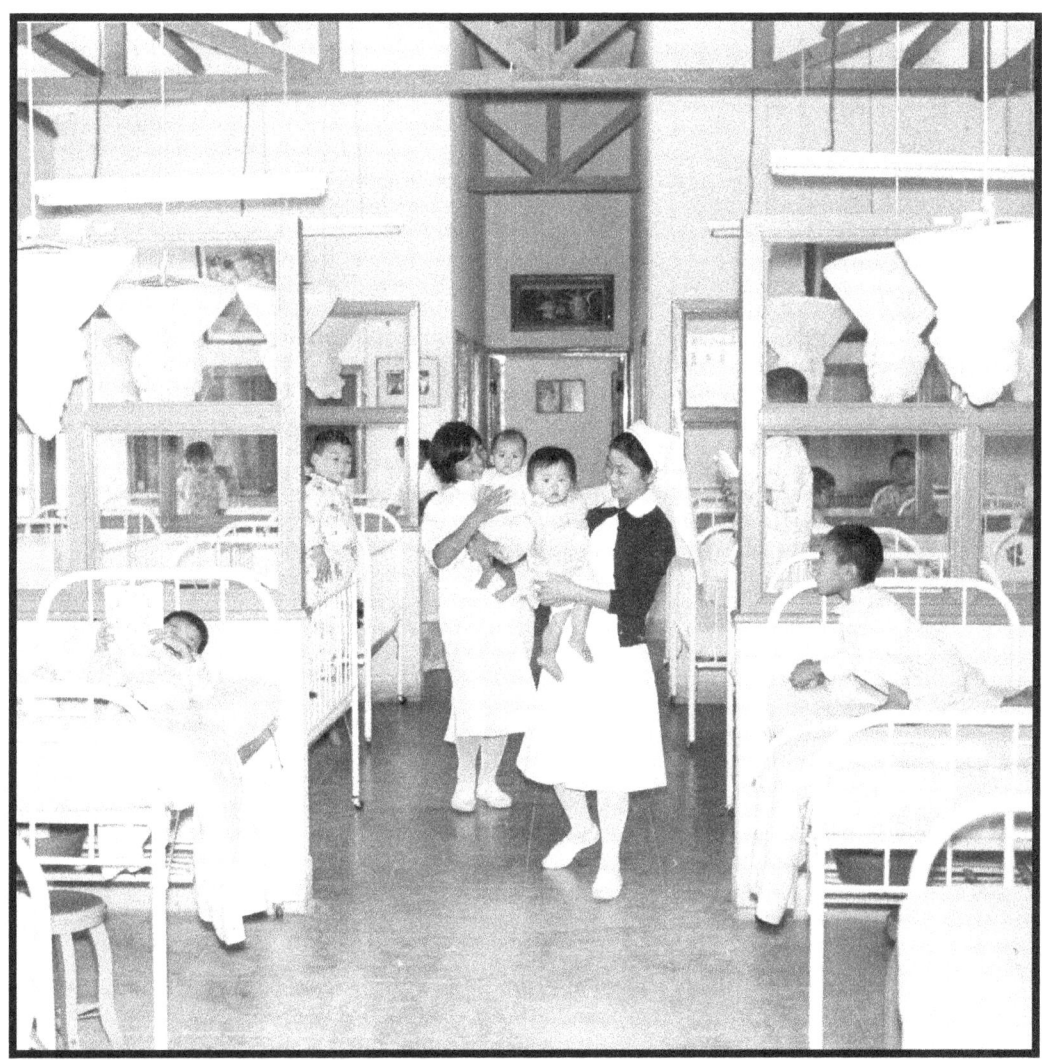

Bibliography

A

Aid Association for Lutherans, ed, **A Week in the Life of the Lutheran Church, Missouri Synod, Concordia Publishing House, St. Louis, 1996
Albrecht, Ardon, **The CELC in Perspective, n.p. Taipei, 1965
Alcorn, Randy, **Safely Home**, Tyndale, Wheaton, 2001
Armentrout, Fred, Ed, **Hong Kong International School: *Celebrating 40 Years of Learning and Service,* AmCham Hong Kong and HKIS, 2007
Arndt, Edward H, **A History of the Evangelical Lutheran Mission for China, n.p., n.d.
_____ **The beginnings of Our Work in China,** CHQ, St. Louis, 1932-3 (4 parts)

B

Bacon, Ursula, **Shanghai Diary,** M Press, Milwaukee, 2004
Baepler, Walter, **A Century of Grace - *A History of the Missouri Synod 1847-1947,* Concordia Publishing House, St. Louis, 1947
Bailey, Steven, **Strolling in Macau**, Things Asian Press, San Francisco, 2007
Baker, Hugh, **Chinese Family and Kinship**, MacMillan, London, 1979
Banham, Tony, **We Shall Suffer There -** *Hong Kong's Defenders Imprisoned, 1942-45*, Hong Kong University Press, 2009
Barr, Pat, **Foreign Devils -** *Westerners in the Far East*, Penguin, Baltimore, 1970
Bays, Daniel, ed, **Christianity in China -** *From the 18th Century to the Present,* Stanford University Press, Stanford, 1996
Bechtel, John, **The Mystery of East Mountain Temple**, Bible Institute Colportage Association Press, Chicago, 1939
Becker, Jasper, **Hungry Ghosts:** *Mao's Secret Famine,* Henry Holt & Co. NY 1996
Benge, Janet & Geoff, **Gladys Aylward: The Adventure of a Lifetime,** Youth With A Mission, Seattle, 1998
Bickers Robert, and Seton, Rosemary, ed, **Missionary Encounters -** *Sources and Issues,* Curzon Press, Richmond, Surry (UK), 1996
Bianco, Lucien, **Origins of the Chinese Revolution 1915-1949**, Stanford University Press, Stanford, 1974
Blumer, Deborah, **Called According to His Purpose – Missionary Letters of George Lillegard, Amazon, ISBN: #978-0-578-01454-8
Board of Control, **Exodus from Concordia: *A Report on the 1974 Walkout,* Concordia Seminary, St Louis, 1977
Bodde, Derk, **Peking Diary -** *A Year of Revolution,* Henry Schuman, New York, 1950
Bonavia, Judy, & Hayman, Richard, **Yangzi -** *The Yangtze River and the Three Gorges,* Odyssey Books, Hong Kong, 2004

Braga, J. M., **China Landfall 1513,** Imprensa Nacional, Macau, 1955
Brauer, Janice, ed, **One Cup of Water - *Five true stories of missionary women in*
    China, International Lutheran Women's Missionary League, St.Louis, 1997
Briner, Bob, **The Management Methods of Jesus**, Thomas Nelson, Nashville, 1996
Buck, Pearl, **My Several Worlds,** Cardinal Giant Pocket books, New York, 1956
Burkee, James, **Power, Politics, and the Missouri Synod - *A Conflict That changed*
    American Christianity, Fortress Press, Minneapolis, 2011
**Buuck, Lorenz, *I Am With You Always,* self-published, Ft. Wayne, 1977(?)

C

Cameron, Nigel, **An Illustrated History of Hong Kong,** Oxford U Press, Hong Kong, 1991
    _____**Barbarians & Mandarins,** Walker/Weatherhill, New York, 1970
Cannon, Terry, & Jenkins, Alan, **The Geography of Contemporary China:**
    The Impact of Deng Xiaoping's Decade, Routledge, London, 1990
Carew, Tim, **The Fall of Hong Kong,** Pan Books, London, 1963
Carroll, John M. **A Concise History of Hong Kong,** Rowman & Littlefield, Lanham, MD, 2007
    _____**Edward Arndt,** graduate paper, Washington University, St. Louis, unpublished, 1991
Cary-Elwes, Columba, **China and the Cross:** *A Survey of Missionary History,* P.J.Kennedy & Sons, New York, 1957
Chang, Leslie, **Factory Girls** -*From Village to City in a Changing China,* Spiegel & Grau, NewYork, 2008
Charbonnier, Jean-Pierra, **Christianity in China - AD 600 to 2000,** Ignatius Press,San Francisco, 2007
Chen Wei Ping, *Autobiography,* n.p. (Hong Kong?), 1965
Cheung, Gary Ka-wai, **Hong Kong's Watershed - The 1967 Riots,** Hong Kong University Press, Hong Kong, 2009
**Chiu, Andrew, *A History of the Research of Exodus 18:1-12*, unpublished ThD
    thesis, Concordia Theological Seminary, St. Louis, 1973
**_____*Short Historical Notes on Concordia Theological Seminary in Hong Kong.* unpublished, n.d.
Chu, Cindy Yik-Yi, **Foreign Communities in Hong Kong, 1840s-1950s,** Palgrave Macmillan, New York, 2005
Clubb, O. Edmund, **Twentieth Century China,** Columbia University Press, New York, 1964
Clyde, Paul, and Beers, Burton, **The Far East** - *A History of the Western Impact and*
    the Eastern Response 1830-1965, Prentice-Hall, Englewood Cliffs, 1966
Coulson, Gail, **The Enduring Church** - *Christians in Hong Kong and China,* Friendship Press, New York, 1996
Covell, Ralph, **Confucious, The Buddha, and Christ** - *A History of the Gospel in*
    Chinese, Orbis Books, Maryknoll, NY, 1986
Cressey, George, **Land of the 500 Million** - *A Geography of China,* McGraw-Hill, New York, 1955
Criveller, Gianni, **From Milan to Hong Kong** - *150 Years of Mission,* PIME House, Hong Kong, 2008
Crow, Carl, **The Chinese Are Like That,** World Publishing Co, Cleveland, OH, 1943
Curran, Thomas, **Educational Reform in Republican China** - *the Failure of Educators*
    to Create a Modern Nation, The Edwin Mellen Press, Lewiston, NY, 2005
Curtis, Claude, **My Cup of Tea**, Gospel Missions Inc, Wahiawa HI, 1979

D

Danker, William, **Two worlds or none - *Rediscovering Mission in the 20th Century,* Concordia, St. Louis, 1964
**Darnell, Laura Lou, *Sen me, Send me!* - *The Story of Laura and Albert Ziegler's Missions to China,*
    Self-published, Henderson, NV, 2005
Davin, Della, **Woman-Work** - *Women and the Party in Revolutionary China,* Clarendon Press, Oxford, 1976
DeFrancis, John, **The Chinese Language:** *Fact and Fantasy*, University of Hawaii
    Press, Honolulu, 1984DePree, Gladis, **The Spring Wind,** Harper and Row, New York, 1970
Dew, Gwen, **Prisoner of the Japs,** Alfred A. Knopf, New York, 1943
Donovan, John, **The Pagoda and the Cross** - *The Life of Bishop Ford of Maryknoll,*
    Charles Scribner's Sons, New York, 1967
DuBose, Francis de, **Classics of Christian Missions,** Broadman Press, Nashville, 1979
Dunn, George H, S.J., **The Missionary in China** - *Past, Present, Future,* Lutheran World Federation, Geneva, 1973

Dutton, Michael, **Street Life China**, Cambridge University Press, Cambridge, 1998

E

Emerson, Geoffrey, **Hong Kong Internment,** 1973
Espey, John, **Minor Heresies** - *Reminiscences of a Shanghai childhood*, Alfred Knopf, New York, 1945
_____**Tales out of School** - *Stories of a boyhood in China,* Knopf, New York, 1947

F

Fairbank, John K., **ChinaBound** - *A Fifty-Year Memoir*, Harper & Row, New York, 1982
_____**The Great Chinese Revolution 1800-1985,** Harper Perennial, NY 1987
Feng Chi-shun, **Diamond Hill** - *Memories of growing up in a Hong Kong squatter village,* Blacksmith Books, Hong Kong, 2009
Fitzgerald, C. P., **Flood Tide in China,** The Cresset Press, London, 1958
Fleming, Daniel, **Living as Comrades**, Foreign Missions Conference of North America, Agricultural Mission Press, NY, 1950
Forman, Harrison, **Report from Red China**, Book Find Club, New York, 1945
Fremantle, Anne, **Mao Tse-tung: An anthology,** Mentor, NY 1962

G

Galster, Leonard, **The Lutheran Church in Hong Kong,** booklet, Hong Kong, n.d.
Gemmels, D. W., and Walter, N E., **Christianity vs Paganism,** Taiwan Missionaries' Conference of the Lutheran Church, Missouri Synod, Taipei, 1958
Giles, Herbert, **A Glossary of Reference** *on Subjects Connected with the Far East,* London, 1878
Gilkey, Langdon, **Shantung Compound**, Harper, San Francisco, 1966, 1975
Gittings, John, **China Changes Face**-*the Road from Revolution*, Oxford, New York, 1989
Gittins, Jean, **Stanley: Behind Barbed Wire,** Hong Kong University Press, 1982
Gleason, Gene, **Hong Kong**, John Day Co, New York, 1963
_____, **Joy to My Heart:** *The true story of nurse Annie Skau*, McGraw-Hill, New York, 1966
**Gockel, Herman, The Cross and the Common Man, Concordia, St. Louis, 1955
Goddard, W. G., **Formosa** - *A Study in Chinese History*, Macmillan, London, 1966
Gowen, Vincent, **Village by the Yangtze**, Douglas-West, Los Angeles, 1975
Grindal, Gracia, **Thea Ronning: Young Woman on a Mission, Lutheran University Press, St. Paul, 2012
Grouch, Archie, **Christianity in China** - *A scholar's Guide to Resources and Archives*, M.E.Sharpe, Inc, Armonk, NY, 1989
Guest, Kenneth J., **God In Chinatown** -*Religion and Survival in New York's Evolving Immigrant Community,* New York University Press, New York, 2003

H

Han, Dongping, **The Unknown Cultural Revolution** - *Life and Change in a Chinese Village,* Monthly Review Press, NY, 2008
Harrop, Phyllis, **Hong Kong Incident,** Eyre & Spottiswoode, London, 1942
Hattaway, Paul, **Operation China** - *Introducing all the Peoples of China*, William Carey Library, Piquant, Pasadena, CA, 2000
Hersey, John, **The Call** - *An American Missionary in China,* Knopf, New York, 1985
Hong Ying, **Daughter of the River**, Grove Press, New York, 1997
Hsiao, Andrew, **A Brief History of the Chinese Lutheran Church, Taosheng Publishing House, Hong Kong, 1999

I - J

Isaacs, Harold, **The Tragedy of the Chinese Revolution**, Athenem, New York, 1951
Jordan, David, **Gods, Ghosts & Ancestors** - *Folk Religion in a Taiwanese Village*,
    University of California Press, Berkeley, 1972

K

Karsen, Wendell, **The Church Under the Cross** - *Mission in Asia in Times of Turmoil*,
    Vol I & II, Erdmanns, Grand Rapids, 2010
Keenan, Barry, **Early Educational Reform and Politics in Early Republican China**,
    Journal of Asian Studies. Vol 33, No 2 (Feb., 1974), pp 225-237
Keinath, H.O.A., **My Church - *A History of the Missouri Synod for Young People*, Concordia, St. Louis, 1947
King, Robert H, ed, **8 Models of Ethnic Ministry, Concordia, St. Louis, 2006
Kohl, David, **Dragon Taels: *Memories of the Golden Age at Hong Kong International Schol*,
    One Spirit Press, Portland, 2007

L

Latourette, Kenneth, **The China That Is To Be** - *The Condon Lectures*, Oregon State
    System of Higher Education, Eugene, 1949
Leck, Greg, **Captives of Empire:** *The Japanese Internment of Allied Civilians in China, 1941-1945*,
    Shandy Press, 2006
Lee, Daniel W., ed, **Lorraine Behling Sonnenberg** - *Handmaid of the Lord*, TheLutheran Church-Hong Kong Synod,
    Hong Kong, 2012
Lee, Vangina (Jean) E., **Bringing Christ to the Chinese - *China. Hong Kong. San Francisco*,
    One Spirit Press, Portland, 2011
Li, Charles N., **The Bitter Sea** - *Coming of Age in China Before Mao*, Harper, New York, 2008
Li Cheng, **Wanderer** - *Beckoned by Eternity*, Ambassadors for Christ Fnd, Paradise, PA, 2002
Liao Yiwu, **God is Red**, HarperCollins, 2011
Lin YuTang, **From Pagan to Christian**, The World Publishing Co, Cleveland, 1959
Llewellyn, Bernard, **I Left My Roots in China**, Oxford U Press, New York, 1953
_____ **With my Back to the East,** Travel Book Club, London WC 2, 1958
Loest, Mark, **How the Missouri Synod was Born, Concordia Historical Institute, St. Louis, 2001
Lodwick, Kathleen, and Cheng, WK, **The Missionary Kaleidoscope** - *Portraits of Six China Missionaries*,
    East Bridge, Norwalk, CT, 2005
Lueker, Erwin, ed, **Lutheran Cyclopedia, Concordia Publishing House, St. Louis, 1954
Lueking, F. Dean, **Mission in the Making - *The Missionary Enterprise Among Missouri Synod Lutherans 1846-1963*, Concordia, St. Louis, 1964
Lutz, Jessie, **Christian Missions in China** - *Evangelists of What?*, Heath & Co, Boston, 1965

M

Mackay, George Leslie, **From Far Formosa**, Fleming H. Revell, New York, 1895
Mackerras, Colin, and Yorke, Amanda, **Cambridge Handbook of Contemporary China**,
    Cambridge University Prtess, Cambridge, 1991
Maier, Paul L, **A Man Spoke, A World Listened, McGraw-Hill, New York, 1963
Malcolm, Kari Torgesen, **We Signed Away Our Lives**, Wm Carey Library, Pasadena, CA, 2004
Manthei, Ben, **In His Majesty's Service, Creative Cottage Publishing, Charlevoix, MI, 2002
Meinzen, Luther, **A Church in Mission - *Identity and Purpose in India*, Concordia Seminary,
    Nagercoil, Tamilnadu, India, 1981
Meyer, Carl S, ed., **Moving Frontiers - *Readings in the History of the Lutheran Church - Missouri Synod*,
    Concordia Publishing, St. Louis, 1964

**Meyer, Richard, *The Missouri Evangelical Lutheran Mission in China*,
    MA thesis, Washington University, St. Louis, 1948
Min, Anchee, **Pearl of China**, Bloomsbury, New York, 2010
Molloy, Robert, **Colossus Unsung** (E.S..Little), Xlibris Corp, print-on-demand, 2012
Moseley, George, **China Since 1911**, Harper & Row, New York, 1969

N - P

Naumann, Cheryl, **In the Footsteps of Phoebe - *A Complete History of the Deaconess Movement in the LC-MS*,
    Concordia, St. Louis, 2009
Neill, Stephen, **A History of Christian Missions,** reprinted Penguin London, 1990
_____, **Colonialism and Christian Missions**, McGraw-Hill, New York, 1966
Nida, Eugene, **Customs and Cultures** - *Anthropology for Christian Missions,* reprinted Wm Carey Library,
    Pasadena, CA, 1986
Pahl, Jon, **Hopes and Dreams of All - *The International Walther League, 1893-1993,*
    Wheat Ridge Ministries, Chicago, 1993
Pankow, Fred & Edith, **The Best is Yet to Come, International Lutheran Laymen's League, St. Louis, 1992
Pollock, David, **Third Culture Kids:** *The Experience of Growing Up Among Worlds*,
    Intercultural Press, Yarmouth, ME, 1999
Pollock, John, **A Foreign Devil in China,** Zondervan, Grand Rapids, 1971
Porter, Jonathan, **Macau** - *The Imaginary City*, Westview Press, Boulder, 2000

R - S

Redwood, Mabel Winefred, **It Was Like This...,** Anslow, Sheffield, UK, 2001
Rowold, Hank, ***Christianity In China* - *class notes*, n.p, Concordia Seminary, St. Louis, 2007
Schell, Orville, **Mandate of Heaven,** Simon & Schuster, New York, 1994
_____ **To Get Rich is Glorious,** Pantheon/Random House, New York, 1984
_____ **Watch Out for the Foreign Guests,** Pantheon, New York, 1980
Schmidt, Otto H, **Globe-Trotting for the Gospel, Vantage Press, New York, 1962
**Schram, Elaine Buuck, *Letters from China*, formatted by Irene Bergman, n.p. 2014
Scovel, Myra, **The Chinese Ginger Jars**, Harper, New York, 1962
Sharlpe, Eric, **Karl Ludvig Reichelt,** Tao Fung Shan, Hong Kong, 1984
Slyke, Lyman, **Yangtze** - *Nature, History, and the River*, Addison-Wesley, Reading, MA, 1988
Smart, Alan, **The Shek Kip Mei Myth:** *Squatters, Fires and Colonial Rule in Hong Kong, 1950-1963,*
    Hong Kong University Press, 2006
Smith, Carl T, **Chinese Christians:** *Elites, Middlemen, and the Church in Hong Kong*,
    Hong Kong University Press, Hong Kong 2005
Stockwell, F. Olin, **With God in Red China** - *The Story of Two Years in Chinese Communist Prisons*,
    Harper & Brothers, New York, 1953
Strege, Paul, **How Small is Small? *From Ludell to Beirut in Christ's Global Mission,*
    Chipmunk Chapel Books, St. Louis, 2002
Strong, Anna Louise, **Rise of the People's Communes in China**, Marzaani and Munsell, NY 1960
Suelflow, Roy A . Challenge in China:** *the Mission Enterprise of the Lutheran Church-Missouri Synod
    in Mainland China 1913-1952,* unpublished thesis manuscript, University of Wisconsin, Madison, 1971
Suyin, Han, **Wind In the Tower,** *Mao Tse Tung 1949-1976*, Triad Panther, England, 1978

T

Taege, Marlys, **WINGS - Women In God's Service, Lutheran Women's Missionary League, St. Louis, 1991
**Thode, Frieda Oelschlaeger, *"In China and Hong Kong with Deth"* unpublished
Todd, Mary, **Authority Vested, *A Story of Identity and Change in the Lutheran
    Church - Missouri Synod,* Erdmann's, Grand Rapids, 2000

Tong, John, **Challenges and Hopes:** *Stories from the Catholic Church in China,* Holy Spirit Study Center, Hong Kong , 2002
Tregear, T. R., **A Geography of China,** University of London, London, 1965
Tuchman, Barbara, **Notes from China,** Collier Books, New York, 1972
Tucker, Ruth, **Daughters of the Church -** *Women and Ministry from New Testament times to the present,* Acadamie Books, Grand Rapids, 1987

Varg, Paul, **Missionaries, Chinese, and Diplomats -** *The American Protestant Missionary Movement in China, 1890-1952,* Princeton U Press, Princeton, 1958
Vickner, David W, **"The Role of Christian Mission in the Establishment of Hong Kong's Education System," Ed D dissertation, Columbia University, NY, 1987

W-Y-Z

Walker, Caroline, **On Leaving Bai Di Cheng -** *The Culture of China's Yangzi Gorges,* NC Press Ltd, Toronto, 1993
White, Theodore, **Thunder Out of China,** Wm Sloane, New York, 1946
Wiesenauer, Stephen, **The Missouri Synod in China, Christian Friends Of China, Minneapolis, unpublished, 2007
Wilson, Kenneth, **Angel at Her Shoulder -** *The Story of"Typhoon" Lil Dickson,* Harper & Row,New York, 1964
Wintle, Justin, **The Timeline History of China,** Barnes & Noble, New York, 2005
Wolf, Arthur. ed. **Religion and Ritual in Chinese Society,** Stanford University, Stanford, 1974
Wright-Nooth, **Prisoner of the Turnip Heads,** Leo Cooper, London, 1994

Yee, Edmond, **Abundant Harvest – *Stories of Asian Lutherans,* Lutheran University Press, Minneapolis, 2012
_____ **The Soaring Crane -** *Stories of Asian Lutherans in North America,* Augsburg Fortress, Minneapois, 2002

Ziegler, Albert , ***Biographies of Missouri Synod Missionaries in China, 1913-52,* unpublished 1981
Zimmer, Robert, **Dreams Come True - *Memories of a Prairie Boy,* Sorrels Printing, Ocala, FL, 2006
Zimmermann, B. Christian, **Hostage in a Hostage World - *Hope aboard Hijacked TWA 847,* Concordia, St.Louis,1985

Periodicals:
China's Millions (China Inland Mission)
Concordia Historical Institute Quarterly
Concordia Theological Monthly
Der Lutheraner
Lu-teh-chiao chien-cheng (Chinese Lutheran Witness)
LWML Quarterly (Lutheran Women's Missionary League)
Walther League Messenger (LC-MS youth)
The Lutheran Witness
The Lutheran Layman

Films:
**In the Wild Mountains*
**Balzac and the Little Chinese Seamstress*
**Eat Drink Man Woman*
**Raise the Red Lantern*
*TaiPan
*Joy Luck Club
**Empire of the Sun*
*The Sand Pebbles
*The Painted Veil
**Postmen in the Mountains*
**Made in China (documentary)*

Inn of the Sixth Happiness
The Children of Huang Shi
The Road Home

Websites:

www.lutheransontheyangtse.com
www.bdcconline.net/en/ - Biographical Dictionary of Chinese Christianity
www.clswebblog.blogspot.tw   hsinshen@cls.org
www.cwef.org.hk - ConcordiaWelfare and Education Foundation
www.gospelherald.net - Gospel Herald news service
www.hklss.hk - HK Lutheran Social Services
www.lcms.org - Lutheran Church-MissouriSynod
www.missioncentral.us - MissionCentral
www.molife.hk - Messengers of Life
www.orientalarchitecture.com
www.vatican2voice.org
www.jesusevangelism.com (Good News About Jesus)

Colophon

Titles and Text Hiroshige
Formatted with Adobe Indesign CC
Photos via Adobe Photoshop CC

History of Hiroshige Font

Hiroshige was designed in 1986 by Cynthia Hollandsworth of AlphaOmega Typography, Inc. The typeface was originally commissioned for a book of woodblock prints by the great nineteenth-century Japanese artist Ando Hiroshige, whose work influenced many Impressionist artists. The typeface has a gentle calligraphic flair that creates an interesting page of text as well as elegant headlines.

One Spirit Press
Portland Oregon

www.onespiritpress.com
onespiritpress@gmail.com

www.ingramcontent.com/pod-product-compliance
Lightning Source LLC
Chambersburg PA
CBHW080536170426
43195CB00016B/2581